Data Visualization

LIBRARY INFORMATION TECHNOLOGY ASSOCIATION (LITA) GUIDES

Marta Mestrovic Deyrup, PhD
Acquisitions Editor, Library Information and Technology Association, a division of the American Library Association

The Library Information Technology Association (LITA) Guides provide information and guidance on topics related to cutting edge technology for library and IT specialists.

Written by top professionals in the field of technology, the guides are sought after by librarians wishing to learn a new skill or to become current in today's best practices.

Each book in the series has been overseen editorially since conception by LITA and reviewed by LITA members with special expertise in the specialty area of the book.

Established in 1966, the Library and Information Technology Association (LITA) is the division of the American Library Association (ALA) that provides its members and the library and information science community as a whole with a forum for discussion, an environment for learning, and a program for actions on the design, development, and implementation of automated and technological systems in the library and information science field.

Approximately 25 LITA Guides were published by Neal-Schuman and ALA between 2007 and 2015. Rowman & Littlefield took over publication of the series beginning in late 2015. Books in the series published by Rowman & Littlefield are:

Digitizing Flat Media: Principles and Practices
The Librarian's Introduction to Programming Languages
Library Service Design: A LITA Guide to Holistic Assessment, Insight, and Improvement
Data Visualization: A Guide to Visual Storytelling for Libraries

Data Visualization

A Guide to Visual Storytelling for Libraries

Edited by Lauren Magnuson

ROWMAN & LITTLEFIELD
Lanham • Boulder • New York • London

Published by Rowman & Littlefield
A wholly owned subsidiary of The Rowman & Littlefield Publishing Group, Inc.
4501 Forbes Boulevard, Suite 200, Lanham, Maryland 20706
www.rowman.com

Unit A, Whitacre Mews, 26-34 Stannary Street, London SE11 4AB

British Library Cataloguing in Publication Information Available

Library of Congress Cataloging-in-Publication Data
Name: Magnuson, Lauren, 1986–, editor.
Title: Data visualization : a guide to visual storytelling for libraries / edited by Lauren Magnuson.
Description: Lanham : Rowman & Littlefield, [2016] | Series: Library Information Technology Association (LITA) guides | Includes bibliographical references and index.
Identifiers: LCCN 2016014587| ISBN 9781442271104 (hardcover) | ISBN 9781442271128 (eBook)
Subjects: LCSH: Library science—Graphic methods. | Library statistics—Computer programs. | Charts, diagrams, etc.—Computer programs. | Information visualization. | Communication in library science. | Visual communication.
Classification: LCC Z678.93.G73 D38 2016 | DDC 020—dc23 LC record available at https://lccn.loc.gov/2016014587

♾™ The paper used in this publication meets the minimum requirements of American National Standard for Information Sciences—Permanence of Paper for Printed Library Materials, ANSI/NISO Z39.48-1992.

Printed in the United States of America

Contents

Illustrations

Figures in photospread, following page 110

1   These two visualizations of the same data show how bar charts can be used
    to solve problems with pie charts. The data used are from a sample data set
    of visitors to catalog pages for an academic library. The categorical variable,
    the first letter of the Library of Congress classification for the catalog item in
    question, has too many categories to be well represented in a pie chart. A bar
    chart shows the data much more effectively.

2   These visualizations illustrate the problem with using bar charts for temporal
    data that have gaps between temporal categories. Charting tools may draw all
    of the bars with equal spacing, ignoring the months that have no data. The
    line chart, instead, correctly shows how the months should be spaced.

3   Three examples of scatterplots. The one-dimensional scatterplot shows the
    distribution of monthly catalog visits over a single Library of Congress class.
    The categorical scatterplot shows the distribution across multiple categories.
    The numerical scatterplot shows two numerical variables, number of visitors
    and number of LC classes, that have a strong positive correlation.

4   Using a grouped bar chart to show the interaction between two categorical
    variables yields a chart with many redundant labels and much wasted space.
    While the bars allow for more precise data lookup, the width of the chart
    and the small bars make it difficult to compare all of the bars of a single
    color. The heat map here offers a much more efficient way of comparing two
    categorical variables. Sorting the countries and LC classes by the grand totals
    for each category makes it easier to see highly active combinations.

5   Two choropleth maps of the counties of the contiguous United States show
    how different color scales can reveal different patterns. On the left, the
    numerical variable—average daily high temperature in Fahrenheit (McClure
    et al. 2013)—is encoded with a rainbow color scale. With this color scale,
    data points that are very close to each other can look very different because
    of the rapid changes in hue. Using a color scale that goes from a very light
    shade to a very dark shade is a more faithful representation and helps focus
    attention on the true regions of interest.

6   Listen to Summon.

Preface

Libraries are embracing the expectation that they demonstrate their effectiveness and be accountable to communities and the institutions they serve. Libraries collect mountains of raw data about how their collections and services are used, but communicating the impact of that data to a variety of audiences can be challenging. Raw data are not enough—data must be carefully prepared and presented in a way that is understandable, transparent, and compelling. Emerging data visualization technologies provide the ability to create engaging, interactive visualizations that effectively tell the story of a library's impact on its users.

Data visualization is interdisciplinary, combining elements of data science, statistics, visual communication, and visual design. Although emerging technologies are making it easier to create complex visualizations using large data sets, data visualization can refer to the design and creation of visuals with or without digital technology. The ultimate goal of data visualization is to help viewers understand data better—by providing context, illustrating trends, showcasing patterns, and enabling interactive exploration of data.

The purpose of this book is to provide guidance and practical-use cases to illustrate how libraries can use data visualization technologies to both understand and communicate data. Case studies in this book discuss a variety of technologies and frameworks that can be used in data visualization, including D3.js (chapter 3), Google Charts (chapters 3 and 4), and visualization libraries for the R programming language (chapters 5 and 9). To create compelling visualizations, you must first acquire a deep understanding of the underlying data. A common theme throughout this book is that a significant amount of work is required to clean, prepare, and transform data to make truly meaningful visualizations, so real-world examples of how this data preparation work can be accomplished are provided.

This book features case studies and examples that can be useful to the total visualization beginner as well as those with some experience using data visualization technologies. Whether you have just started creating visualizations using charting tools like Excel or Google Charts or you have used sophisticated front-end data visualization code libraries, you will find useful case studies and inspirational applications of visualization technologies in this book.

The scope of this book covers core principles of data preparation and visualization and describes how libraries apply data visualization technologies and strategies to improve library services, enhance accountability, and understand collections and users. Also included are practical strategies for incorporating data visualizations, data literacy, and visual literacy into information literacy and instructional services.

The book begins with Eric Phetteplace's chapter, "Sculpting Data for a Successful Visualization," which provides a practical overview of methods for cleaning and preparing data for visualizations. In "Designing Public Visualizations of Library Data," Angela Zoss discusses essential principles of visualization design and provides a comprehensive overview of common data visualization types and techniques.

The following chapters discuss case studies and examples of creating visualizations using data about library services, from discovery and web analytics to interlibrary loan data. In "Tools and Technologies: Visualizing Research Activity in the Discovery Layer in Real Time," Godmar Back and Annette Bailey describe how they created a series of innovative visualizations to better understand and communicate search behavior in their Summon discovery system. In "Using Google Tools to Create Public Analytics Visualizations," I provide a step-by-step tutorial for setting up a service that enables querying Google Analytics data for a website to create publicly accessible, constantly updating visualizations. Roger Taylor and Emily Mitchell, in "Minding the Gap: Utilizing Data Visualizations for Library Collection Development," provide a comprehensive overview of how collection circulation data can be mined and visualized to provide guidance in making collection decisions. In "A Picture Is Worth a Thousand Books: OBILLSK, Data Visualization, and Interlibrary Loan," Ryan Litsey, Kenny Ketner, and Scott Luker describe the creation of a tool that gathers and renders interlibrary loan data from across a library consortium to provide greater accountability for interlibrary loan services.

Several chapters in the book focus on visualizing archives metadata, institutional repository collections, and scholarly research activities. David E. Polley's chapter, "Visualizing the Topical Coverage of an Institutional Repository Using VOSviewer," presents a detailed exploration of how an institution's faculty research can be visualized in an innovative way using term co-occurrence maps. In "Visualizing Archival Context and Content for Digital Collections," Stephen Kutay discusses how visualizations can enable users to better understand digital archival collections and details strategies that can be used to effectively identify, curate, and present visualizations using a digital archives platform. Tim Dennis, in "Using R and ggvis to Create Interactive Graphics for Exploratory Data Analysis," explores how data visualization packages for the R programming language can generate a range of visualizations using data sets such as gate counts, circulation statistics, and article-level metrics.

As libraries become more advanced creators of data visualizations, they can also play a role in educating their users to become data literate consumers and producers of visualizations. Data literacy and visual literacy are increasingly important to information literacy instruction, as explored in chapters by Charissa Jefferson and Caitlin A. Bagley. In "Integrating Data and Spatial Literacy into Information Literacy Instruction," Charissa Jefferson provides a comprehensive overview of strategies that libraries can use to incorporate open data and geospatial data into library instruction and educate library users on finding, understanding, and using data to create effective visualizations. Caitlin A. Bagley, in her chapter "Using Infographics to Teach Data Literacy," describes how using the infographic service Piktochart enhanced information literacy instruction and empowered students to create their own unique visualizations from research data.

Creating effective data visualizations requires a wide variety of skills, including a thorough understanding of math and statistics, knowledge of data storage and mining methods and front-end design, and development knowledge. This book provides an overview of how these skills can be applied in a library context to create better libraries, better services, and better instruction and to showcase the impact libraries have on their users and their communities. It is my hope that after reading this book, you will have the knowledge and tools needed to begin transforming your library's data into a compelling, meaningful story.

1

Sculpting Data for a Successful Visualization

Eric Phetteplace

There are many prerequisites for successful information visualization, not the least of which is meaningful data. Ben Fry's *Visualizing Data* breaks down the process of creating a visual into seven steps: acquire, parse, filter, mine, represent, refine, and interact (Fry 2008). Importantly, we do not even begin to work with something visual until step five (represent); the first four steps all relate to manipulating data. We must first acquire and hone meaningful information that can be used to answer a pressing question about library services, to demonstrate value, or to simply serve as a launch pad for exploration. While much has been written about how to evaluate library value or what data libraries should be collecting, this chapter focuses on the procedures of preparing data for visualization.

What is at stake when refining our data? Poorly processed information can make creating an insightful visualization impossible or, even worse, mislead its audience. Consider figures 1.1 and 1.2. In figure 1.1, the data's trend is not evident at all because an outlier distorts the chart. The chart's vertical range has to be extended so much to accommodate one aberration that the rest of the data seem, by comparison, near identical in their Y values. The same data source is used in figure 1.2 except that the outlier has been removed; suddenly, a general downward trend is evident. The two figures demonstrate how a solitary point can completely obscure the distinctions present within the rest of our data.

Does that mean we are justified in removing the obnoxious outlier? Not in the least. That a datum is inconvenient is not cause to remove it. We must ask *why* the outlier exists, which in turn involves knowing what our data describe and how they were collected. Consider that our data represent returns at a slot machine, with the x-axis representing money and the y-axis time. As the gambler plays, he slowly loses money, occasionally slightly rebounding. But suddenly he hits the jackpot, surging his winnings for the session. It would be massively misleading to simply discard the

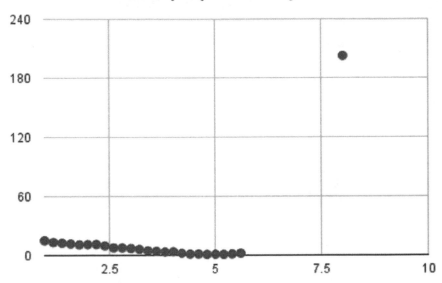

Figure 1.1. A single data point greatly influences the chart's boundaries.

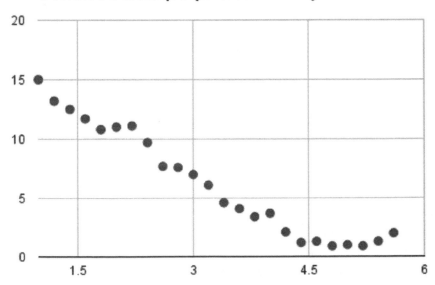

Figure 1.2. Removing the single point allows the chart to intensify its focus.

jackpot spin due to its extremity. In this example, the outlier must be retained if we are to accurately represent the phenomena being studied. If we are unhappy with our visualization, perhaps we should ask whether the data set itself is sufficient. Is a single gambling session a meaningful sample? Would it not be more sensible to gather the results of many sessions or else scrap the investigation if that's not obtainable?

On the other hand, not all outliers belong. Some represent errors in the data collection process and should be removed. Identifying errors within our data set and handling them appropriately requires familiarity with the data and good judgment. It is an ethical issue as well as a technical one. Data processing is arguably a less interesting topic than data visualization. It is dry, and tedious, and difficult. But it is also essential. This chapter explores the multifarious facets of manipulating the raw clay of a troublesome data set into a gorgeous sculpture.

TERMS

Before we discuss the various pieces of data manipulation and some specific case studies, it is important that we have a shared understanding of vital terms. Some of these terms will no doubt be familiar, acronyms you have at least seen or heard before. Please feel free to skip terms you are already acquainted with; this chapter does not provide any sterling insight into their essence but rather a basic outline of their primary properties.

API (Application Programming Interface)

"Application Programming Interface" is a most unhelpful expansion of this term, divulging little of its meaning. For the purposes of this chapter, APIs are sources of structured data. They provide us with information that can help illuminate or refine our data set in a format that we can use (often JSON or XML; see descriptions below). For instance, perhaps we have a list of our most circulated titles that we want to visualize. To provide more context for the data set, we can use a bibliographic data API (our catalog, Open Library, or the WorldCat API all come to mind), sending it a series of requests for our titles and retrieving related information such as publisher, date of creation, and creator.

CSV (Comma-Separated Values)

CSV is a data format that is easy to read and edit—even manually in a text editor—which makes it a popular interchange format for many purposes. It consists of rows of text separated by line breaks, with smaller cellular segments of data that are optionally wrapped in quotation marks and separated by commas. CSV is so easy to parse that we might as well take a look at one:

```
"Title","Circulation Events","Year of Publication"
"Beloved",103,1987
"The First Cities",88,1968
"Ulysses",12,1922
```

The one caveat to the CSV format is that it truly is a row-based, delimited data set in which the delimiter can vary; tabs are also common. Most visualization applications have a means of reading in and exporting to delimited data formats such as CSV.

JSON (JavaScript Object Notation)

JSON is an important and popular data format. Although JavaScript is mentioned in its name, functionality for reading and writing JSON is present in nearly every programming language. JSON has an astonishingly simple standard that clocks in at only fourteen pages, several of which are blank or front matter (ECMA International 2013). The JSON.org website describes it best:

> JSON (JavaScript Object Notation) is a lightweight data-interchange format. It is easy for humans to read and write. It is easy for machines to parse and generate. It is based on a subset of the JavaScript Programming Language, Standard ECMA-262 3rd Edition - December 1999. JSON is a text format that is completely language independent but uses conventions that are familiar to programmers of the C-family of languages, including C, C++, C#, Java, JavaScript, Perl, Python, and many others. These properties make JSON an ideal data-interchange language. (JSON 2015)

JSON is important because a number of web service APIs return JSON data. Furthermore, the ease with which programming languages can manipulate it makes it easier to process than many other formats. Finally, if we want to build a visualization that lives on the web, it's likely that JSON will be our desired format due to the many JavaScript visualization tools, such as the D3.js library,[1] that consume it.

Regular Expressions

Regular expressions are magical incantations used to extract patterns from text. They are bewildering jumbles of punctuation understood by few but used by many, since their power is great. With luck, we will not need to know much about regular expressions to perform the text processing we so require. Indeed, the mystic expressions needed to match such common strings as an email address or URL can often be found by searching online, though we should verify them against our data sets before trusting them. To learn more about regular expressions, you are best served by searching the Internet.[2]

Spreadsheet

By spreadsheet data I mean data that are present in a spreadsheet application, such as Apple's Numbers, Google Drive's Sheets, Microsoft Excel, or Libre/OpenOffice Calc.

It is perhaps misleading to separate these from other formats, as they can be created from CSV files and are often implemented as XML documents of a particular structure (as is the case with Excel and Calc). However, spreadsheet data are distinct in that they are primarily most useful in their native application and suffer elsewhere. One can export between formats or to a more neutral form such as CSV, but some features may be lost in the transition. For this reason, most sophisticated visualizations are done in simpler and more open formats that are easier to interchange between applications. If we intend to create a visualization using a tool like Processing or D3.js, we will not be able to use spreadsheet data but must export them first.

Unix

Unix is an amorphous concept. As I use it in this chapter, it stands less for a family of computer operating systems than a systems design philosophy. Unix programs are small and perform one task well but use text as a universal interface to exchange data. The output of one program can always be used as the input of another. Thus Unix is less about a specific era in the history of computers than the idea of small, interlocking parts that form a greater whole. In terms of the importance of data processing, well-established Unix tools allow us to chain together a suite of simple operations to accomplish tasks of arbitrary complexity.

XML (eXtensible Markup Language)

XML is a markup language, similar to the HTML of the web, which is composed of angle bracket–encased tags that house attributes and text. As the first word of its acronym belies, XML is extraordinarily flexible and can represent virtually any data structure because of that. However, XML's popularity is waning as JSON becomes a preferred mode for data interchange. Still, particularly in libraries, XML is popular and sometimes the only data format provided by certain sources.

Personally, I find XML data difficult to work with. It lacks both the columnar features of CSV and spreadsheet data, while also missing the programming language constructs of JSON (e.g., arrays). Code written to process XML is often more verbose and difficult to follow than JSON processing. However, XML shines when it truly is being used as a *markup* language to enhance text, such as adding annotations, hyperlinks, or formatting. It also has a robust conception of namespaces, which is useful when working with linked data concepts where every term must be associated with the domain from whence it came.

FOUR PLATEAUS

Fry's aforementioned stages of information visualization are an important guiding point, but they should not be taken as gospel. Instead, we will discuss four intermingled plateaus of data preparation: the acquisition and collection, the filtering and refinement, the processing and formatting, and the publishing of data.[3] These plateaus are interleaved; they do not occur in cleanly discrete *stages*. For instance, we might start immediately with the publishing stage by declaring our research interests and data collection methodology publicly. As we collect more data, we continually publish, perhaps on a website that allows prior versions to be viewed and compared to present work, such as the software version control service GitHub.[4] Thus the publishing plateau is not a final pinnacle to be reached *after* we obtain and process data but is present simultaneously alongside those other terrains.

Acquire/Collect

Acquiring data is increasingly becoming the easiest step in the data visualization process, as libraries monitor more and more of their services and sources of open data continue to grow. However, it is by no means straightforward to obtain *the* data we are interested in. Depending on our position within our institution, some data sets may be restricted. Departments may be possessive of their data or legitimately worry about misrepresentation. It takes social tact and negotiation skills to secure access to data outside our position's immediate responsibilities. In these situations, I find that assuring data owners that they will have a chance to review any work done with their information—and that they will likely benefit from my work—to be a strong stance.

On the other hand, open data are widely available through sites such as data.gov, wikidata.org, and datahub.io. Library-specific data sets can be found through OCLC or Open Library, to name but two major services. However, while open data make *acquisition* easier, they can complicate the other plateaus we discuss in this section. Data may be incomplete, inconsistent, in an odd format, or undocumented. Thus the work of filling in missing data, normalizing values, converting to a usable format, and discerning the data's internal structure is increased.

Thus far we have discussed obtaining fully formed data sets, but what about collecting our own data from scratch? Defining our own data collection procedures is incredibly powerful because we know the strengths and weaknesses of the collection methodology and can adjust subsequent work accordingly (for instance, by filtering out known inaccuracies). Collecting one's own data lets data processing inform collection. Were we unable to answer a research question with our available information? Was it a struggle to process the raw data into a meaningful summary? Then we can improve how data are gathered to make future efforts more successful.

Finally, data stewarding is worth discussing alongside issues of collection. Libraries often collect data with personally identifiable information (PII) included; consider circulation records attached to a patron's identity or a recording of a patron's voice during a web usability study. Even supposedly anonymized data can potentially be linked back to an individual via their patterns; the release of anonymized AOL search logs in 2006 stands as an infamous example of how inadequate naïve anonymization is (Hafner 2006). For that reason, we should avoid working with data at a level that can be linked to individuals, instead seeking aggregated forms. If we *must* work with PII, a timescale for data retention should be defined. We should keep strict standards on how long we will maintain access to the data and how securely they are stored.

Filter/Refine

Altering the data post acquisition is perhaps the hardest area to discuss in the abstract, because its nature will vary so greatly with each project. Data sets may need to be supplemented, pruned, or aggregated. We must always keep in mind that we refine our data sets to *enhance* their objectivity, not discard it. Discarding data points simply because they are problematic is unethical and distorts the meaning of the set as a whole. Rather, we should discard a datum if we can prove it to be erroneous or outside the scope of our particular investigation. Are we researching a library's virtual reference services that occur online? Then we filter out interactions with an unsuitable mode of communication, such as telephone or in person. Are we researching print circulation? Then ILS records describing DVDs are ignored. While these are two examples of *filtering* data outside our scope, *refinement* refers less to narrowing our data than improving their quality. For instance, we can utilize our knowledge of the library's hours of operation to delete inexplicable data; an in-person reference interaction at 2:00 a.m. when all library branches are closed is clearly an artifact of poor data entry. Similarly, two separate and near-identical bibliographic records for the same title need to be de-duplicated for our circulation study to be accurate.

Whatever our methods and reasoning when filtering data, documentation is utterly vital. We should maintain a running narrative of the alterations we make and their rationale. The value of this document is manifold: formally justifying our decisions strengthens them and makes us less likely to rely on indefensible personal preferences. With a detailed guide we, or anyone else, can re-create our study and generate longitudinally comparable data in the future, and we can ask others to critique our decision making to gain perspective.

Format/Process

While perhaps similar to Filter/Refine, here we are more concerned with the technical procedures of converting data from their original format to the one that our visualization software utilizes. While we may be handed an Excel file full of equations, macros, and cell references, that is rarely the most suitable form for our final product. We may need to convert equations into their raw values, export multiple worksheets into separate tabular data files, and normalize character encodings from a common Windows encoding (e.g., Windows-1252) to the more ubiquitous UTF-8.

Any nontrivial format conversion should be verified to some extent. It's easy to grab a random sample of data points to verify that all values were translated sensibly. We can perhaps inspect a random subset of ≈10 percent of our data to confirm that everything converted accordingly. Often, it's possible to verify via aggregation methods that data were transformed appropriately. For instance, if we convert from CSV to JSON, we can compute the average of a numeric field before and after conversion to virtually ensure that nothing was distorted in that particular column.

As we go along converting data from one format to another, it behooves us to keep intermediary copies of the data as they transition. If we discover down the line that something has become corrupted, we had better be able to pinpoint where in the formatting procedures this occurred and determine a fix. As mentioned at the start of this section, an ideal tool for saving snapshots of our data after each transformation is version control software such as Git. If we download an Excel file, export to CSV, and convert from CSV to JSON, we can record each alteration in a "commit" that can easily be reverted to later. Version control software is also another argument for simple, text-based file formats. Programs such as Git have a much easier time tracking the changes in a line-oriented text file than in more complicated formats meant to be read by a particular application, such as Excel spreadsheets.

Publish

Many volumes could be written on publishing data alone. Rather than devote a substantial segment of this chapter to the subject, I will simply emphasize that publishing data is important. If we want our research study to be verifiable, we *must* publish the data in some form alongside our final visualization. Beyond verifiability, publishing our data means that others can correct errors in the event that our filtering/refining was imperfect, remix our data by applying it to another visualization technique, or reuse it as part of a larger study that takes our data as but one of several sources.

There are a few major considerations when publishing data. For one, we should be wary of publishing any PII or data with strong patterns that could be linked to individuals, as discussed in the Acquire/Collect section. One value that sets libraries apart in the digital age is our commitment to patron privacy, and that absolutely extends to how we treat potentially sensitive data. If in doubt, we should not share or publish data that could reveal information about an individual without his or her explicit permission. Returning to our dual examples of reference interactions and circulation totals, it is easy to see how disaggregated data could be abused. Knowing that the library answered 73 email reference questions in the month of July is likely an unrevealing level of aggregation; knowing that one of the emails was answered at 7:05 p.m. on July 3 on the subject of illegal fireworks is potentially incriminating and could clearly be used by local law enforcement. Circulation records are an even more obvious liability, with the classic example of exposing a patron's checkout history that includes *The Anarchist's Cookbook*.

If we do publish data, it is our duty to document them thoroughly and provide them in a useful format. A raw data set with no description of its schema, data types, or collection procedures is often worse than no data at all because of the ease with which it is misinterpreted. Rather, we now find a use for all the documentation created during our Filter/Refine plateau. Furthermore, presenting a formal data schema is of immense value to potential consumers. Knowing whether a particular field is composed of integers, unique ID numbers, or floating point values has implications for how others perform their own processing of our information. While documenting a data schema is a somewhat nascent field, there is a datapackage.json standard that lets us describe our data with a lightweight metadata file we place alongside our published product (Pollock and Keegan 2015). Standardized efforts to describe data structure have the added advantage of making our data set more accessible to machines; while we do want individual researchers to be able to ascertain the meaning of our data, machine-readable documentation again enables larger meta-studies that quickly process our data via code (Phetteplace 2015).

A SERIES OF STUDIES

No single case study can easily encompass the range of work involved in preparing data for visualization. Rather, we will work through a number of small issues in a variety of projects to capture an expansive view of the topic.

Character Encoding

In our smallest case study, we can convert from uncommon or proprietary character encodings to more usable, web-friendly formats with command line tools or other software services. If you are unfamiliar with character encodings, they are essentially reductions of character sets (e.g., the Western alphabet, Arabic, Wingdings symbols) to digital representations like binary or octets. When a piece of software opens a document in an unanticipated character encoding, errors or misinterpreted characters can occur, often indicated by replacement characters. Recently, I was provided with a set of metadata files in a reusable CSV format but encoded in Mac OS Roman; inspecting the data in my terminal showed replacement characters, and the bulk metadata tool I intended to use expected UTF-8 data. I was able to convert the metadata with the "iconv" command line program that comes preinstalled on Mac OS X: (iconv(1) Mac OS X Manual Page 2015):

```
iconv -f MACROMAN -t UTF-8 metadata.csv > utf-8-metadata.csv
```

The short "-f" and "-t" flags stand for "from" and "to" respectively, while the greater than sign indicates that I am piping the converted output of the iconv command into a new file named "utf-8-metadata.csv." The iconv program knows well over a hundred different character encodings, which are listed with the "iconv --list" command.

Unix Text Processing

The Unix command line offers an incredible set of tools for processing text. What's more, the Unix philosophy of small programs that perform one task well and operate on text input has proven to be a solid historical base on which many modern tools choose to operate. For this reason, learning basic command line operations can greatly enhance our ability to meld data from a troublesome format into a useful one. For instance, say we are given a text file of author names, only there are duplicates in the file, which has no ordering logic, and we need a list of all unique names to seed our network diagram. A short chain of Unix commands produces the desired data:

```
sort authors.txt | uniq > unique-authors.txt
```

Here we first use the "sort" program to sort our text file alphabetically. Next we "pipe" the output of the sort program to the "uniq" program with the vertical bar character. The uniq program then de-duplicates identical, adjacent lines in our text file. This sorted text output is redirected into a new "unique-authors.txt" file, where it is ready to be used, using the same greater than symbol we saw in the character encoding section. This example, while trivial, demonstrates the elegant power of Unix text processing; though each program does only a simple task, the ability to chain together the output of one as the input of the next allows us to create complex text manipulation procedures. For instance, what if our author names followed the common format in authority files and had a birth and death date following them? We could use the "stream editor" sed to search for and remove date sequences from our list of names:

```
sed -e 's| [[:digit:]]*-.*||' unique-authors.txt > unique-
authors-without-dates.txt
```

The above sed command is more mysterious than those we have seen previously, but only because of the presence of regular expressions. The sed program, like sort and uniq before it, operates on a text file and has its output redirected to a new text file. The "-e 's| [[:digit:]]*-.*||'" string tells sed to perform an edit, specifically a substitution ("s"), which substitutes an empty string (the final pair of adjacent vertical bars "||"; if we wanted to replace with something instead of nothing, the replacement is set between these two characters) for character patterns like "1983-," "500-600," or "999-1020."[5] As a short aside, our process of saving the result of each procedure as a new file is good practice for an initial processing run-through. Until we are certain that our procedures are flawless, saving the inchoate results helps us rewind to a safe point if we make a tragic mistake later. The most surefire, formal way of saving our progress is by fully versioning our data using a program such as Git, Mercurial, or Subversion, but relying on meaningful files conventions is a cheap method of accomplishing the same.

But what if we have our data in the fine CSV format but want to perform slightly more complicated spreadsheet-like operations? Procedures that are conceptually simple, such as "extract all the values from the second column of our data," can become extraordinarily complex if we limit ourselves to standard command line tools such as sed, sort, and uniq. However, the csvkit suite of tools written in Python can solve these problems with ease: the in2csv tool converts from Excel or JSON to CSV; csvcut allows us to slice particular columns out of our data; csvgrep mimics the powerful Unix "grep" command except it searches over the contents of cells; csvstat reports summary statistics on our columns; csvlook renders our data as a readable table right in our terminal (Csvkit 0.9.1 — Csvkit 0.9.1 Documentation 2015). These are but a few examples of useful csvkit tools.

Returning to our earlier example, what if we had a CSV of circulation transactions and wanted to extract a list of unique authors? We know how to perform this sort of extraction with a simplistic text file, but now we can do the same with our CSV:

```
csvcut -c "Author" circulation-events.csv | tail -n +2 | sort
| uniq > unique-authors.txt
```

Assuming the column we want is labeled in the header row as "Authors," this string of procedures first extracts the authors column, removes the first line with "tail" to delete the "Author" header, sorts it alphabetically, and then de-duplicates as before. The csvkit tools are powerful and comprehensive, extending all the usual line-oriented text operations to everyone's favorite delimited data format.

While many applications can perform the operations described in this section, the strength of utilizing common Unix tools lies in the ability to write long scripts that flawlessly perform the exact same operation in the future. If we are publishing our data, it is easier to include a four-line shell script that converts our list of authors than to describe a series of Excel sorts and equations that achieve the same outcome but are less universal. We—or other parties—can update the backing data of a visualization in mere seconds by downloading a fresh batch of author names and running our script, confident that the output will be consistent with prior versions.

Custom Scripting

EZproxy is a ubiquitous piece of library technology; virtually every library needs a proxy server to provide authenticated access to its subscription databases outside of the physical library building, and a large majority choose to employ OCLC's software to do so. But what if we want to investigate our proxy server's usage patterns to inform purchasing decisions, argue for the library's value, or modify our services? EZproxy logs are packed with informative data but they are not immediately useful. Here's an example of one line from a log file:

```
12.123.23.32 - wp0Zort3D7B5a2w [20/Jan/2014:07:56:40 -0500]
"GET http://global.ebsco-content.com:80/embimages/c964b0e32e61
67277108703cad5e9f2d/52dd1d01/imh/upi/thumbnail/wax20100604733_
lg.jpg HTTP/1.1" 200 2244
```

If you can read that and garner useful clues from it, great! You can skip this section. But if you are utterly baffled at what half of the pieces mean, then it might require more work to make the raw data usable. EZproxy data are most similar to CSV format; each piece is separated by a single space. But then there are strange oddities; the timestamp is wrapped in brackets while the HTTP request details are in quotes. Even a simple conversion to the more universal CSV format is nontrivial in that respect. Furthermore, EZproxy can be set to log every HTTP request that clogs up the data with tons of lines representing rather minor events, such as the loading of a thumbnail (which is what's happening above). If we have a huge text file of thousands of HTTP requests, how can you distill it down to a metric our administrators care about, such as an individual person's session?

One method of converting EZproxy data is to write a custom script that recognizes the meaning of each element in a single line of a log file. Robin Camille Davis, emerging technologies and distance services librarian at John Jay College of Criminal Justice (CUNY), wrote a piece of code in the Python programming language to do just such a thing (2015). The script takes a directory of EZproxy log files and produces a series of aggregate statistics, such as the total number of connections, number of on-campus connections, percentage of connections that were on campus, number of connections from within the library building, number of student sessions from off campus, and number of faculty or staff sessions from off campus. It should be immediately evident how much more useful those figures are in comparison with the raw data that a particular IP address requested a certain thumbnail image at 7:00 a.m. on January 20. Camille Davis's script not only provides a high level of insight into our EZproxy usage but also enables rapid bulk processing of large sets of logs that would be cumbersome and time consuming to perform otherwise.

The Python language is ideally suited to many kinds of data processing. For one, it is meant to be a readable and easy-to-learn language that mimics the English language, more so than other languages that sometimes rely on arcane combinations of punctuation as shorthand for certain operations. Furthermore, Python has an "all batteries included" philosophy, which means that the language comes with a large number of built-in features for handling common tasks. Inspecting the EZproxy parsing script, the utility of these features is obvious: regular expressions are used to search for patterns in each line of the logs, a system module is used to accept user-entered arguments on the command line such as which directory to process the files within, and the "glob" feature makes iterating over said files straightforward. The full script is powerful yet only 124 lines long, many of which are explanatory comments and not computer code. Python's prowess is not limited to only text-based processing like this, as it has tools for manipulating numeric and scientific data as well. While Python is a strong choice for custom data processing, it is not the only one. Many scripting languages exist that aim to offer the programmer extensive control of his or her data in just a few lines of expressive code. Other languages, such as Ruby, JavaScript, and Perl, could perform the same logs analysis with ease.

Coding a custom script is certainly not the only means for processing EZproxy logs. In a blog post, Lauren Magnuson and Robin Camille Davis outline several approaches to squeezing delicious lemonade out of sour lemon server logs (2014). Besides scripts they provide several potential options for the aspiring analyst and outline the pros and cons of each, noting that AWstats, Piwik, EZpaarse, and Splunk are all useful for these purposes. I have used Sawmill to quickly summarize EZproxy data myself, extracting useful information such as what is my library's busiest month of the year, busiest day of the week, or busiest time of day and which databases are utilized disproportionately from off campus given their overall usage statistics.

While it's by no means necessary to code a custom processing solution, the ability to do so provides *full control* over our data. Particularly if we have obtuse data that are specific to our institution, coding may be the absolute best method we have of ensuring they are processed properly. EZproxy is actually not a great example due to its ubiquity; EZproxy logs are not too dissimilar from other formats of web server logs, and thus a few pieces of software come with an understanding of the log format. However, if we are faced with locally maintained vocabularies, heavily modified metadata schemas, or simply the desire to approach a common data set in a novel manner, coding knowledge is invaluable.

Normalization with OpenRefine

Names are difficult data. Whether of people, places, or institutions, names often come in a variety of forms. There is a reason that authority control is such an important concept in library science. We keep carefully maintained lists of authoritative forms of proper nouns specifically because our data would lose a substantial amount of value without them. Knowing that the strings "Samuel Clemens," "Mark Twain," and "Twain, Mark, 1835-1910" all refer to the same person allows us to provide a single access point to a set of metadata records that share a relation to that person. Consider a data set with the following entries:

```
"King, Augusta Ada, 1815-1852"
"Morrison, Toni"
"Morrison, Toni, 1931-"
"King, Augusta Ada"
"Morrison, Toni 1931-"
"Lovelace, Ada"
```

To a machine, these are six distinct entities and if we attempt to construct a visualization without combining like entities it will fail to be an accurate representation. The total times that a given entity appears will be reduced by the varied forms it takes. Given just six lines, we can easily use our human cognition to sort them into two identities. But at a large scale this sorting becomes arduous. Even a series of search-and-replace operations in a common text editor are not viable. We may miss a subtle difference, like the missing comma after "Toni" in "Morrison, Toni 1931-." Repeating our exact same set of replacements on a new data set would still be tedious and require that we painstakingly document each change. It is simply not scalable to normalize a large batch of names over and over again without specialized software to assist us.

Luckily, there is software that shines in this area. OpenRefine is an incredible piece of open source software designed to make bulk transformations on data sets easy and repeatable. In fact, OpenRefine performs many of the actions we have seen in other sections of this chapter. It can use values in one column to pull in and parse information from an external web service API. It can accept data in a variety of formats and character encodings, translating them into a spreadsheet-like interface. However, OpenRefine does not focus on graphs and equations the way that other spreadsheet software typically does. Rather, it focuses on facets and filters that allow us to combine and parse our data quickly. Most valuably, it comes with several built-in algorithms for identifying likely duplicates; OpenRefine acts almost like a human in seeing that "Morrison, Toni" and "Morrison, Toni, 1931-" should be clustered together as the same entity.

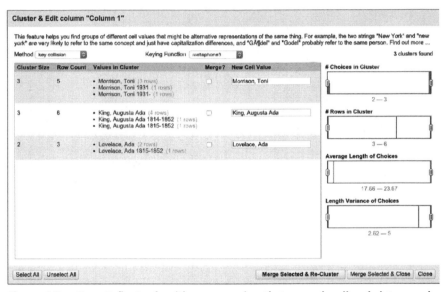

Figure 1.3. **OpenRefine's algorithms recognize that several cells of data can be combined.**

Even in the instances where OpenRefine's algorithms are insufficient, we can create custom facets that combine terms. So we can write our own facet to tell the software that "Lovelace, Ada" and "King, Augusta Ada" are indeed identical. This may seem like a step backward to the manifold search-and-replace activities I disparaged earlier, but the true beauty of OpenRefine lies in how it stores a history of our operations in an exportable file. Remember my emphasis on documenting our data processing as we go about it? OpenRefine does that for us but in a machine-readable format. This means that applying a long series of intricate, order-sensitive operations on a huge data set suddenly becomes trivial when we have done it once; we can save the operations in OpenRefine to repeat them later in the future and ensure that future data processing is identical to past instances. Not only that, we can share sets of effective transformations with colleagues or other researchers working with similar data sets.

OpenRefine, like many of the tools discussed in these brief case studies, is flexible and capable of much more than just ensuring a set of names conform to a consistent standard. It can perform common text cleanup across an entire column of tabular data with a single click, trimming leading or trailing whitespace or transforming text into a particular case (lowercase, title case, etc.). For some reason, many systems and data formats adhere to the bad practice of stuffing multiple pieces of information into a single field. For instance, consider a course information system that handles a single course with multiple faculty members by stuffing their names into a single field and separating them with a comma. When dealing with difficult data such as this, OpenRefine's ability to split or join multivalued cells becomes a big timesaver. Rather than expend time and mental energy writing a custom procedure (whether in code or as an Excel equation) to break up this data, we can import it into Open-Refine and export a more workable CSV in minutes.

ASSESSING IMPACT

To discuss the impact of data cleanup, I present one final case study. At a prior institution, a small community college where many students drove from their homes to class, I was a member of a sustainability committee. We were tasked with estimating the total carbon emissions of the college as part of our participation in the American College and University Presidents' Climate Commitment (Home | Presidents' Climate Commitment 2015). Many pieces of the puzzle could be put together with information from our facilities or budgetary offices, but calculating student commute mileage was a challenge. We knew that it was likely a large portion of our total emissions, but there was no easy way to determine it given the data at hand, which was course schedules for all our students.

First of all, student course schedules are obviously personal information. It would be highly troubling were someone to gain access to a schedule without authorization. So I created a data retention plan to delete all but the aggregated data totals and equations used to derive them three months after the project was completed. I also introduced another layer of anonymization into the data, removing student ID numbers that could be traced to individuals and replacing them with different unique identifiers. My eventual goal was to derive an approximation of how many miles each student drove during the academic year from a course schedule and home zip code. To do so, I utilized many of the approaches discussed in this chapter. I filtered out extraneous data that didn't relate to automobile emissions: online classes, classes taught to local high schools, and inexplicable data such as classes that apparently never met. I had to adjust for factors such as students dropping out midsemester; hybrid classes that had only half of their sessions in person; finals; classes that met twice on the same day, thus implying only a single trip to campus (e.g., science laboratory courses); and students who took what limited public transit was available in the area.

With an estimation of the number of trips each student took to campus, I still needed to derive the distance from their homes to each of our campuses. So I employed a Google Maps API that accepted a "from" and "to" zip code and returned a distance in miles. But eyeing over the mileage data, I spotted some strange results. We had students commuting from Texas and the middle of the German countryside! It turned out that some of our students listed zip codes that do not exist in our system, which Google Maps interpreted as foreign addresses, and others listed a home address where they clearly did not live during the academic year. I had to further filter our data set by removing rows that met an arbitrary standard of feasibility; no one was commuting from hundreds of miles away. The final piece of the equation—taking mileage and converting it into emissions—was actually done for me by a spreadsheet application designed exclusively for the purpose of calculating an institution's emissions. It uses an average gas mileage of American automobiles to produce a number of metric tons of carbon dioxide.

There were many assumptions made throughout the process of estimating carbon emissions from student commuting. I had to repeatedly adjust my ideas of how classes were scheduled and where students were coming from by performing a data transformation and inspecting its effects. The final product, however, was quite worth it; we produced a few bold graphics to demonstrate the primary sources of the college's emissions and displayed them prominently at a major campus event. These figures further informed policy decisions at the college and how best we could begin approaching carbon neutrality. Knowing student commuting totals, even as the rough estimate we had, was a key ingredient in our planning. Besides leaving behind a series of spreadsheets with painstakingly developed equations, I also wrote a long narrative document describing each operation, the rationale behind the equations, and the assumptions made. This document makes it easier to re-create my steps and inspect my assumptions for flaws.

Often, the difficulty with data cleanup is knowing when to stop. If our goals are strictly defined at the start—we just need the data in a slightly different format, we want to normalize certain values, etc.—then completing them is no challenge. In this case, the value of our work is often obvious since without it the creation of a corresponding visual would be impossible. But if our objective is more nebulous, we can spend much time endlessly tweaking our data set in an attempt to perfect it. Much as writers struggle with endless revisions, we need to stop at some point and publish. I could have spent years fine-tuning our commuting data, but deadlines demanded I do the best I could within a restricted timeframe. Luckily, the open-ended nature of data processing works well with iterative design; we clean up our data, experiment with a visualization, consider its efficacy, and repeat. Only once our visual is compelling can we claim that our data cleanup is complete.

CONCLUSION

Data cleanup is a difficult and perilous task. It requires not only variegated skills, from statistical analysis to coding to knowledge of sophisticated software, but also subjective decision making. The line between removing irrelevant noise from a data set and introducing bias is often razor thin. While the visual steps that follow early stage data sculpting are more glamorous and yield more interesting results, they are not necessarily more important. Edward Tufte (1990) famously said, "If the statistics are boring, then you've got the wrong numbers." Investing time and effort in the earliest stages of data visualization to ensure that your collection and filtering procedures are top notch is the best way to obtain the *right* numbers.

NOTES

1. D3.js refers to the Data-Driven Documents JavaScript library, which is a widely used code library for creating data visualizations. Examples of D3.js will be discussed in chapter 3 of this volume. For more information, see https://d3js.org.

2. I would be remiss not to mention two of my favorite sources for learning regular expressions: Kim, Bohyun. 2013. "Fear No Longer Regular Expressions." *ACRL TechConnect Blog*. July 31. http://acrl.ala.org/techconnect/?p=3549; Verou, Lea. 2012. "/Reg(exp){2}lained/: Demystifying Regular Expressions." Presented at the O'Reilly Fluent, San Francisco, CA, May 29. https://www.youtube.com/watch?v=EkluES9Rvak.

3. I use the word *plateau* deliberately, following philosophers Gilles Deleuze and Felix Guattari in conceiving it as a medium to be passed through and returned to, not a final destination. See: Deleuze, Gilles, and Félix Guattari. 1987. *A Thousand Plateaus: Capitalism and Schizophrenia*. Minneapolis: University of Minnesota Press.

4. GitHub is a repository hosting service that is used for storing and sharing code and version control information through the Git version control system. Accounts can be created for free at https://github.com.

5. I do not claim that this pattern sufficiently captures the possible forms of dates in authorized name formats; for instance it does not accommodate AD/AH/BC/BCE calendar abbreviations, which might precede a date. The best way to identify an appropriate pattern is by inspecting one's own data and seeing what works sufficiently, as the possible formats for any string of text (whether it be a name, date, etc.) are incredibly diverse.

REFERENCES

Camille Davis, Robin. 2015. "Robincamille/ezproxy-Analysis." *GitHub*. Accessed August 2, 2015. https://github.com/robincamille/ezproxy-analysis.

"Csvkit 0.9.1 — Csvkit 0.9.1 Documentation." 2015. *Csvkit 0.9.1*. Accessed July 27, 2015. https://csvkit.readthedocs.org/en/0.9.1/.

Deleuze, Gilles, and Félix Guattari. 1987. *A Thousand Plateaus: Capitalism and Schizophrenia.* Minneapolis: University of Minnesota Press.

ECMA International. 2013. *The JSON Data Interchange Format.* 1st ed. Geneva. http://www .ecma-international.org/publications/files/ECMA-ST/ECMA-404.pdf.

Fry, Ben. 2008. *Visualizing Data.* Beijing; Cambridge: O'Reilly Media, Inc.

Hafner, Katie. 2006. "Researchers Yearn to Use AOL Logs, but They Hesitate." *The New York Times,* August 23, sec. Technology. http://www.nytimes.com/2006/08/23/ technology/23search.html.

"Home | Presidents' Climate Commitment." 2015. Accessed August 2, 2015. http://www .presidentsclimatecommitment.org/.

"iconv(1) Mac OS X Manual Page." 2015. *OS X Man Pages.* Accessed July 20, 2015. https:// developer.apple.com/library/mac/documentation/Darwin/Reference/ManPages/man1/ iconv.1.html.

"JSON." 2015. Accessed July 11, 2015. http://json.org/.

Kim, Bohyun. 2013. "Fear No Longer Regular Expressions." *ACRL TechConnect Blog.* http:// acrl.ala.org/techconnect/?p=3549.

Magnuson, Lauren, and Robin Camille Davis. 2014. "Analyzing EZProxy Logs." Blog. *ACRL TechConnect Blog.* http://acrl.ala.org/techconnect/?p=4684.

Phetteplace, Eric. 2015. "A Forray into Publishing Open Data on GitHub." *ACRL TechConnect Blog.* http://acrl.ala.org/techconnect/?p=5084.

Pollock, Rufus, and Martin Keegan. 2015. "Data Packages." *Data Protocols Lightweight Standards and Patterns for Data.* http://dataprotocols.org/data-packages/.

Tufte, Edward R. 1990. *Envisioning Information.* Cheshire, CT: Graphics Press.

Verou, Lea. 2012. "/Reg(exp){2}lained/: Demystifying Regular Expressions." Presented at the O'Reilly Fluent, San Francisco, CA. https://www.youtube.com/watch?v=EkluES9Rvak.

2

Designing Public Visualizations of Library Data

Angela M. Zoss

As in many other organizations and fields of inquiry, the data generated by libraries becomes ever more complex, and the need to communicate trends both internally and externally has also been increasing. As visualizations become increasingly embedded in library assessment and outreach, it is crucial to take into consideration the audience of the visualizations and to design visualizations that are easy to interpret. This chapter will walk readers through the process of selecting a visualization based on a particular data representation need, designing that visualization to be optimized to its specific purpose, and combining visualizations into larger narratives to engage a public audience.

The process of choosing, designing, and combining visualizations in a way that is engaging to a broader public requires an understanding of how visualizations convert data into shapes or spatial arrangements that can be analyzed and understood. Various types of visualizations have been developed over the centuries to take advantage of human skills and acuities. To understand why some work better than others in certain situations, it helps to first examine the components of these graphs and how well they match up with what humans are good at.

Several studies have been done to explore how well individuals read different components of visualizations. Cleveland and McGill (1985) conducted a seminal study in which users were asked to evaluate two data elements in terms of the proportion one represented of the other. This task was performed using multiple visual representations: position, length, angle, slope, and area. The results suggested that individuals are much better at assessing numerical data using position and length encodings than they are using slope or area of a shape. This study was replicated and extended by Heer and Bostock (2010), who confirmed that position and length afford more accuracy than slope or area, including both circular and rectangular areas.

A quote from Moritz Stefaner (2012), a professional visualization designer and researcher, summarizes this and related academic and professional work around designing data visualizations: "position is everything, color is difficult." The following section will explore how these studies and inherent properties of different types of visualizations can be used to select an appropriate visualization for a data need.

VISUALIZATION SELECTION

This section will review common types of charts and maps and discuss their strengths and weaknesses in relation to different types of data and audiences. For example, some visualizations are matched well with the visual acuities of humans, some are good at filling space on a page, and some can be especially engaging for a public audience. Additional visualization-specific design suggestions will accompany the discussions of each visualization type.

Basic charts and graphs[1] (as opposed to custom/novel visualizations or highly scientific plots) are the easiest visualizations to produce, as well as the easiest visualizations for a broad audience to understand. Their ubiquity does not, however, mean that all chart types can be equally well understood by all people. First, different charts use different visual encodings, and those encodings match up differently with human perceptual abilities. Second, people do not have equal exposure to all chart types. Depending on someone's educational background, she or he may have more or less practice interpreting a particular chart type. Third, the data being visualized may have properties that do not match well with a particular chart type, making the resulting chart difficult or impossible to read effectively.

Choosing an appropriate chart type requires familiarity with the chart options available, as well as with the properties of the data and the purpose of the chart. What trends in the data are most important? What chart will best show those trends? Who is going to be reading the chart? The following section will review six basic chart types: bar charts, pie charts, line charts, scatterplots, bubble charts, and heat maps. Each chart will be presented with a discussion of the best uses of the chart, the most common concerns with the chart, and any additional suggestions about the use of the chart.

Bar Chart

Bar charts are a staple of data visualization—especially those that are intended for a broad audience. They are some of the most general types of charts, with few limits on the kind of data that can be used. Here are just a few basic design tips to watch out for to make sure you're taking full advantage of how powerful they can be.

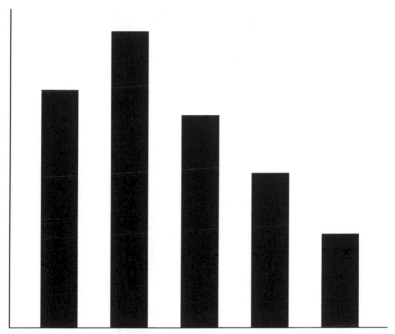

Figure 2.1. A basic bar chart.

Data. The most basic form of a bar chart[2] involves one categorical variable and one numerical variable. The categories from the categorical variable are each given a bar, and the quantities from the numerical variable are used to determine the length of the bar. An optional, additional categorical variable can be added to make either a grouped bar chart (where several bars appear next to each other for each category in the original categorical variable) or a stacked bar chart (where the original bar is split up into several colored segments, stacked on top of each other).

Strengths. Bar charts are especially good for times when it's important to be able to read numbers accurately off the chart. The reason for this lies in the human visual system. Humans have excellent perceptual acuity for differences in alignment and line length (Cleveland and McGill 1985, Ware 2013). Bar charts are also extremely common. They are some of the first charts we learn to read and produce. Comparing the individual bars to each other or exploring the overall trend across categories are both good uses for a bar chart.

Weaknesses. Bar charts have a few common concerns, however. First, labeling the bars with long phrases can cause design problems. If the bars are vertical, it can be difficult to make the bar labels horizontal; the words will be much wider than the bars, leaving large gaps or awkward line breaks in the labels. If, on the other hand, the bars are horizontal, it is very easy to have long labels for each bar. The text height and the bar height can be very similar, and the wide format for the chart fits much better with the aspect ratio of screens nowadays.

Sometimes one or two bars will be much longer than the others; consider creating a second chart in which you exclude the long bar and zoom in on the shorter bars (Few 2012) or investigate whether several categories can be combined into an "other" category. Also consider what comparisons or evaluations are most important for your bar chart; if alphabetical order is not relevant for your data, for example, it might make sense to sort the bars instead by length (Cleveland 1994).

Most important, however, is to pay attention to the numerical axis of the bar chart. Because humans are so good at perceiving differences in length between bars, having the axis start at anything other than zero will distort how the length corresponds to the data. This renders the bars, which are a powerful visual cue, inaccurate and hard to ignore. The numerical axes for bar charts should always start at zero (Few 2012, Yau 2013).

Pie Chart

Along with bar charts, pie charts are also very common in infographics, reports, etc. They are the subject of much discussion and often criticized because of the many problems associated with them, but they are still a valuable chart in certain contexts.

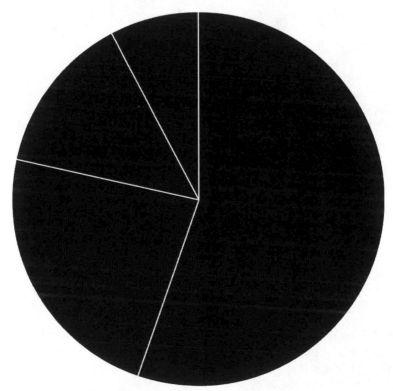

Figure 2.2.   A basic pie chart.

Data. Like a bar chart, a pie chart is built from one categorical variable and one numerical variable. In a bar chart, each category becomes a separate bar. In a pie chart, each category becomes a separate wedge of the pie. The proportion of the total data associated with each category is represented by the area of the wedge. Typically, programs that create pie charts will start the first wedge at the "12:00" position of the circle and proceed clockwise. Programs also typically assign a different color to each wedge; this color is then used to match a wedge with the legend entry for the wedge. If wedges are instead labeled directly, they can each have the same color, provided a contrasting border color is used to show the wedge boundaries (Wong 2010).

Strengths. Pie charts are a favorite when people want to show a part-to-whole relationship. That is, when you have data on the total amount of some variable, like a budget, it is natural to want to represent the subdivisions of that total in a way that shows that all of the parts add up to the total. Pie charts also are quite common and easy to produce, so audience familiarity should be relatively high.

It has been said that the best data set for a pie chart is a single number. Focusing on one category and how much of the total data it represents can be very compelling. This technique is used more frequently in an infographic context—one where data are reduced to bite-sized pieces—rather than a reporting context, where completeness may be important.

Weaknesses. Humans are notoriously bad at reading data values from pie charts. Our perceptual system is not very precise at evaluating angles, orientations, or two-dimensional areas (Cleveland and McGill 1985, Heer and Bostock 2010). With each wedge rotated in space, it is incredibly difficult either to read precise values or to compare wedges, especially those that do not appear next to each other.

This problem is compounded if the differences between data values are very small. For example, if you have five categories and each is only slightly above or slightly below 20 percent of the total, the fine distinctions will be lost to chart readers. If the goal of your chart is to help readers understand small differences, the pie chart may not be the better choice; consider switching to a bar chart. If, on the other hand, there are noticeable differences in the sizes of most of your wedges, you can make sure to help your readers as much as possible by putting the wedges in decreasing order by size (i.e., left-hand edge of largest wedge at "12:00," followed on the right by next largest wedge, etc.).[3] Sorting by size can aid readers in making relative estimates of data values.

Also beware of data that do not have a true part-to-whole relationship. One example might be data that change over time—for example, where each "category" is a single year. In this case, there is a mismatch between the visual encoding or the visual metaphor (one that joins parts of the chart into a solid shape) and the nature of the data (one where a single variable is changing over time). Combining multiple years does not often result in a meaningful total, so encoding that total as a visual element (a completed circle) is seldom necessary or natural. Time-based variables are often a good match for line charts, which will be discussed next.

Pie charts have another notorious concern—the use of three-dimensional special effects. Some programs allow the chart's creator to add a special effect that renders charts as though they are 3D objects. This may simply involve drawing a 2D pie chart to look like it is popping forward, but it may also involve actually tilting the chart "away" from the reader. This tilting effect causes an extreme distortion of the visual area of the chart (Skau 2011). The wedge at the bottom of the chart will end up taking up much more of the chart space than it would in a 2D version, and the wedges at the top will take up much less chart space than they should. Thus, in a tilted pie chart, neither the angle nor the area of the wedges accurately corresponds to the data values in question. An already difficult chart to read has become highly distorted. Consider settling for the more boring, but much more faithful, 2D version (Few 2012).

The final problem with pie charts occurs when there are a large number of categories (see figure 1 in the photospread), which can result in very small slices, including ones that may even be invisible depending on the size of the chart. A large number of categories can also lead to difficulties with color if the program you are using assigns a new color to each wedge. If the program has to repeat the same color multiple times, it becomes hard to match a wedge to the correct entry in the legend. If wedges are labeled directly to solve the color problem, the many labels can add a lot of visual complexity to the chart. If the data have a natural grouping, you could combine wedges into larger categories or simply create an "other" category for wedges under a certain size.

Line Chart

Line charts are more limited than bar charts and don't necessarily match well with proportional data, but they are very well suited to visualizing continuity and temporal data. The main concerns involve data complexity or consistency.

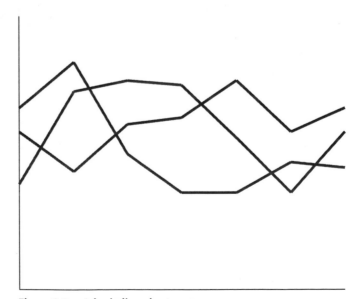

Figure 2.3.   A basic line chart.

Data. Line charts typically show change over time. As such, they often use one date variable (for the horizontal axis) and one numerical variable (for the vertical axis). If your software program does not require line charts to use dates, the program might treat that axis as a series of ordered categories (like days of the week) or just as another numerical variable (like treating years as integers). An extra categorical variable can be used to split the line into multiple lines, one for each category.

Strengths. The continuity of the line in a line chart is a great match for data that change continually over time. Pie charts, as previously discussed, should be used for only separate categories that add up to a meaningful whole. A bar chart is a good general chart and can be used either for parts of a whole or for quantities that change over time, but the separations between bars do not reinforce the idea that data are changing in a more fluid manner.

The line chart also offers practical features beyond a bar chart. First, the line chart can be more elegant than a bar chart when you add a category variable. Imagine looking at a data set over time with a grouped bar chart. For each time point, you will have several bars, but they have to be placed next to each other. This will add width to the chart and make it difficult for the eye to connect the bars that represent a single category. The other option, a stacked bar chart, makes it very difficult to read the exact value of each category because all but the bottom-most category start at a value other than zero.

A line chart can fix both of these problems. Each data point is positioned from the bottom of the y-axis;[4] data points within a single category are clearly connected by lines; and the data points from all categories line up vertically at each time point, keeping the width of the chart manageable.

A final benefit of using a line chart is that the date measurements do not have to be evenly spaced. Bars default to even spacing, which would distort how quickly data are changing if, say, some dates are a single year apart while others are two or three years apart. With a line chart, the horizontal position of the data points is (or should be) precise, corresponding exactly to the date and accurately representing the distance between measurements. (See figure 2 in the photospread.)

Weaknesses. The strengths of the line chart become its weaknesses when it comes to data overlap. Unlike bar and pie charts, line charts have nothing that prevents the lines from covering each other up. Typically line charts use color to differentiate the lines, which can help when lines cross a lot, but this also makes it more difficult for users to read the chart. Users end up needing to look back and forth between the chart and the legend to identify the lines. Where possible, placing labels on the chart, next to the lines, can improve readability and potentially even eliminate the need to use color for identifying categories.

Depending on the software being used, you may still need to worry about the problem of uneven spacing between date measurements. If your dates look more like categories—for example, if you are using the names of months, you may have to create the complete list of all possible months and then leave "null" values or zeroes for the months that have no data. (For a good discussion about how to deal with missing data in a line chart, see Kandel et al. [2011]).

Finally, if you use a simple style (i.e., a plain line) for your line chart, you may find that it is hard to tell where the data points are. The measured data will be visible only if the line bends one way or the other at that particular point. If the slope of the line is relatively consistent, it is hard to tell how evenly spaced the data are. Consider adding small dots on top of the line to clarify where the measurements are, especially if they are unevenly distributed (Few 2012). It is typically not necessary to use multiple shapes for these dots; a single shape (e.g., a circle) for all lines will help maintain a consistent style and ensure that each data point is equally visible.

Scatterplot

Scatterplots are some of the most precise and data-dense charts available for visualization. Special patterns in scatterplots can reveal strong trends in a data set or even suggest errors or outliers in the data (Yau 2013). Scatterplots are a great match for our perceptual system, but they can fall short in terms of audience familiarity.

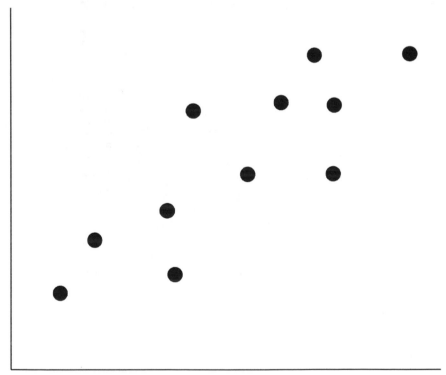

Figure 2.4.   A basic scatterplot.

Data. Scatterplots are typically used to show the relationship between two numerical variables. Each variable is assigned to an axis, and a point is placed in space so that it lines up with the correct values on each axis. An additional categorical or numerical variable can be added to change the color or shade of the dots in the scatterplot. A slight variation on the scatterplot, often called a bubble chart, will change the size (specifically, the area) of the dots according to yet another numerical variable.

Strengths. Scatterplots offer a visual representation of the correlation of two numerical variables. If there is a strong (linear)[5] relationship between these variables, the dots will form something like a line, angled either from top left to bottom right (negative correlation) or from bottom left to top right (positive correlation). Scatterplots are also useful for showing clusters of data points (i.e., data points that are much closer to each other than they are to other data points) or outliers (i.e., individual data points that are very different from the rest of the data points) (Yau 2013).

A scatterplot also can be used as a general form to make other types of charts. Take, for example, a data set where you want to see the distribution—or range of values—for a particular variable. Maybe you have the number of pages each user read of a particular ebook. You don't necessarily need to know the name of each user; you just want to see how the different users varied from each other, what the lowest and highest values were, etc. Instead of making a bar chart, which could take up a lot of space, you could use a scatterplot in which one axis is the number of pages read and the other axis is a single value—basically, a fake integer representing the name of the book. This is called a one-dimensional scatterplot (Cleveland 1994), or strip plot (Few 2012), and all of the dots representing the users will be places in a single vertical or horizontal line. This will help you see clearly whether there is a pattern across these ebook readers or if they vary wildly, and the chart itself will be very compact. The distribution of a variable can also be shown with a histogram (see previous note), which may be a better option if you have a lot of data points or if many of the data points lie on top of each other.

Note, however, that this simplified scatterplot technique would also work for multiple books. You could assign a different fake number to each book, and the data points for each book would then show up in parallel lines on the chart. More generally, this is how you can use a categorical variable, like book title or genre, with a scatterplot. This can even be used as a replacement for a bar chart. Each category is assigned to a different integer, and each category has a single numerical value, or a single dot. Because the dot is not visually powerful in the same way as a bar, this type of chart—often called a dot plot—does not require a full numerical axis that goes all the way to zero (Cleveland 1994, Few 2012). See figure 3 of the photospread for examples of using scatterplots with different combinations of variables.

Weaknesses. One of the primary weaknesses of scatterplots is that they are less common than bar charts, pie charts, and line charts. It does require some training to be able to detect and make sense of trends in dot patterns, and the sheer number of data points may also be overwhelming.

Likewise, the more data you have, the greater the chance that dots will cover each other up. Unlike the line chart, where lines coming into and out of data points can help users infer an obscured data point, scatterplot points can simply disappear when drawn on top of each other. Some solutions involve using transparency to show when multiple dots are stacked, using logarithmic axes to space dots out more toward the lower ends of the data values, or even using aggregation to total up the number of points that are in exactly the same spot (Cleveland 1994). This gives you an additional variable that you can encode as either color or size to make a bubble chart.

Bubble charts, though, have an additional weakness. Like a pie chart, a bubble chart requires users to compare the areas of different shapes to understand trends in the data. Comparing the areas of circles has been found to be extremely difficult (Cleveland 1994), and bubble size is thus not a good match for data that need to be interpreted precisely. If you have three numerical variables and you would like to show them all on the same chart, it is best to use the axes for the two that are most important or that require the most precision.

Heat Map

Heat maps are much less common than the other types of charts, but they can be extremely useful for representing a large amount of data. They are more appropriate for general trends than for precise data lookup.

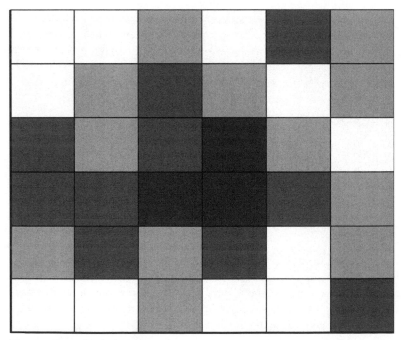

Figure 2.5. A basic heat map.

Data. Heat maps show data in rows and columns, much like a standard table. The difference between a table and a heat map is that every number in a table cell is converted to a color. The grid of a heat map can be created with categorical or numerical variables. For categorical variables, each category becomes a separate row (or column). For numerical variables that are easily separated, such as integers, the values can be treated just like categories. For continuous numerical variables, though, it is typical to create number ranges (see previous note on histograms). Within the grid, a third numerical variable (often the number of data points associated with that particular row and column) is encoded as the color of the cell.

Strengths. While not a common data visualization, heat maps fill a gap in the ability of visualizations to highlight the relationships between two categorical variables. Grouped or stacked bar charts can also visualize two categorical variables along with a numerical variable, but both make it difficult to see interesting interactions between the categories, and both prioritize one variable over the other (see figure 4 of the photospread). Laying two categorical variables out on a grid gives both of those variables equal focus. Finally, heat maps are also very space efficient; they can compress an amazing amount of data into a small area (Munzner 2014).

Weaknesses. The primary weakness of a heat map is that the numerical variable cannot be read precisely. The color encoding may give a sense of what categories are consistently high or low or where the interaction between two categories results in a high point or a low point. Like area encoding, however, (numerical) color encoding does not allow data to be matched precisely to a data value. Humans are simply not proficient at detecting small changes in the brightness or saturation of a color and matching the changes to a data range.

Another weakness of heat maps is that they are relatively uncommon. While they can be produced even in common spreadsheet programs, they do not appear as an official chart type. This makes them harder to produce than other chart types, and the lack of popularity also means that users will be less familiar with them.

Finally, heat maps are highly dependent on the order of the rows and columns to reveal similarities between different categories within the same variable. If the categories do not have a natural ordering—say, if they are institution names instead of months of the year—you may wish to inspect the data to see whether some of the categories should be placed next to each other (Yau 2013).

MAPS

Data often include a spatial component. Maps can be a very powerful way to engage an audience and to highlight patterns in data that relate strongly to location. Sometimes, however, location data are a red herring. Sometimes the patterns in your data are not inherently spatial (Wong 2010). Even if location is important, sometimes a map is too constraining to show the data well.

For example, you may have data on where website traffic is coming from (see figure 2.6). In all likelihood, most of the traffic is coming from the country in which your university is located. Maybe a few other countries are represented, but there may be no spatial pattern to where those other requests are coming from. There may be a small number of those external requests, and they might be scattered across the rest of the globe, hard to see among the many countries without data and the large oceans. That would be a lot of space devoted to showing a very small amount of data, and unless location turns out to be important somehow (e.g., requests are coming only from places in a particular time zone), there may be a better visualization type than a map. Remember—position is everything in data visualization. When you use a map, you lose the ability to encode a variable (or two!) by position.

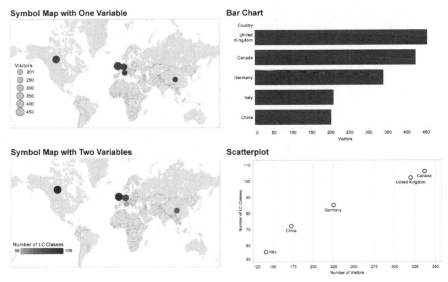

Figure 2.6.   Two symbol maps focusing on locations.

If spatial patterns are important, however, maps can often immediately pull users in by helping them "find themselves" in the data. Different types of maps allow for different types of data analysis. This chapter will focus on the two most common types of maps for data presentation: choropleth maps and (proportional) symbol maps.

Choropleth Map

Choropleth maps are a basic and common map type. They fill the borders of geographic regions (e.g., countries and states) with colors that represent data. They are easy to create with a variety of tools and easy to read. While there are some problems to be aware of, knowing how to use these maps well can lead to maps that are very easy to read.

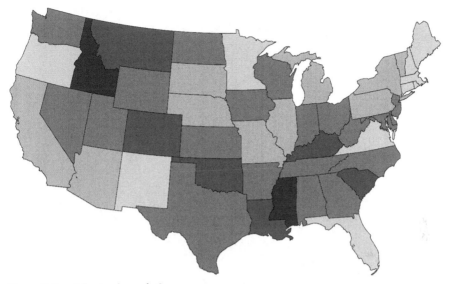

Figure 2.7. A basic choropleth map.

Data. Choropleth maps typically take two variables—the name of the region of interest and a numerical or categorical variable that gets converted into a color. When using a numerical variable with a choropleth map, cartographers often use number ranges (see the note on histograms) instead of a continuous color scale. This is a way to adjust for unevenness in the numerical variable. For example, if your data values are very skewed and you have a lot of very low values, you might want to limit how many of those low values show up as a very light color. You can set up number ranges that start out very narrow and gradually get larger, grouping together enough data points in the upper ranges that the map shows a good amount of differentiation.

Strengths. Choropleths are especially good for making sure that data points do not overlap each other. Map regions can get very complicated, but in most cases it is easy to draw boundaries and keep data separate from one region to another. Choropleths can also take advantage of audience familiarity with particular region shapes; the shape of a county, state, or country can sometimes stand on its own, without the need for a label, which could add visual complexity.

Weaknesses. The major weakness of a choropleth map is that sometimes large regions take up a huge amount of visual space but don't necessarily warrant that much attention. On the iconic "red state/blue state" maps that emerge around election times in the United States, large but sparsely populated states such as Montana end up making the country look like a lot of the population leans "red." In truth, the densely populated areas such as large cities take up very little visual space but can have a much larger effect on the results of an election.

The other major weakness of a choropleth map is that the only variables are a location variable and a single extra variable. Being wedded to both the accurate position and the accurate size of regions means that both of these encodings are unavailable. Special maps called "cartograms" play with this notion by changing the size of the regions while trying to keep them looking approximately the same as the true regions. For example, Montana might shrink down in proportion to the number of Electoral College votes it has, while New York and California would swell quite a bit. The distortion can make these difficult to read, depending on how different the region ends up looking, and it is also hard to find software that will create cartograms.

Symbol Map

Symbol maps use a standard map in the background, but the data are encoded in circles that are placed on top of the correct locations. These maps are becoming more common, but they fall prey to some of the same problems experienced by scatterplots and bubble charts.

Figure 2.8.   A basic symbol map.

   Data. Symbol maps, or proportional symbol maps, place a circle on top of a location of interest. The circles can then be sized by a (positive) numerical variable and colored by a numerical or categorical variable.
   Strengths. Symbol maps avoid the limitations of choropleths and can encode two separate variables, in addition to location. They also make it easier to draw attention to small regions on the map that are more important than large regions, without distorting the underlying map. Finally, symbol maps are the standard way of creating maps for data related to cities. While cities do have borders and could be filled,

typically the borders of a city are not recognizable, and most cities are so far apart that the filled regions would be much too small to show the data trends.

Weaknesses. When changing filled borders for area-encoded circles, however, the danger of overlapping circles arises. As with a scatterplot, there are a few possible solutions. Transparency and aggregation are possible solutions. Also, this map requires making comparisons based on area, which is not an easy task. Precision judgments would be better served by a bar chart.

GENERAL DESIGN SUGGESTIONS

In addition to the visualization-specific design suggestions mentioned above, there are other design suggestions that apply across visualizations. This section will focus on the color and text used within visualizations. Color is one of the most complex considerations in the design of visualizations, and careful color selections are essential to the success of the visualization. Text may seem like a strange focus for a section on visualization design, but the text of a visualization plays an integral role in its interpretation.

Color

How color is used in a chart or map has a huge effect on both how the audience engages with the chart and how easily and accurately the data are interpreted. If chosen carefully, color differences can be perceived almost instantaneously and used easily for data interpretation. On the other hand, color that is chosen poorly can severely impede how well individuals can read the chart, either by creating optical illusions or by obscuring genuine trends in the data. Color contrast is an important consideration for all chart elements, but there are also specific concerns when color is used to encode either numerical or categorical variables.

Color Contrast

The first aspect of color to consider is how well the colors of the chart or map show up against the background of the chart. This is called contrast, and it is a way of ensuring that, at a very basic level, the elements of your chart will be visible and clear (Few 2012). In general, elements that have the most contrast with the background color will draw the most attention.

For light backgrounds, this means that the most important elements of your chart should be the darkest. Supporting elements, like grid lines, axes, etc., are typically not the most important parts of the chart. It often works well to make these elements lighter and thinner to allow users to focus on the data elements. For some charts and tasks, it is even possible to remove nondata elements entirely; if precise data lookup is not important or if data points are labeled with the precise data values, it may even be possible to remove the axis.

After the contrast of the nondata elements has been reduced, you can begin to make choices about the chart itself. If you are not currently using color to visually encode a variable, you may have a completely monochromatic chart—all blue bars, for example. Consider using a medium contrast color for this default color. This creates an opportunity to use a high contrast color to highlight one area of the chart or one special data point (Few 2012). Say you want to compare your institution to other similar institutions. You could color the bars for the other institutions in a medium gray color and color the bar for your institution in a darker color (e.g., blue or red).

Even if you are using color to visually encode a variable, there are still choices to make. Contrast between the background color and the foreground (data) element colors must be maximized, but there must also be some contrast between data elements of different colors. The purpose of data visualization is to be able to quickly tell the difference between data elements that are, in fact, different. When data colors are too close to each other, especially for categorical data, the user will have to spend more time and attention to evaluate the patterns in the data. With proper contrast between the data colors, this process becomes what is called "pre-attentive," or something that happens so fast that we perceive it almost immediately and don't have to focus on it (Healey and Enns 2012).

Keeping data colors distinct from each other is much easier when the colors are mostly dark than when they are mostly light. That is, it is much easier to perceive differences between reds and purples than pinks and lavenders. In truth, some variation in lightness greatly helps both for readability and the ability to print color graphics in grayscale, but data colors should typically be mostly dark or mostly light in order to select an appropriate background color. Because staying with mostly dark colors increases contrast options, using light backgrounds and dark colors is typically safe. Black on white charts may look boring and antiquated, but there are good perceptual reasons for dark on light rather than light on dark. (Note, however, that yellow is always perceptually light, even though we normally consider it to be a primary color like blue and orange. Yellow does not offer enough contrast against a white background to be visible.) The next two sections focus specifically on choosing colors for encoding either numerical or categorical variables.

Color for Numerical Variables

Using color to represent a numerical variable is not common for basic charts and graphs. Aside from heat maps, most basic charts use color only for categorical variables. Choropleth and symbol maps, on the other hand, very commonly use color encoding for numerical variables. If your favorite software tool does allow you to encode numerical data as a color, these suggestions should apply equally well to maps and charts.

When converting a numerical variable to a color, there are several choices to make. First, does the variable have a natural middle, such as a variable that starts negative, goes through a zero point in the middle, and finishes positive? If so, you may want to emphasize both extremes as if they are two categories and deemphasize values around the middle. In terms of contrast, that usually means the colors you use for the extremes should have both high contrast with the background of the chart and high contrast against each other. The middle values, instead, should have relatively low contrast against the background.[6] This type of color scale is called a "diverging" color scale because two colors diverge from the center color.

When choosing the colors to use for the extreme high and low values, remember that a significant portion of the general population experiences red-green color blindness. Combinations such as red-blue, orange-blue, orange-green, and red-purple avoid this problem.

If there is no natural middle to your data, which side of the variable is more important—the upper extreme or the lower extreme? Say you are making a map that is supposed to reveal areas of low income. You may want users to focus on high values if your variable is the percentage of people under the poverty line, but you may want users to focus on low values if your variable is average income. Use the most contrast for the end of the number scale that is more important.

If you have ever seen a weather report that shows the temperature across the country, you have likely seen a map that uses the wavelength spectrum, or a "ROYGBIV" rainbow, to encode a numerical variable. Figure 5 in the photospread shows an example of the wavelength spectrum using the average daily high temperature per county in the contiguous United States (McClure et al. 2013). Reds indicate high temperatures, blues or purples indicate low temperatures, and the temperatures in the middle go through yellows and greens. Unfortunately, despite how common this is, using a rainbow for numerical variables is a terrible match for human perceptual abilities. Many excellent analyses of rainbow color scales have already been written (e.g., Borland and Taylor 2007, Munzner 2014), but the arguments that relate most to information visualizations such as this are the arguments about visual artifacts, loss of detail, and salience.

Visual artifacts are like optical illusions; they look like real data, but using a different color scale would show a different pattern, or show that there is no real pattern there. When you use a rainbow color scale, the data tend to look striped—like there are big jumps in the values in certain parts of the number range (Borland and Taylor 2007). On weather maps, this usually shows up as a sharp line between red and yellow, yellow and green, and so on. If your data don't have sharp breaks, for the color scale to add them for you certainly isn't helpful.

Loss of detail happens in some parts of the rainbow because of some of the properties of certain colors. The range that is especially problematic is the yellow to light green range (Borland and Taylor 2007). As we mentioned earlier, two light colors are not as easy to differentiate as two dark colors. Rainbow color scales can devote as much as a third of the color scale to the colors yellow and light green, and sometimes cyan. The data points that fall into this range will be very difficult to tell apart, making them look much more similar to each other than they really are.

The final problem with rainbow color scales is salience (Wong 2011). Salience is a way of talking about how much a particular color "pops out" and draws attention. Salience is related to contrast; light colors against a dark background are an iconic example of visual salience. The rainbow color scale has a built-in salience problem—the yellow and light greens, again, will always draw attention away from the ends of the scale, which are typically dark reds and dark blues. You may notice that this makes the rainbow sound more like a diverging color scale. Indeed, using a rainbow can create a similar effect to using a diverging color scale, but rainbows are seldom used on data with a natural middle point, and even having a natural middle point does not resolve the striping and data loss issues.

For a numerical variable with no natural middle point, consider using a color scale that goes from white to a dark color (black, purple, red, etc.). The continuously increasing (or decreasing) lightness is incredibly important for accurately representing data. If your data are not evenly distributed, though, you might consider using number ranges to give yourself more control over how data values are associated with shades of a color (see the previous section on choropleths for more information). Note that there is a limit to the number of different shades humans can differentiate. It is usually safe to use between five and seven discrete shades of a color for numerical variables (Gilmartin and Shelton 1990), assuming that the darkest version of that color is quite dark.

Color for Categorical Variables

Using color to encode a categorical variable is quite common. The discussions above show that color occurs in almost every basic chart type. In charts such as pie charts and line charts, color often simply stands in for the name of a data point, and each color is used only once. In bar charts and scatterplots, more likely the category will appear multiple times, and color is the only thing connecting the various data elements within the category.

In either case, however, what matters is that the data colors can easily be distinguished from each other. The basic rules of contrast are the primary focus for categorical variables. Again, using a light background and dark data colors offers the most options. With numerical variables, we talked about shades of a single, dark color. With categorical variables, we are talking about different color classes, or "hues." Humans begin to have trouble distinguishing between hues when there are more than about seven separate hues (Healey 1996). Even at seven hues it is difficult to ensure high foreground/background contrast—seven hues often require using a fairly light color such as yellow, which will begin to introduce salience concerns on top of the differentiation concerns.

Choice of color will be highly dependent on the patterns and features in your data. Some categorical data have culturally determined colors; in the United States, we often use pink and blue for female and male or red and blue for Republican and Democrat. If your data have these associations, reinforcing them with color can improve the readability of your chart (Lin et al. 2013). It can even increase the number of categories you can represent; if you have a map of different types of natural resources, you may be able to use three different shades of green for different types of forests or wooded areas. This works best if the shades are positioned close to each other; if you have two different light green colors and they are on two different sides of your visualization, it will likely be difficult to tell them apart.

Text

Many people don't think about text as being a major component of a chart or a map, but good use of text can make or break a visualization. Especially when you are sharing data with a broad audience, informative text can help users understand how to read the chart and what trends in the data are most important.

Text Design

Text design can enhance or detract from the look and feel of the chart. Paying attention to font choice, font size, and text rotation can create a professional look for your chart and even make the chart easier to understand.

Font choice is a way of influencing the style of your charts. If the chart appears in a report, article, or poster, there may already be a chosen font that you would like to continue to use or complement. If you are selecting a font from a blank slate, you just need to pay attention to the "mood" of the font. Try not to pick anything too stylized or too informal if you are going for a more professional look.

When choosing font size, it is essential to consider the final size and context of the visualization. It is much more likely that you will discover your fonts are too small rather than too large. For example, when you use a visualization in a slideshow presentation, the chart needs to be easy to read from a long distance, possibly in an improperly lit space. The same is true for posters. For reports and papers, visualizations may need to fit into a single column on a two-column page, or they may be resized to help the report flow better. Err on the side of very large text.

Having text that is easy to read means that text will act in service of the visualization, instead of distracting from it. Ways to make text easier to read include making sure text is horizontal wherever possible (Byrne 2002). As mentioned previously, rotated text problems occur often with bar charts. Try using a horizontal bar chart instead of a vertical bar chart so the labels will not have to be rotated or wrapped onto multiple lines. Rotated text is also common for y-axis labels. While leaving the text rotated for the axis label is less problematic than for category labels—users typically need to read an axis label only once—it is worth trying to keep the text horizontal if the words are short.

Active Titling

One safe rule of thumb is to make sure that every axis (or visual encoding) is labeled. Sometimes chart designers will use the title of the chart to describe the variables in the chart and leave the axes unlabeled. If you label the axes directly, however, it actually becomes unnecessary to duplicate this information in the chart title. Instead, the chart title becomes an opportunity to help users understand the chart better.

Consider using a practice called "active titling." With active titling, the standard boring chart title transforms into an active statement of the importance of the chart. Instead of "Change in ebook transactions over time," you can make a concrete statement about the change *was* over time—for example, "ebook transactions have been doubling each year."

Annotations

Annotations, or special informative text or reference points that have been added to visualizations, take the principle of active titling one step further. Annotations can offer users additional contextual information, focus attention on a single data point or specific trend, or add an additional reference against which to evaluate the data. Examples include paragraphs of text placed on or near the chart, special labels for points, additional lines or boxes added to areas of graphs, or even a "callout" box that zooms into or out of the data in the chart. While it's important not to overwhelm the reader or create too much visual complexity, it's also important to make sure the chart is understandable, especially if it is being designed for a broad audience (Yau 2013).

Different publication venues may limit the use of annotations, however. For example, a paragraph of explanatory text may not be appropriate for a PowerPoint presentation. Instead, consider creating several versions of the chart, each focusing on a small aspect or adding one small annotation at a time. On the other hand, web-based visualizations may offer wonderful opportunities for "on-demand" annotations. Perhaps annotations can appear when the mouse hovers over a data point and go away again when they are no longer needed, thus reducing visual complexity.

Most programs that create visualizations will allow you to customize the text on the charts or maps. If not, consider removing all of the text from the chart and adding it back in later with a graphic design program or even a simple drawing or presentation program. The same is true for most annotations; even if you are adding a reference line, it may be easier to figure out how to add it in with a drawing program than to figure out how to get a visualization program to do it. Just make sure any manual edits look professional and are in the same style as that of the original chart.

STORYTELLING WITH DATA

These days, it isn't quite enough to produce a well-designed and accurate visualization. The focus is increasingly on storytelling with data, or on creating some kind of narrative arc that ties multiple visualizations together into a clear and compelling progression. This can happen sequentially over time, as in a digital slideshow, or by arranging the visualizations in space, as with an infographic, online dashboard, or poster.

Narrative Design

Designing a narrative with separate visualizations is much like studying how a user explores data with a single visualization. For many years, the field of data visualization has subscribed to Ben Shneiderman's "visual information seeking mantra" (1996), which states that the following information-seeking tasks should be prioritized in the design of interactive visualization systems: "overview first, zoom and filter, then details-on-demand." Several additional tasks, including a "relate" task defined as "viewing relationships among items" (p. 2), are listed in the paper but not included in the mantra.

Applying these tasks to a narrative, it makes sense to start with an overview of the data you want the user to understand. Where in an interactive visualization you could literally zoom into parts of the visualization, in a narrative you would create a separate visualization that is already zoomed or filtered—that is, limited in numerical ranges or categories or time periods. Perhaps to show this different level of detail, you will also want to change the chart type. For details on demand, you may be able to generate a series of small, highly focused charts that allow users to focus on the details that are most interesting to them. Finally, to summarize what the data suggest, using the additional "relate" task to build back to an interpretation of the data will help users understand why you are drawing certain conclusions from the data.

There are other ways to structure narratives across multiple visualizations. Few (2012) recommends designing visual communication by following this organizational process: "1. Group (i.e., segment information into meaningful sections), 2. Prioritize (i.e., rank information by importance), 3. Sequence (i.e., provide direction for the order in which information should be read)" (p. 144). Going through this process is especially helpful when determining the spatial layout of your visualizations, which will be addressed in the next section.

Finally, a recent study by Hullman et al. (2013) presents a survey of transition types found within a sample of narrative visualizations, as well as visualization blogs and repositories, from the field of journalism. The study found six transition types (presented in decreasing order of frequency): temporal, granularity, comparison, causal, spatial, and dialogue. Some kind of temporal transition, or moving from one time period to another, appears in almost 90 percent of the examined narratives. Transitions in granularity (i.e., from general to specific or vice versa) closely mirror the "overview first, zoom and filter" components of the visual information-seeking mantra (Shneiderman 1996). The final transitions—those of comparison, causality, spatial proximity, and dialogue—each extends the normal approach to designing a user experience with a visualization by exploring the different types of connections that can occur between different visualizations. When considering how to organize visualizations into a larger narrative, it may be necessary to move back and forth between general questions of organization ("What are my priorities?") and specific questions of arrangement ("What transition makes the most sense here?").

Arrangement of Visuals

After the content of the visualizations has been selected and the visualizations have been generated, it's important to lay the visualizations out in an appealing and understandable arrangement. Especially for posters, infographics, or dashboards, the size and arrangement of visualizations have a huge effect on how users read the display.

The arrangement of panels in a graphic novel or comic book offers a great example (McCloud 1993). The size and arrangement of the panels must guide the reader's eye so that he or she follows the narrative in the correct order. Cultural differences can also play a part here: Is your audience likely to start in the upper left corner or the upper right corner? Is the primary reading directly horizontal or vertical? When you have a diverse audience, you will want to use visual elements to help guide the eye and encourage users to follow the narrative in the way or ways that will make the most sense. Typically, in Western cultures, the most important elements are placed at the top left, and additional elements follow left to right first and then top to bottom. Consider using size as well as position to emphasize which elements are most important.

Gestalt principles explain some of the native tendencies of humans when they are interpreting visual elements (Ware 2008). For example, the Gestalt principle of enclosure says that visual elements that are all contained within an enclosing shape will be seen as more similar to each other than to elements outside of that shape. To apply this principle, any elements contained within a box or circle will be interpreted together, separately from others. Another Gestalt principle, the principle of proximity, states that objects that are close together will seem more similar than those that are far apart. This offers another practical solution: You can actually simply use whitespace in your arrangement to guide the eye between elements. Make the spacing tight between elements that should be interpreted as a single group and then increase the space between that group and any other groups (Few 2012).

Finally, the arrangement of elements in your layout should take into consideration graphic design principles such as the rule of thirds and the golden ratio (see figure 2.9). When arranging elements in visual space, having perfectly centered and symmetrical arrangements is not always considered the most aesthetically pleasing. The rule of thirds suggests that the focal point of an arrangement should be determined by dividing a space into thirds, both horizontally and vertically, and then placing visual elements along or at the intersections of those divisions. The elements of interest in the display thus get placed slightly off center but not all the way at the edge of the visual field.

Rule of Thirds

Golden Ratio

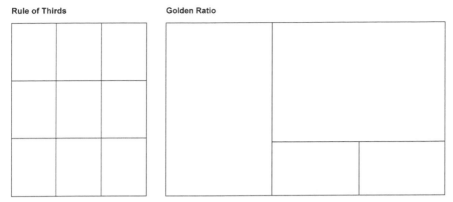

Figure 2.9. Rule of thirds or grids made up of the golden ratio.

The golden ratio is used to create rectangles where the long end is about 1.618 times the length of the short end, or almost two thirds longer. The exact ratio is perhaps less important than the idea that nestling golden ratio rectangles within other golden ratio rectangles creates another type of arrangement that keeps elements slightly off center and encourages changes in size, which in turn encourages users to focus their attention differently on different elements. Combining the golden ratio and the rule of thirds with more basic grids can generate very visually appealing narrative visualizations.

Design Consistency

In any situation where you are combining multiple visual elements, however, it is important to use graphic design to ensure consistency across all elements. This will present a more professional output, but it will also aid comprehension by allowing users to learn design conventions once and apply them successfully to multiple visualizations (Wainer 2008).

Design consistency extends from using the same or compatible fonts across all text and visual elements to the use of the same color scheme (or same specific colors) from one chart to the next. A special case of design consistency arises when you create multiple visualizations from the same variables. Small multiples, also known as trellis plots or lattice plots, are created when a complex chart such as a line chart with too many lines is split up into a series of nearly identical charts, each showing one category. In this situation, it is essential that not only any data colors be kept consistent but also the range on the axes, grid lines, and other reference marks (Cleveland 1994). To make accurate judgments about how the data differ from one category to another, the reference systems for each chart have to be identical.

CONCLUSION

The considerations presented in this chapter will hopefully provide a foundation for developing visualizations that can appeal to a broad public. The process, however, is likely to be much less linear than the information here suggests. You may find while building a narrative that a new chart is necessary for a particular transition. You may realize that you have several different charts all using color in different ways and decide to try to re-encode at least one of those variables in some other type of graphic element. Specialized visualization software such as Tableau (http://www.tableau.com) can be especially helpful during planning phases because of the ease with which additional charts can be created. The best advice for creating great visualizations is often to create as many draft visualizations as possible and to seek out feedback on your ideas. With practice, you will develop your own style and intuitions, and your visualizations will become increasingly clear and engaging.

NOTES

1. Some authors make distinctions between charts and graphs. For example, Börner (2015) uses "chart" for visualizations that lack a formal reference system (e.g., word clouds). Both Börner (2015) and Few (2012) reserve "graph" for visualizations that do use a reference system—typically a Cartesian or polar reference system. In many software applications, however, these terms are used interchangeably, and this chapter will follow that convention.

2. Sometimes bar charts are incorrectly referred to as "histograms." A true histogram visualizes only a single numerical variable. The "bars" in a histogram are actually numerical ranges (e.g., 0 to 4.99, 5 to 9.99), dividing the values of the variable into a series of chunks or "bins." The number of data points that fall within the range becomes the length of the bar for that bin. You can usually tell the difference between a histogram and a bar chart by looking for gaps between the bars. In a histogram, the lower value of one bin starts right where the upper value of the previous bin leaves off so that the bars in a histogram usually do not have any gap between them.

3. Wong (2010), however, recommends placing the largest wedge to the right of the 12:00 position and then starting the second largest wedge to the left of 12:00, continuing counterclockwise after that. This places the two most important wedges at the top of the chart, instead of placing the most and the least important wedges at the top. If wedge sizes are similar, however, it may not be obvious to readers that this nontraditional ordering is being used.

4. There is some debate about whether the y-axis of a line chart should start at zero. Because there is no bar representing the number as a continuous visual area, it may be appropriate to limit the y-axis to the range of interest, effectively "zooming in" on the line chart (Cleveland 1994). This can be especially useful for data series where small variations are important or significant.

5. Two numerical variables could be related to each other nonlinearly, as well. Scatterplots can also show this, but broad audiences are less likely to understand nonlinear relationships.

6. This actually may differ between maps and charts, where the data are less densely positioned. In a choropleth map, for example, the fact that the background behind the map is

white may not matter if you are filling in every state with a color. Each state will be surrounded by other states filled with some kind of color. If a state filled with a light color is surrounded by states filled with dark colors, that state may actually draw more attention instead of less attention. You may sometimes want to choose a darker center color—say, a medium gray—so it doesn't pop so much in context.

REFERENCES

Borland, David, and Russell M. Taylor. 2007. "Rainbow Color Map (Still) Considered Harmful." *IEEE Computer Graphics and Applications* 27(2): 14–17.

Börner, Katy. 2015. *Atlas of Knowledge: Anyone Can Map*. Cambridge, MA: MIT Press.

Byrne, Michael D. 2002. "Reading Vertical Text: Rotated vs. Marquee." Proceedings of the Human Factors and Ergonomics Society 46th Annual Meeting, Santa Monica, CA.

Cleveland, William S. 1994. *The Elements of Graphing Data*. Murray Hill, NJ: AT&T Bell Laboratories.

Cleveland, William S., and Robert McGill. 1985. "Graphical Perception and Graphical Methods for Analyzing Scientific Data." *Science* 299(4716): 828–833.

Few, Stephen. 2012. *Show Me the Numbers: Designing Tables and Graphs to Enlighten*. 2nd ed. Burlingame, CA: Analytics Press.

Gilmartin, Patricia, and Elisabeth Shelton. 1990. "Choropleth Maps on High Resolution CRTs: The Effects of Number of Classes and Hue on Communication." *Cartographica* 26(2): 40–52.

Healey, Christopher G. 1996. "Choosing Effective Colors for Data Visualization." Proceedings of the 7th Conference on Visualization '96 (VIS '96), San Francisco, CA.

Healey, Christopher G., and James T. Enns. 2012. "Attention and Visual Memory in Visualization and Computer Graphics." *IEEE Transactions on Visualization and Computer Graphics* 18(7): 1170–1188.

Heer, Jeffrey, and Michael Bostock. 2010. *Crowdsourcing Graphical Perception: Using Mechanical Turk to Assess Visualization Design*. New York: ACM.

Hullman, Jessica, Steven Drucker, Nathalie Henry Riche, Bongshin Lee, Danyel Fisher, and Eytan Adar. 2013. "A Deeper Understanding of Sequence in Narrative Visualization." *IEEE Transactions on Visualization and Computer Graphics* 19(12): 2406–2415.

Kandel, Sean, Jeffrey Heer, Catherine Plaisant, Jessie Kennedy, Frank van Ham, Nathalie Henry Riche, Chris Weaver, Bongshin Lee, Dominique Brodbeck, and Paolo Buono. 2011. "Research Directions in Data Wrangling: Visualizations and Transformations for Usable and Credible Data." *Information Visualization* 10(4): 271–288.

Lin, Sharon, Julie Fortuna, Chinmay Kulkarni, Maureen Stone, and Jeffrey Heer. 2013. "Selecting Semantically-Resonant Colors for Data Visualization." Proceeedings of Eurographics Conference on Visualization (EuroVis) 2013, Leipzig, Germany.

McCloud, Scott. 1993. *Understanding Comics: The Invisible Art*. New York: HarperPerennial.

McClure, Leslie, Mohammad Al-Hamdan, William Crosson, Sigrid Economou, Maurice Estes Jr., Sue Estes, Mark Puckett, and Dale Quattrochi Jr. 2013. North America Land Data Assimilation System (NLDAS) Daily Air Temperatures and Heat Index (1979-2011). CDC WONDER Online Database.

Munzner, Tamara, ed. 2014. *Visualization Analysis & Design*. Boca Raton, FL: CRC Press.

Shneiderman, Ben. 1996. "The Eyes Have It: A Task by Data Type Taxonomy for Information Visualizations." Proceedings of IEEE Symposium on Visual Languages, Boulder, CO.

Skau, Drew. 2011. "2D's Company, 3D's a Crowd." *Visual.ly blog*. http://blog.visual.ly/2ds -company-3ds-a-crowd/.

Stefaner, Moritz. 2012. Data Stories Episode #5: How to Learn Data Visualization (with Andy Kirk). In *Data Stories*, edited by Enrico Bertini and Moritz Stefaner.

Wainer, Howard. 2008. "Improving Graphic Displays by Controlling Creativity." *Chance* 21(2): 46–53.

Ware, Colin. 2008. *Visual Thinking for Design*. Burlington, MA: Morgan Kaufmann Publishers.

Ware, Colin. 2013. *Information Visualization: Perception for Design*. 3rd ed. Waltham, MA: Morgan Kaufmann Publishers.

Wong, Bang. 2011. "Points of View: Salience to Relevance." *Nature Methods* 8(11): 889–889.

Wong, Dona M. 2010. *The Wall Street Journal Guide to Information Graphics: The Dos & Don'ts of Presenting Data, Facts, and Figures*. New York: W. W. Norton.

Yau, Nathan. 2013. *Data Points: Visualization That Means Something*. Indianapolis: Wiley.

3

Tools and Technologies

Visualizing Research Activity in the Discovery Layer in Real Time

Godmar Back and Annette Bailey

During the past decade, the role of academic and public libraries alike has been steadily shifting. The vast majority of circulation today is electronic, and thus many libraries have reduced the amount of physical space dedicated to print resources. Physical library space is increasingly used to provide collaborative space for students and faculty. Libraries are repurposing themselves to create information commons (Bailey and Tierney 2008), which are physical and online spaces dedicated to information and knowledge accumulation and discovery. Small- and large-scale wall displays for instruction or exhibition purposes are becoming ubiquitous. Digital signage has emerged as a managed aspect of public relations in many libraries, serving to share upcoming events and to offer another venue for library displays.

Libraries have been replacing their traditional, outdated online public access catalogs (OPACs) with modern discovery systems, which are full-text, index-based search engines that match the convenience and ease of use of general-purpose search engines, yet provide users with access to scholarly materials selected by their library. The resources users click on in their search results in a discovery interface represent a transaction similar to that of the traditional checking out of books and other resources in the OPAC. Examples of library discovery systems currently available in the library marketplace include ProQuest's Summon, Ex Libris's Primo, and EBSCO's EBSCO Discovery Service (EDS).

These changes are exciting for the new opportunities they offer, but they also pose a number of risks to the future relevance of libraries. For instance, if interaction with the library becomes entirely private, the communal character of the transaction, once so common at the circulation desk, is forfeited. Consequently, library resources are viewed as commodities for which the library is no longer seen as a selector and provider. This effect leads some to doubt the library's relevance, particularly in the face of declining print circulation, and makes it difficult for libraries to justify their collection budgets.

Notwithstanding the emergent use of such standards as COUNTER (counting online usage of networked electronic resources) and the desire of most libraries to carefully compile, process, and publish usage statistics, such statistics are often delayed, incomplete, or used only for internal purposes. No major discovery system provides real-time statistics on its use, and those systems that do collect search statistics do so in a way that places this information in a silo that makes it difficult for libraries to analyze easily; cross-institutional analyses are nearly impossible.

This chapter describes the LibFX technology developed by the authors, which collects and processes real-time usage data from a library's discovery system (powered by ProQuest's Summon discovery system) and creates compelling real-time visualizations. We gather the interactions of users (while protecting their privacy) with their library's discovery system, collect this information in real time on a web-based server, perform real-time processing, and broadcast the processed data to data visualization applications. These applications can drive small or large public displays with which users can interact, and they can also be integrated into existing or new web offerings. We chose the name LibFX for our system to emphasize its ability to visualize the data in an engaging manner.

RELATED WORK

Hilary Davis wrote an influential blog article in 2009 for *In the Library with the Lead Pipe* about why visualization of library data matters to libraries (Davis 2009). According to Davis, libraries have many sources of data, and the challenge in communicating that data to outside stakeholders has become increasingly complex. Visualizations can provide a compelling way to communicate with stakeholders. Several projects have used visualizations for library data, some of them to gain a deeper understanding to aid in collection management and others to collaborate with artists to display library data to the public.

The Harvard Library Explorer project uses a variety of visualizations in a single window to demonstrate aggregate data about the circulation of the library's collections over a fixed period of time (Harvard 2012). Using the visualizations, the user can drill down to more specific data about how many times books under a Library of Congress Subject Heading circulated during each year. Color gradients are used to show "popularity" so that one can see at a glance the level of interest in particular subjects. Another graph demonstrates the number of books published in a given year on a subject. This display effectively visualizes a cross-section of data that inform both librarians and users about past publication and circulation activities.

The Seattle Central Library installed large-scale displays in its circulation and other public areas that display aggregate data about how many transactions had transpired over a period of time, along with other information (Legrady n.d.). Aptly named "Making the Invisible Visible," the library's data visualizations are known for being a key part of its community members' experience in the physical space of their library. It allows the user community that creates the data to see these data, which are typically looked at by only librarians.

Indianapolis's Museum of Art (IMA) uses a dashboard to communicate with its community members about their interactions with it and its art collection (IMA 2010). Using a tiled display, IMA tells visitors at a glance how many Facebook friends the museum currently has and other real-time data, such as the current attendance at its physical museum space. This real-time data enrich the museumgoers' experience by sharing with them the community's current activities.

The Filament Mind project (Lee and Brush 2013) in the Teton County Library is a striking art installation that taps in real time into every library catalog search in the state of Wyoming, using 1,000 light filaments. These 1,000 light filaments correspond to 1,000 Dewey Decimal classifications. The filaments are lit based on the Dewey Decimal classification of the search results users see. The choice of physical strands of fiber creates an experience that powerfully unites the "real" with the "virtual" world.

To the best of our knowledge, our project is the only project that focuses on the real-time visualization of discovery system activity.

ARCHITECTURE

Extracting real-time data and creating visualizations using LibFX involves multiple steps, which are depicted in figure 3.1. Users interact with a modified front end when they use Summon for discovery. A number of server components record a user's interaction with Summon results and then log the results. A log watcher com-

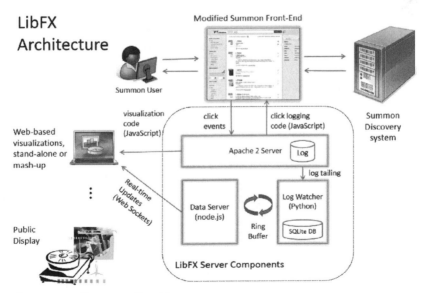

Figure 3.1. LibFX overall architecture.

ponent processes the metadata associated with each user event and prepares them for broadcasting by the data server to the web-based visualizations. We discuss each of these components in turn.

Front-End Modifications

Although Summon provides usage statistics via the back-end configuration interface (known as the Client Center), they are aggregate only and not retrievable in real time. Thus, to record which Summon results our users clicked on, we needed to modify the Summon search page. Such modifications are possible because Summon allows its clients to specify a URL pointing to a JavaScript file that is loaded into the page when search results are displayed. This feature is both powerful and rudimentary: powerful because it gives clients full control over the web page including the ability to add, remove, or change any content displayed and to intercept and record any user interactions with the page, but also rudimentary because there is no vendor support for any of these actions—the vendor code is undocumented, provides no public APIs at this level, and is subject to change without notice!

Since we possessed a significant amount of JavaScript experience from past projects, we reverse engineered the user interface and identified the elements we needed to monitor. When Summon upgraded from 1.0 to 2.0, the entire front-end implementation changed, and we had to start from scratch. Reverse engineering Summon 2.0 was significantly more difficult than modifying Summon 1.0 because it uses higher-level libraries (e.g., AngularJS [Hevery 2009]) with significantly higher levels of abstraction. We ended up publishing the technical details of how we modified Summon 2.0 in a separate paper (Back and Bailey 2014).

Briefly put, our modifications identify which search results are displayed on the results page. For each result, we retrieve the unique Summon ID of the associated displayed item, which is embedded in information to which our JavaScript code has access. We install an on-click event handler for each hyperlink a user may click on when accessing the displayed link to the item, and there are multiple hyperlinks for each item. When users click, we send the IDs of the items on which they clicked to our server, which then logs them. Similar to what Google Analytics does, we exploit a request to a 1 × 1 GIF image for this purpose and send along the ID in the request's query parameters. We use a standard Apache server installation to serve these images, but we configured it such that requests for those images are logged in a separate log file. Dedicating a separate log file to these requests allows the subsequent tools in our chain to focus on only this log file, eliminating the need to extract requests from a shared log file and avoiding polluting the same.

Metadata Collection

The click logging results in a time-stamped log of (time, Summon ID) pairs, each referencing an event in which a user accessed a Summon result. For the purposes of analysis and visualization, we need the metadata associated with each Summon ID. The Summon API (Serials Solutions 2009) allows us to retrieve this metadata using the ID. An edited excerpt of a typical record is shown below using JSON (Bray 2014) notation:

```
{
"Abstract": [ "Data-Driven Documents (D3) is a novel
representation-transparent..." ],
"Author": [ "Heer, J", "Ogievetsky, V", "Bostock, M" ],
"AuthorAffiliation": [ "Comput. Sci. Dept., Stanford Univ.,
Stanford, CA, USA" ],
"ContentType": [ "Journal Article" ],
"Copyright": [ "1995-2012 IEEE", "2010 IEEE" ],
"DOI": [ "10.1109/TVCG.2011.185" ], "DatabaseTitle": [
"PubMed", "CrossRef" ],
"Discipline": [ "Engineering" ],
"EISSN": [ "1941-0506" ],
"EndPage": [ "2309" ],
"Genre": [ "orig-research", "Journal Article" ],
"ID": [ "FETCH-LOGICAL-c900-3917ebf7400b0992ef397b577022eff784f
41b08302ff0c446ef0440fe8ac9a33" ],
. . .
}
```

As of this writing, the Summon index contains well beyond one billion entries, many of which were created by automated metadata processing algorithms. A general lack of authority control resulted in records that are very heterogeneous, both in terms of the types of fields they contain and their content. This inconsistency constitutes a challenge for our data processing and visualization tools.

In implementing the processing of these metadata records we encountered the problem that Summon IDs are short-lived. As new records are being added to the Summon index and merged with records already in the index, new IDs are created for the new, merged records while the old IDs are removed and can no longer be retrieved. To circumvent this problem, and also to avoid frequent accesses to the Summon API, we retrieve and keep a copy of each record in a local SQLite database (Hipp 2015). The database contains a single table that maps an ID to a JSON encoding of the record's data retrieved via the API. For our institution, this method resulted in the retrieval of 1.3M unique records stemming from about 1.7 million clicks during the 30.5-month period from mid-January 2013 to August 2015, during which time the SQLite database grew to 9.7GB in size. Recently, ProQuest introduced a PermaLink feature, which may alleviate the need to keep a copy of the metadata.

From a software engineering perspective, we decoupled the click logging and metadata collection and analysis by performing all log-related activities in a separate, continuously running Python program, which we refer to as *log watcher*. The log watcher is suspended while there is no activity. When a user clicks on a result, an entry is added to the log file, which wakes up the log watcher via the Linux inotify interface (McCutchan 2006), which will then read the added line from the log file. After extracting the ID, the log watcher will check whether the metadata associated with that ID are already contained within our local database. If they are not, they are fetched from the Summon API and added to the database.

The log watcher program also needs to be able to interact with standard log rotation, which is controlled by a system program and occurs at the end of each month. To prevent log files from growing too large, the existing log file is renamed and a new log file is started. We use inotify to detect this situation and continue our data collection seamlessly with the new log file.

Metadata Aggregation

To be meaningful, most of our visualizations require processing and aggregation of the metadata contained in multiple records. In our architecture, this processing takes place within the log watcher process, which maintains a number of *tabulators*, which tabulate frequencies related to different metadata fields in the time-stamped stream of click events.

To provide greater flexibility to our visualizations, we simultaneously maintain several tabulators. Each tabulator is responsible for one or more metadata fields, whose contents are aggregated over some past time frame. Tabulators can count the frequencies of either entire fields or a specified combination of fields. In addition, they may first split a field's content into words, whose frequency is then counted. We tabulate the discipline, source type, content type, publication year, keyword, and subject terms fields. We split and then tabulate the title and abstract fields. In addition, we tabulate the combination of keyword and subject terms and the combination of abstract and title.

Since our visualization is expected to run unattended during times of both heavy and light use of the Summon discovery system, the choice of time frame over which to aggregate proved challenging. At first, we considered using time periods only (e.g., the last minute, five minutes, hour, day, and week) because these periods provide observers with a time frame to which they can easily relate. However, this approach does not work well during periods of light use (e.g., when there are only a few clicks per minute) because the resulting aggregate frequencies can be zero or near zero. For this reason, we also added tabulators for event periods, whose length is determined by a given number of events, regardless of when they occurred. We keep track of aggregations over the last 50, 100, 200, 500, 1,000, and 2,000 events.

Tabulators process new events and update their aggregations incrementally; each update involves two steps. First, the metadata record associated with the new event is retrieved, and the field contents are extracted and added with their respective frequencies. Then the tabulator examines whether any events need to be removed from the aggregation because they have expired. Event period tabulators must always expire a single old event for each new event (e.g., an event period tabulator with a period of 200 events must retrieve and expire the 200th last event). Time period–

based tabulators must remove all events with a time stamp that is older than the time period they are aggregating.

To decouple the metadata aggregations from their later use in the visualizations, a snapshot of the aggregated metadata during each time or event period is saved after each click event. We use a ring buffer with 100 entries to keep the last 100 updates. To keep the implementation simple, this ring buffer is implemented using subdirectories numbered 0 to 99, each of which contains JSON files that represent a snapshot of the aggregation after the last event, the next to last, the -2nd, and so on. A symbolic link named now points to the most recently processed subdirectory.

We maintain 10 tabulators over 5 time periods and 6 event periods, for a total of 110 aggregations. These tabulators require roughly 450KB of disk space; the entire ring buffer thus takes about 45MB of space. As a concrete example, a snapshot of the frequencies of the words occurring in the Title fields of the last 50 clicks might look like this:

```
{
"timestamp" : "2015-08-03T12:00:27-04:00",
"Title" : [
[ "legionella", 5 ],
[ "robotics", 4 ],
[ "anatomy", 4 ],
[ "boltzmann", 4 ],
[ "lattice", 4 ],
[ "handbook", 4 ],
[ "sciences", 3 ],
[ "mathematical", 3 ],
[ "groundwater", 3 ],
[ "relationships", 3 ],
[ "shear", 3 ],
[ "writing", 3 ],
[ "dynamics", 2 ],
[ "tissue", 2 ],
[ "brain", 2 ],
[ "experimental", 2 ],
[ "education", 2 ],
[ "invariance", 2 ],
[ "vascular", 2 ],
[ "range", 2 ],
. . .
```

Data Server

The data server component broadcasts real-time updates to the visualization clients. We chose to build the data server on top of the node.js platform (Dahl 2009). The node.js platform is a server-side version of Google's V8 JavaScript virtual machine, which also powers the Google Chrome browser. It provides an environment that supports an event-based programming style, which allows for efficient network communication and efficient access to files on disk but requires that the programmer arrange his or her program in the form of many event handlers, which are executed in response to I/O events. Node.js network applications hold the promise to support large numbers of simultaneous clients while using limited resources.

We decided to use node.js for three reasons: first, for its aforementioned promise of efficiency and the resulting scalability; second, because it is a JavaScript environment and thus provides natural support for operating on JSON data, including reading, writing, manipulating, sending, and receiving; and, third, because it supports the Socket.io library in its ecosystem of packages (Rauch 2015), which provide real-time, bidirectional, and event-based communication with the visualization clients in which the actual visualization is implemented.

Clients connect to our data server after bootstrapping a JavaScript file, which provides the code to create a Socket.io[1] connection. On most modern browsers, this connection is based on the HTML5 Web Sockets transport protocol,[2] although Socket.io has the ability to fall back on older technologies such as AJAX-based long polling. Clients first send a message to subscribe to one or more channels. Channels correspond to one of the 110 metadata aggregations computed by the log watcher, plus one additional channel that simply broadcasts the most recent metadata record. The data server obtains this data from the ring buffer, into which the log watcher places records and aggregated data. Changes in the ring buffer are recognized via inotify when the now symbolic link is updated, which signals an advance to the next subdirectory. Thus, the log watcher and data server programs communicate solely via the file system; no other form of interprocess communication is necessary. The data server can also be started and stopped independently of the log watcher.

After a client subscribes to one or more channels, the data server sends the client updates for each subscribed channel whenever a new event is processed by the log watcher and added to the ring buffer. From the server's perspective, the data associated with each event is read once and then broadcast to all connected clients while respecting their individual subscriptions.

A number of our visualizations use some form of animation to advance from one visualization state to a new visualization state in response to a new event. To test these animations, our data server supports a feature that allows a client to request the data resulting from past events for each channel to which the client subscribes. These data are sent after a connection has been established and can be processed by the client in the same way as if the events had occurred in real time. Besides testing, this feature is also useful for demonstrating our visualizations and animations.

VISUALIZATIONS

This section describes the implementation of the different visualizations we have built and discusses the underlying technologies. All the visualizations execute inside modern, standards-compliant browsers, which require the visualizations to be programmed using HTML5, CSS, and JavaScript. We reuse widely available open source and proprietary libraries and modules where appropriate. An example is the powerful visualization library D3.js (Bostock, Ogievetsky, and Heer 2011). In keeping with adapted terminology and to emphasize the aspect that our code can be integrated into an existing web page, we refer to some of the visualization implementations as *widgets*.

Speed Gauge

The speed gauge is a simple visualization that visualizes one number, the current speed of discovery (see figure 3.2). To implement the speed gauge display, we reused the "Just Gage" library by Bojan Đuričić (2012), which in turn relies on the Raphaël JavaScript library (Baranovskiy 2013).

The displayed speed is computed by subscribing to the Record channel and recording the time stamps of the last n clicks in an array. The difference D (in ms) between the most recent time stamp and the nth last time stamp is converted into an hourly estimate using the formula:

$$S = \frac{n}{D} * 3,600 * 1,000$$

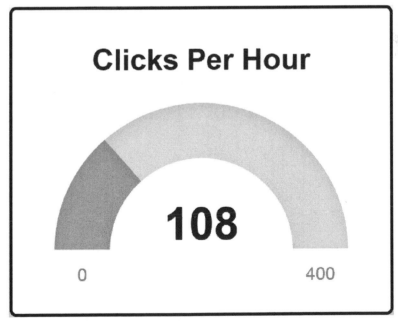

Figure 3.2. The Speed Gauge visualizes discovery speed.

We found that setting $n = 10$ works well. Whenever a new event is broadcast on the Record channel, the widget adds its time stamp to the array, discards the 10th last time stamp, applies the above formula, and updates the gauge. The entire widget is implemented in ~40 lines of JavaScript.

Discipline Ticker

The discipline ticker is a simple visualization widget that provides historical context on which disciplines users currently do research in. The ticker is a moving animation, updated on each new event, that summarizes trends. A snapshot is shown in figure 3.3.

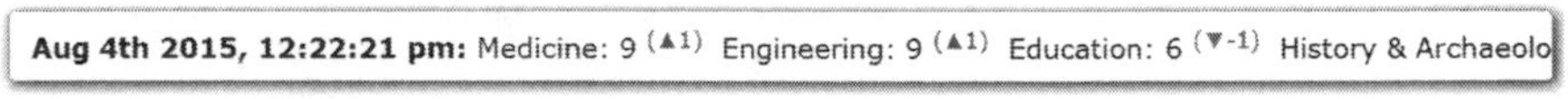

> **Aug 4th 2015, 12:22:21 pm:** Medicine: 9 [▲1] Engineering: 9 [▲1] Education: 6 [▼-1] History & Archaeolo

Figure 3.3.   The Discipline Ticker.

The data for the discipline ticker are computed by comparing the aggregate frequency of each discipline at the most recent event with the aggregate frequency count 10 events ago. To do that, the widget subscribes to the Discipline.last50 channel. For each discipline with a non-zero frequency, the difference is computed and noted as a delta using an appropriate color.

The ticker was implemented from scratch via CSS3 transitions (Jackson, Hyatt, Marrin, and Baron 2013). CSS3 transitions provide a way to have the browser change CSS attributes over time, resulting in an animated transition. For instance, via CSS3 transitions, a browser can be instructed to change an element's position from (0, 0) to (100, 0) over the time frame of 2 seconds, making the element move on the screen. Before the widespread support and use of CSS3 transitions, such animations were accomplished using JavaScript code, which needed to be invoked repeatedly in small time steps and which then set those attributes to their interpolated values (for instance, moving the x-value from 0 to 100 over 2 seconds might result in 100 calls, one every 20 ms, each incrementing the x-value by one). CSS3 transitions simplify this process by off-loading it onto the browser without the need for any JavaScript code. This provides the additional advantage that the browser can use the built-in capabilities of modern graphic processing units (GPUs), which are now found in all desktop computers. Without CSS3 transitions, the CPU can quickly become a bottleneck, limiting the number of elements that can be simultaneously animated.

We implemented the ticker effect by positioning two rectangular div elements relative to their container, which in CSS is accomplished by setting the position to absolute and choosing appropriate values for the top, left, bottom, and right attributes. The container is chosen so that extraneous content is clipped (see figure 3.4).

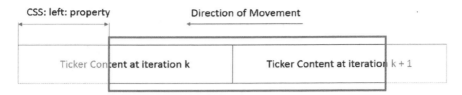

Figure 3.4.   Implementing a scrolling ticker via CSS3 transitions.

After determining the width of the ticker content we wish to display, we use a CSS3 transition on the left property to move the ticker band to the left, behind the visible area. To achieve the effect of an infinite ticker, we associate an event handler with the end of the transition. At this point, we append new content (if any was received from the server) to the right end and restart the transition. If no new content was received, we repeat the last content. In addition, we check whether any content has completely disappeared from view; if it has, we remove this content from the band and adjust its left property accordingly. These manipulations require knowledge of how long the ticker band is, which is the sum of the widths of each piece of content. We compute these widths by laying out each content piece in a hidden div element and retrieving its CSS width attribute.

Implementing the ticker revealed an interesting design and programming challenge that recurs in the other visualizations we implemented: the animation of the ticker occurs concurrently with the receipt of new events, yet we need to coordinate the two. We accomplish this by queuing events on receipt and then checking the queue of received but not yet processed events whenever a CSS3 transition ends (i.e., when new content has to be added to the band on the right).

The Summon Cube

The Summon Cube visualization projects the metadata records of the most recently accessed items onto a 3-dimensional cube (see figure 3.5). As a new item is being accessed, the cube rotates around one or more of its axes and stops with a new face pointing forward (figure 3.5 displays a snapshot in the middle of such a rotation). The face is populated using the metadata of the most recent record. We include book images (if the record contains them), along with metadata such as title, author, publication date, and publisher. If the record contains an abstract, we display it. For books, we also include snippets provided by Bowker.

Our implementation of the rotating cube was inspired by a CSS 3D tutorial that implemented a continuously rotating cube (Crombie 2015). This rotating cube uses CSS3 animations. CSS3 animations are, like CSS3 transitions, geometric transformations that are computed and rendered by the browser's layout engine with the help of a GPU, without requiring continuous JavaScript code to run during the animation. Animations are specified using key frames that represent states that correspond

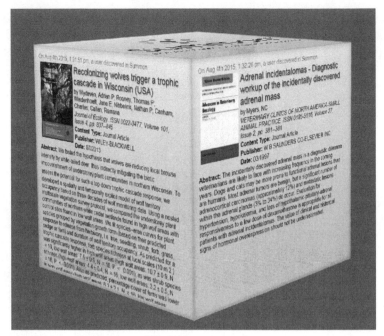

Figure 3.5.   The Summon Cube.

to a set of CSS properties. For instance, the following key-frame declaration specifies an animation with two key frames (labeled from and to):

```
@-webkit-keyframes spincube4 {
from { -webkit-transform: rotateY(-180deg) rotateZ(90deg); }
to { -webkit-transform: rotateY(90deg) rotateX(90deg); }
}
```

If this animation is applied to an element, the element rotates around three axes simultaneously: the *x*-axis from 0 to 90 degrees, the *y*-axis from −180 to 90 degrees, and the *z*-axis from 90 degrees to 0 degrees. To make the rotating cube work, we had to decompose the key frames describing a continuously animated cube into six separate states (and animations that move from one to the next state in a circular fashion).

Unlike the ticker, which is continuously running, the cube moves only in response to new records arriving. A question that arises is how long should each record on a face be displayed before displaying the next face. During periods of low activity, it is reasonable to simply move to the next face, as a viewer will have ample time to read the information displayed. During bursts of high activity, however, advancing to the next face should not occur in lockstep, or else a viewer might not have enough time to read the displayed information, similar to how a bad presenter might advance slides too fast for his or her audience to read. On the other hand, if the burst of high activity persists for too long and the per-face pause is set too high, the animation might eventually be too far out of sync.

We used a variable delay queue to mitigate this problem. As new records arrive, they are placed in a queue that releases items only after a delay. The delay depends on the number of elements in the queue before it. The more elements, the smaller the delay, down to a set minimum. For instance, a [6,4,2] queue might have a delay of six seconds if there is only item in the queue when a new one is added or four seconds if there are two items, and the delay may be reduced to two seconds if more than two items are already in it. In this way, if two records are accessed at nearly at the same time, the first one to arrive will not cause a "flashing" of the animation but rather will be visible for six seconds before the next one is displayed. In the event that several records are accessed near simultaneously, they will be displayed at a pace of one every two seconds, which then will increase to four and then to six as soon as the burst ebbs off.

Word Cloud

D3.js is a JavaScript library for providing dynamic, interactive data visualizations in web browsers. It was developed by Mike Bostock and Jeffrey Heer (Bostock, Heer, and Ogievetsky 2011; Bostock, Ogievetsky, and Heer 2011). It is based on manipulating web documents that consist of HTML, CSS, and, in particular, scalable vector graphics (SVG) in concordance with data coming from a source. Such *data binding* allows data-driven transformations: for example, a given data element might be bound to an HTML div element's height CSS attribute, which represents a bar in a bar chart. As the data are updated, the bar changes its height accordingly.

D3.js provides a number of higher-level abstractions to facilitate this programming style and make it suitable for arbitrary, dynamic sets of data. In addition, it allows the creation of smooth transitions as data change and simplify the creation of interactive applications that respond to user input. The true power of D3.js, however, lies in the components and plug-ins built by its avid developer community that support many possible different styles of visualizations (Bostock n.d.).

We implemented a dynamic word cloud visualization based on a D3.js plug-in written by Jason Davies (2013). An example is shown in figure 3.6, based on terms found in the titles of retrieved items over the last 50 events. A word cloud is a popular way to visualize the frequency of words in a text. More frequently occurring words are displayed using a larger font. The words are arranged to fill a given area in a nonoverlapping way. To achieve maximum cover, words are laid out in a spiral starting from the center until a gap is found that is large enough so that a word will fit. This layout logic is implemented in the plug-in we are using.

The plug-in is written using D3.js's model of separating data (also known as model) and view. The data comprise the words and their frequency. The view is a set of svg:text elements (W3C 2001) along with a set of attributes that is computed

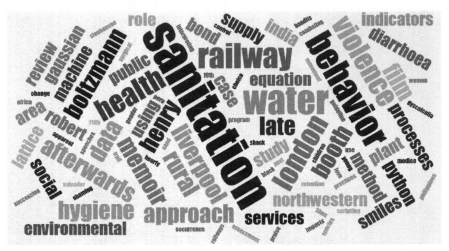

Figure 3.6.   Word Cloud Visualization.

by the layout algorithm and include the x, y positions, where the text element is placed inside the SVG canvas; an angle of rotation; and the font size at which the text element should be displayed. At its basic use (for a static word cloud), the set of words must be provided to the layout algorithm, which will create the corresponding text elements and initiate the computation of their layout. Computing the layout is time intensive (may take several seconds for large word clouds) and for that reason is performed using a programming pattern that spreads the computation over multiple chunks to allow the interleaving of other work necessary to ensure that a web page does not lose interactive responsiveness. When the last chunk is finished, a callback function is invoked. In that callback function, the computed attributes are applied to the text elements that correspond to the model.

The code becomes more complicated if we wish to implement a word cloud that changes as new aggregated data arrive. In this scenario, some words are in both the old and the new set (although their frequency may change), some words are in only the new set, and some old words are no longer in the set. Visually, the words that stay transition from their old positions and sizes to their new positions and sizes. The words that are removed will fade away, and new words will fade in at their new positions. These three transitions take place simultaneously over a given time span. We expressed this logic using the idioms required by D3.js's programming model. As we do for the Summon cube visualization, we use a variable delay queue to ensure that the word cloud does not update immediately during bursts of click events.

Building dynamic word clouds, as opposed to designing and tweaking a word cloud for a static set of words obtained from a text, poses another challenge, namely, how to choose the function that maps frequencies to font size. If the font size is too large, only a few words will fit on the page (the algorithm will discard any word it cannot place without overlap). If the font size is too small, the smallest words will be hard to read and/or there may not be enough words in the set to fully cover the given area, which makes the word cloud look empty. We developed a heuristic to address this problem. We determine the maximum and minimum frequencies occurring in the set, then provide a font size function that logarithmically maps this [min, max] range to a range of font in the size [h/40, h/5], where h is the height of the provided area into which the word cloud is drawn. This heuristic is based on the idea that if the words of the cloud were laid out in simple horizontal lines, the entire area would be filled with five lines of the most frequent words or 40 lines of the least frequent words.

Listen to Summon

Another visualization is an adaptation of the well-known Listen to Wikipedia visualization, which was created by Mahmoud Hashemi and Stephen LaPorte (LaPorte and Hashemi 2013). A snapshot of the Listen to Summon visualization can be seen in figure 6 in the photospread.

The Listen to Wikipedia visualization provides a visual and aural depiction of real-time updates to Wikipedia. After a Wikipedia article has been edited, a circle appears at a random location on a canvas whose size is proportional to the size of the edit. In addition, a semitransparent ring grows around the circle, creating a ripple-like effect. The title of the Wikipedia article is displayed over the circle and hyperlinked to point to the actual article. Colors are used to differentiate between edits by unregistered contributors, Wikipedia editors, and bots. Sound is used to denote the type of edit: bells signal additions and string plucks subtractions. The sounds come from an array of sounds with varying pitch, and the pitch chosen is based on the size of the edit. To avoid cluttering the animation, older entries fade away after a set time period.

We adopted the Listen to Summon code and modified it to suit our purposes. The visualization code subscribes to the Record channel and displays new circles when new records are broadcast. A variable delay queue is used to avoid overwhelming the viewer during bursts of events. We map the number of pages of a book or article (if provided in the record) to the size of the circle. We map the first discipline listed in the record so that it determines the color. We use the two types of instruments to distinguish records that came from our original catalog from others. We use the publication year if it is given to determine the pitch of the sound. Unlike Listen to Wikipedia, which removes entries after a set time period, we fade old entries out only if needed to keep the number of displayed circles constant.

Google Chart API

We also used the Google Chart API[3] to visualize some data. Google Charts is a proprietary library created by Google, subject to the Google API Terms of Service. It supports a closed set of chart types, the code for which is owned and hosted by Google. These chart types include column charts, bar charts, pie charts, and several other types. These charts are highly customizable.

An example is shown in figure 7 in the photospread, which displays a pie chart of the ContentType.last100 aggregation channel. Integrating Google Charts into our visualization required us to transform our data into the table-based model required by the Chart API, which was largely straightforward. However, the Chart API also supports animated transitions when a new data set arrives. For these animated transitions to work well, we needed to retain the row assignment for each discipline category between updates. This required some programming to remember the assigned row index for each category. To handle bursts, we again used a variable delay queue.

A second use of the Google Chart API is for the creation of QR Codes. Our QR Code widget subscribes to the Record channel; for each record, the widget retrieves the same URL to which the user who clicked on the Summon result was led and encodes it as a QR Code, which can then be embedded in the visualization. This feature allows passersby to retrieve any items that may pique their interest.

PUTTING IT ALL TOGETHER

The visualizations we have presented so far exist as code that requires a combination of HTML, CSS, and JavaScript (our code as well as that of the libraries we are using). Integrating these visualizations into existing web pages requires moderate effort—a user must copy and paste the corresponding <script> and <link> tags and ensure that those files are accessible.

To deploy some of our visualizations in a public space we have prototyped a Chrome app (Google Inc. 2014). Chrome applications are prepackaged bundles that combine HTML, CSS, and JavaScript and can be invoked by simply installing and launching them in the Chrome web browser. This packaging results in a streamlined process for the person deploying them on the computer connected to a public display and should enable integration into digital signage systems, something we are in the process of testing.

Our Chrome application is an arrangement of visualizations designed for a newly installed large display in the main entrance of the Newman Library at Virginia Tech. This large display consists of four 60-inch screens arranged in a 2 × 2 pattern. Due to technical limitations, the display supports only HD resolution (1920 × 1080); the bezels separating the four screens are also large. For this reason, we split the application into four quadrants; each quadrant displays a frameless top-level window. Each window contains a single <webview> element that displays a different page (see figure 8 in the photospread).

A webview element can load and render a web page loaded from an external source. This external source is our server, which provides the actual code so that code updates do not require access to the machine that physically drives the display. As a noteworthy technical detail, we needed to assign each webview element a different "partition" property when we open it. By doing so, we instruct the Chrome browser that the code running in the four windows will not attempt to communicate with each another (despite being loaded from the same domain), which in turn enables Chrome to place the four windows into four separate operating system processes. These processes can in turn be placed onto four different CPU cores, which allows their code to execute in parallel. This separation allows us to exploit multiprocessing for CPU-intensive JavaScript portions. As a result, the layout computation in the window displaying the word cloud does not affect the other windows; we are able to drive smooth animations in all four quadrants smoothly, even on a commodity PC.

SHORTCOMINGS AND IDEAS FOR FUTURE WORK

Our technology is basically at the prototype stage and can be improved in multiple ways. Several engineering challenges still lie ahead, such as improving the ease of packaging of the log watcher and data server components. A second goal is to improve the ease with which visualizations can be embedded into our web pages.

There are also numerous ways to improve the visualizations themselves. For instance, the word extracting algorithm that determines the frequency of words in titles or abstracts currently does not take collocations into account; we are working on integrating a multiword extractor (MWE) from a text processing library. Such an extractor could rely on a dictionary but ideally would be trained by the records it sees as it processes the event logs to learn which groups of words form multiword expressions.

A second improvement would be to perform deeper longitudinal processing of the data. For instance, it may be interesting to visualize research activity during longer time frames than just the recent past. This will require improvements to the data processing stage to compute and store aggregations over longer periods.

We are also considering accessing external sources with which to enrich the data. A possible example is the use of altmetrics (Priem, Taraborelli, Groth, and Neylon 2010), which can provide enriching information to items being accessed. Our visualization system could itself become a source of altmetrics, particularly if it were deployed at multiple institutions.

CONCLUSION

We have developed LibFX, which is a web-based technology that taps into our library's discovery system, collects user interaction in real time, and creates several visualizations that can be deployed on wall displays or integrated in web pages.

We believe that deploying LibFX has the potential to amplify our library's effect in its community. Particularly on academic campuses, libraries remain highly frequented physical centers of their institutions. Engaging and lively visualizations of their discovery system's activities could rekindle the public's awareness of the library's mission as a hub for the discovery and provision of information. Such displays could spark conversations about the use of books, ebooks, and journals and unveil hot spots of research interest. Visitors would recognize libraries as active places that connect the on- and offline activities of their users, which would in turn reinforce the physical and virtual ties that bind an academic community.

NOTES

1. See http://socket.io/.
2. See http://tools.ietf.org/html/rfc6455.
3. See https://developers.google.com/chart.

REFERENCES

Back, Godmarand, and Annette Bailey. 2014. "Hacking Summon 2.0 the Elegant Way." *The Code4Lib Journal* (26).

Bailey, D. R., and B. Tierney. 2008. Transforming Library Service through Information Commons: Case Studies for the Digital Age. Chicago, IL: American Library Association.

Baranovskiy, Dimitri. 2013. "Raphael—JavaScript Library." Accessed August 3, 2015. http://raphaeljs.com/.

Bostock, Mike. n.d. "D3 Gallery." Accessed August 3, 2015. https://github.com/mbostock/d3/wiki/Gallery.

Bostock, Mike, Jeffrey Heer, and Vadim Ogievetsky. 2011. "D3.js." Accessed August 3, 2015. https://d3js.org.

Bostock, Mike, Vadim Ogievetsky, and Jeffrey Heer. 2011. "D3 Data-Driven Documents." *IEEE Transactions on Visualization and Computer Graphics* 17(12): 2301–2309.

Bray, Tim. 2014. "The JavaScript Object Notation (JSON) Data Interchange Format." http://www.rfc-editor.org/rfc/rfc7159.txt.

Crombie, Duncan. 2015. "CSS 3D Transforms and Animations." Accessed August 3, 2015. http://www.the-art-of-web.com/css/3d-transforms/.

Dahl, Ryan. 2009. "Node.js." Accessed August 3, 2015. https://nodejs.org/.

Davies, Jason. 2013. "How the Word Cloud Generator Works." Accessed August 3, 2015. http://www.jasondavies.com/wordcloud/about/.

Davis, Hilary M. 2009. "Not Just Another Pretty Picture." http://www.inthelibrarywiththeleadpipe.org/2009/not-just-another-pretty-picture/.

Đuričić, Bojan. 2012. "JustGage." Accessed August 3, 2015. http://justgage.com/.

Google Inc. 2014. "What are Chrome Apps?" https://developer.chrome.com/apps/about_apps.

Harvard University. 2012. "Harvard Library Explorer." http://librarylab.law.harvard.edu/toolkit/.

Hevery, Miško. 2009. "Building Web Apps with Angular." Paper presented at the OOPSLA. Retrieved from http://www.oopsla.org/oopsla2009/program/demonstrations/254-building-web-apps-with-angular-2-of-2.

Hipp, D. Richard. 2015. "SQLite." https://www.sqlite.org/.

Indianapolis Museum of Art (IMA). 2010. "Dashboard Indianapolis Museum of Art." Accessed August 3, 2015. http://dashboard.imamuseum.org/.

Jackson, Dean, David Hyatt, Chris Marrin, and L. David Baron. 2013. "CSS Transitions."
    Accessed August 3, 2015. http://www.w3.org/TR/css3-transitions/.

LaPorte, Stephen, and Mahmoud Hashemi. 2013. "Listen to Wikipedia." Accessed August 3,
    2015. http://listen.hatnote.com/.

Lee, Yong Ju, and Brian Brush. 2013. "Filament Mind." Accessed August 3, 2015. http://
    www.eboarch.com/Filament-Mind.

Legrady, George. n.d. "Making Visible the Invisible, 2005–2014." Accessed August 3, 2015.
    http://www.mat.ucsb.edu/~g.legrady/glWeb/Projects/spl/spl.html.

McCutchan, John. 2006. "inotify(7)—Linux Man Page." http://linux.die.net/man/7/inotify.

Priem, Jason, Dario Taraborelli, Paul Groth, and Cameron Neylon. 2010. "altmetrics: a mani-
    festo." Accessed February 2, 2014. http://altmetrics.org/manifesto/.

Rauch, Guillermo. 2015. "Socket.IO." http://socket.io/.

Serials Solutions. 2009. "API Documentation Center." http://api.summon.serialssolutions.com/.

W3C. 2001. "Scalable Vector Graphics (SVG)." Accessed August 3, 2015. http://www
    .w3.org/Graphics/SVG/.

4

Using Google Tools to Create Public Analytics Visualizations

Lauren Magnuson

Libraries offer access to a huge range of digital resources through their websites, and gathering meaningful data about how those resources are used can be a significant challenge. At the same time, both internal and external library stakeholders increasingly expect to be able to easily access up-to-the-minute information about how library web resources are used. While many libraries have adopted Google Analytics as a free, convenient way of tracking user behavior on their websites, the ability to easily share up-to-date data and trends from Google Analytics with library staff and stakeholders is limited. Users can share Google Analytics data through Google Accounts, but this requires that they log in to view the data and that the Google Analytics account administrator grants individual access. Understanding analytics data through Google Analytics interfaces also requires users to have some working knowledge of how Google Analytics works and how to navigate its administrative menus.

This chapter will describe how the Google Analytics Application Programming Interface (API) can be used to create and share data visualizations that can be published on public-facing web pages or intranets. Beginning with creating a Google Analytics account and setting up a web property, this chapter will provide a step-by-step guide for using the Google Analytics API, a Google superProxy application, and the Google Charts API to create a public-facing dashboard to share Google Analytics data with your library's stakeholders.

GOOGLE ANALYTICS AND THE GOOGLE ANALYTICS API

Google Analytics gathers web usage behavior by placing a small JavaScript snippet into each web page for which usage data is desired. Once the tracking code has been installed and starts returning data to Google Analytics (which may take between twenty-four and forty-eight hours), analytics data can be accessed through the Google Analytics web interface, which requires access through a Google Account. Each domain or site tracked by Google Analytics is referred to as a distinct *property*. Account access to a particular web property can be shared and configured by the Google Analytics administrator under each web Property's Admin > User Management section (Google 2015d). To create visualizations through the methods described in this chapter, you must have a Google Account with *Read and Analyze* access to at least one Google Analytics property.

While Google Analytics data are most commonly accessed through the Google Analytics native interface, the same data are accessible via the Google Analytics Core Reporting Application Programming Interface (API) (Google 2015e). An *API* is a mechanism through which software components can communicate with each other. When using the Google Analytics Core Reporting API to power a public-facing dashboard, requests are sent from the dashboard viewer's browser to the Google Analytics service, which returns data from the analytics property to the user's browser. JavaScript or other client-side methods (such as the Google Charts API) can then be used to generate an array of interactive charts and graphs. The Google Analytics Core Reporting API can be used in conjunction with a Google App Engine application, known as the Google Analytics superProxy, to create a publicly accessible dashboard to show trends and patterns in your library's web traffic.

THE GOOGLE ANALYTICS SUPERPROXY

In 2013, Google Analytics released a method of accessing Google Analytics API data that doesn't require end users to authenticate to view data, known as the Google Analytics superProxy. Prior to the superProxy, it had been possible to build a custom application that could fetch Google Analytics data through the Google Analytics API, but for end users to access the data, they must first sign into Google Analytics through Google's OAuth 2.0 framework. This meant that every user who wished to view your Google Analytics data would have to be individually authorized to view them through the Google Analytics Admin interface. To get around this, the superProxy method was released. The superProxy facilitates the creation of a query engine that retrieves Google Analytics statistics through the Google Analytics Core Reporting API, caches the statistics in a separate web application service, and enables the display of Google Analytics data to end users without requiring individual authentication. Cacheing the data has the additional benefit of ensuring that your application will not exceed the Google Core Reporting API request limit of 50,000 requests per day. The superProxy can be set up to refresh a limited number of times per day, and in many cases a daily refresh of data is sufficient.

The required elements of this method are available on the superProxy GitHub page (Google 2015a). There are four major parts to the setup of the superProxy: (1) setting up Google App Engine hosting, (2) preparing the development environment on your local computer, (3) configuring and deploying the superProxy to Google's App Engine Appspot host, and (4) writing and scheduling queries that will be used to populate visualizations.

The following steps assume that you are logged into a Google account that has access to Google Analytics data. It is important to use the same Google account to authenticate all Google services discussed.

Set Up Google App Engine Hosting

First, enable your Google Analytics account credentials to access the Google Developer's Console at https://console.developers.google.com/start. The superProxy application you will be creating will be supported by the Google Developers Console. Click the *Use Google APIs* to create your application and designate an *Application Identifier* that will serve as the end point domain for queries to your Google Analytics data. Ultimately, the application itself will run from Google's App Engine service, and your Application Identifier will be used to construct the URL of the application (e.g., *mylibrarycharts.appspot.com*). If your chosen project ID is not entirely unique, Google may append numbers to the end of the project ID (e.g., mylibrarycharts-1124; see figure 4.1).

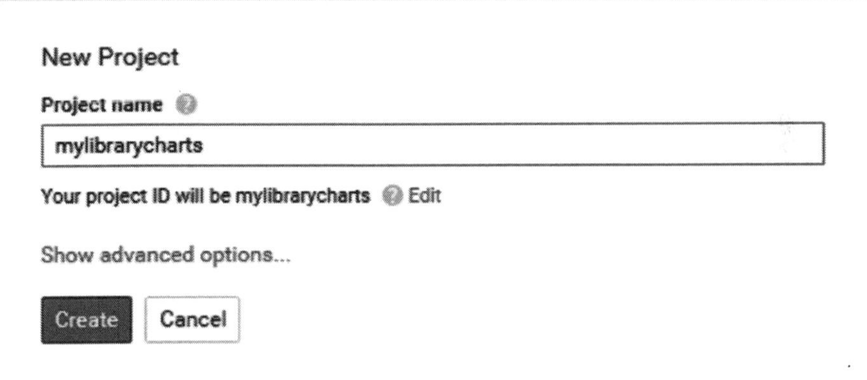

New Project

Project name ⓘ

mylibrarycharts

Your project ID will be mylibrarycharts ⓘ Edit

Show advanced options...

Create   Cancel

Figure 4.1.   Creating an Application with the Google App Engine.

Once your project has been created, you will have access to settings for the project. Navigate to the *APIs and auth* section and perform a search for Analytics to locate the Analytics API. Click on the Analytics API and click *Enable*. Then visit the *Credentials* menu to set up an OAuth 2.0 Client ID. You will be prompted to configure the *Consent Screen* menu and choose an email address (such as your Google account email address), fill in the product name field with your Application Identifier (e.g., *mylibrarycharts*), and save your settings. If you do not include these settings, you may experience errors when accessing your superProxy application admin menu.

Next, set up authentication credentials. Your application type is likely to be a *Web application*. Set the *Authorized JavaScript Origins* value to your appspot domain (e.g., *http://mylibrarycharts.appspot.com*). Use the same value for the *Authorized Redirect URI*, but add /admin/auth to the end (e.g., *http://mylibrarycharts.appspot.com/admin/auth*). Note the OAuth Client ID, OAuth Client Secret, and OAuth Redirect URI that are stored here, as you will need to reference them later before you deploy your superProxy application to the Google App Engine.

Prepare the Development Environment

To configure superProxy and deploy it to Google App Engine you will need two pieces of software installed on your local computer: Python 2.7 and the Google App Engine Launcher. Download the appropriate Python library for your operating system[1] and then install the Google App Engine SDK/Launcher for Python.[2] These pieces of software will enable you to configure and deploy your superProxy application to the Google App Engine host.

Configure and Deploy the superProxy

The superProxy application is available from the superProxy GitHub page.[3] Download the .zip files and extract them onto your computer into a location you can easily reference (e.g., C:/Users/yourname/Desktop/superproxy or /Applications/superproxy). Use a text editor such as Notepad or Notepad++ to edit the src/app. yaml to include your Application ID (e.g., *mylibrarycharts*). Then use Notepad to edit src/config.py to include the OAuth Client ID, OAuth Client Secret, and OAuth Redirect URI that were generated when you created the Client ID in the Google Developer's Console under the *Credentials* menu. Detailed instructions for editing these files are available on the superProxy GitHub page.

After you have edited and saved src/app.yaml and src/config.py, open the Google App Engine Launcher application previously downloaded. Go to File > Add Existing Application. In the dialogue box that appears, browse to the location of your superProxy app's /src directory (see figure 4.2).

Click *Add*. Then click the *Deploy* button in the upper right corner of the App Engine Launcher. You may be asked to log in to your Google account, and a log console may appear informing you of the deployment process. When deployment has finished, you should be able to access your superProxy application's Admin screen at http://[yourapplicationID].appspot.com/admin, replacing [yourapplicationID] with your Application Identifier. You must have an authenticated Google session (in other words, your browser must be logged in to your Google account) to access your app's superProxy settings. If you are logged in, you will see an option to Authorize Access, which you will need to do only once.

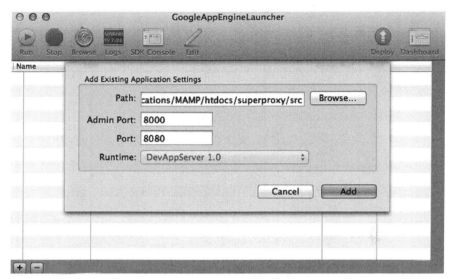

Figure 4.2.   Using the Google App Engine Launcher.

CREATING SUPERPROXY QUERIES

superProxy queries request data from your Google Analytics account and return those data to the superProxy application. When the data are returned, they are made available to an end point that can be used to populate charts, graphs, or other data visualizations on any web page. Most data available to you through the Google Analytics native interface are available through superProxy queries.

An easy way to get started with building a query is to visit the Google Analytics Query Explorer (https://ga-dev-tools.appspot.com/explorer/). You will need to log in with your Google Analytics account to use the Query Explorer. This tool allows you to build a sample query for the Core Reporting API, which is the same API service that your superProxy application will be using. It is helpful to experiment with creating queries using this tool before attempting to create a query with your superProxy app (figure 4.3).

When experimenting with the Google Analytics Query Explorer, make note of all the elements you use in your query. For example, to create a query that retrieves the number of users who visited your site between July 4 and July 18, 2015, you will need to select your Google *Account*, *Property* and *View* from the drop-down menus and then build a query with the following parameters:

ids = this is a number (usually eight digits) that will be automatically populated for you when you choose your Google Analytics *Account*, *Property* and *View*. The ids value is your *property ID*, and you will need this value later when building your superProxy query.

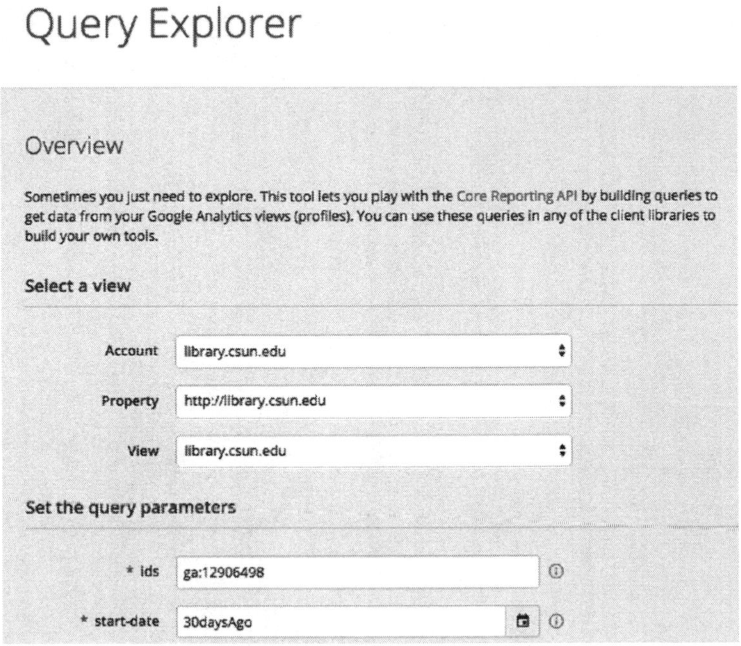

Query Explorer

Overview

Sometimes you just need to explore. This tool lets you play with the Core Reporting API by building queries to get data from your Google Analytics views (profiles). You can use these queries in any of the client libraries to build your own tools.

Select a view

Account	library.csun.edu	⬍
Property	http://library.csun.edu	⬍
View	library.csun.edu	⬍

Set the query parameters

| * ids | ga:12906498 | ⓘ |
| * start-date | 30daysAgo | 📅 ⓘ |

Figure 4.3. Running sample queries through the Google Analytics Query Explorer.

dimensions = ga:browser
metrics = ga:users
start-date = 07-04-2015
end-date = 07-18-2015

You can set the max-results value to limit the number of results returned. For queries that could potentially have thousands of results (such as individual search terms entered by users), limiting to the top ten or fifty results will retrieve data more quickly. Clicking on any of the fields will generate a menu from which you can select available options. Click *Get Data* to retrieve Google Analytics data and verify that your query works (figure 4.4).

Underneath the results of your query, you will see a field labeled API Query URI. This URI is an encoded query that you will be able to use in your superProxy application to schedule automatically refreshed data from the Google Analytics API. The encoded URI will look something like this:

```
https://www.googleapis.com/analytics/v3/data/ga?ids=ga%39999999
&start-date=30daysAgo&end-date=yesterday&metrics=ga%3Ausers&
dimensions=ga%3Abrowser&max-results=10
```

Results showing: **23**   Total results found: **23**
Contains sampled data: **No**   ↓ Jump to bottom

Browser	Users ▼
Chrome	57512
Internet Explorer	14215
Safari	14096
Firefox	6074
Edge	850
Safari (in-app)	227
Android Browser	131

Figure 4.4. Successful Google Analytics Query Explorer query result.

Note that this URI, if entered into a browser, does not result in any data being re-turned. Instead, entering this URI will result in an error because a log-in is required. This is because the URI can return data only if the request is wrapped in an authenti-cated API request via the superProxy. Return to your superProxy application's admin page (e.g., http://[yourapplicationid].appspot.com/admin and select *Create Query*). Name your query something to make it easy to identify later (e.g., Users by Browser). The *Refresh Interval* refers to how often you want the superProxy to retrieve fresh data from Google Analytics. For most queries, a daily refresh of the data will be suf-ficient, so if you are unsure, set the refresh interval to 86400. This will refresh your data every 86,400 seconds, or once per day (figure 4.5).

You can use the Google Analytics API Explorer to generate encoded URIs, or you can write them yourself to retrieve nearly any data from your Google Analytics ac-count. Building an encoded URI for the query may seem daunting, but understand-ing the various pieces of the URI can simplify creating custom queries (figure 4.6). Here is an example of an encoded URI that queries the number of users (organized by browser) who have visited a web property in the past 30 days:

```
https://www.googleapis.com/analytics/v3/data/ga?ids=ga:99999991
&start-date=30daysAgo&end-date=yesterday&metrics=ga:users&
dimensions=ga:browser&sort=-ga:users&max-results=5
```

Create Query « Admin Home

Setup your query

Query Name	Users by Browser
Refresh Interval (seconds)	86400	(1 hour = 3600, 1 day = 86400)

Encoded URI for the query

`https://www.googleapis.com/analytics/v3/data/ga?ids=ga:999999&metrics=ga:users&dimensions=ga:browser&max-results=10&start-date={30daysago}&end-date={today}`

Supported date parameters are {today} and {Ndaysago}.
Relative dates are resolved to actual dates during query execution and are currently configured to use the Pacific timezone.

E.g. A query for the last 7 days would use the following start and end dates:
https://www.googleapis.com/analytics/v3/data/ga?ids=ga%3A12345&start-date={6daysago}&end-date={today}

Tip: Use the Google Analytics Query Explorer to build a valid Query URI.

[Save Query] [Save & Schedule Query] [Test Query]

Figure 4.5.   Creating a superProxy Query.

All encoded URIs will start with https://www.googleapis.com/analytics/v3/data/ga?. The encoded URI also contains the following elements:

ids. The ids value is equal to the eight-digit Property ID of your Google Analytics property. This can be retrieved through the Google Analytics API Query Explorer.

```
https://www.googleapis.com/analytics/v3/data/ga?ids=ga:99999991
&start-date=30daysAgo&end-date=yesterday&metrics=ga:users&
dimensions=ga:browser&sort=-ga:users&max-results=5
```

metrics. The metrics property of the encoded URI determines the quantitative measure you wish to have returned from Google Analytics. For example, metrics might include the number of users, the number of sessions, or the number of new users.

```
https://www.googleapis.com/analytics/v3/data/ga?ids=ga:99999991
&start-date=30daysAgo&end-date=yesterday&metrics=ga:users&
dimensions=ga:browser&sort=-ga:users&max-results=5
```

dimensions. An optional, usually qualitative characteristic you wish to return from Google Analytics. While a metric may return the number of users who have visited your site, a dimension can organize the number of user visits by browser type, state, country, or other user characteristic.

```
https://www.googleapis.com/analytics/v3/data/ga?ids=ga:99999991
&start-date=30daysAgo&end-date=yesterday&metrics=ga:users&
dimensions=ga:browser&sort=-ga:users&max-results=5
```

sort. This element enables the data returned to be sorted by either the data's metrics or dimensions. In this example, dimensions are sorted by number of users in a descending pattern, which provides us the top browsers by number of users:

```
https://www.googleapis.com/analytics/v3/data/ga?ids=ga:99999991
&start-date=30daysAgo&end-date=yesterday&metrics=ga:users&
dimensions=ga:browser&sort=-ga:users&max-results=5
```

max-results. A limit to the number of results returned, resulting in quicker responses.

```
https://www.googleapis.com/analytics/v3/data/ga?ids=ga:99999991
&start-date=30daysAgo&end-date=yesterday&metrics=ga:users&
dimensions=ga:browser&sort=-ga:users&max-results=5
```

start-date and end-date. The time frame for which you want data returned. This query example returns data for the past thirty days, but you could set this to retrieve data for the past six months (e.g., start-date={179daysago}) or the past week (e.g., start-date={6daysago}). When data are returned through today, today's data will be included, so a start date of six days ago will return seven days of data.

```
https://www.googleapis.com/analytics/v3/data/
ga?ids=ga:99999991&start-date=30daysAgo&end-date=yesterday&metr
ics=ga:users&dimensions=ga:browser&sort=-ga:users&max-results=5
```

Before saving, be sure to run *Test Query* to see a preview of the kind of data that are returned by your query. A successful query will return a *JSON* (JavaScript Object Notation) string, which is a raw form of your Google Analytics data expressed as an array. A snippet of this array is shown below:

```
{u'kind': u'analytics#gaData', u'rows': [[u'Chrome',
u'57512'], [u'Internet Explorer', u'14215'], [u'Safari',
u'14096'], [u'Firefox', u'6074'], [u'Edge', u'850']],
u'containsSampledData': False, u'totalsForAllResults':
{u'ga:users': u'93442'}, u'id': u'https://www.googleapis.com/
analytics/v3/data/ga?ids=ga:12906498&dimensions=ga:browser&
metrics=ga:users&sort=-ga:users&start-date=30daysAgo&end-date
=yesterday&max-results=5', u'itemsPerPage': 5, u'nextLink':
u'https://www.googleapis.com/analytics/v3/data/ga?ids=ga:129064
98&dimensions=ga:browser&metrics=ga:users&sort=-ga:users&start-
date=30daysAgo&end-date=yesterday&start-index=6&max-results=5',
. . .
```

The JSON array contains data showing the number of users who accessed your site organized by browser. Once you've tested a successful query, save it, which will allow the JSON string to become accessible to an application that can help to visualize these data. After saving, you will be directed to the management screen for your API, where you will need to click *Activate Endpoint* to begin publishing the results of the query in a way that is retrievable on the web from any web page. Then click *Start Scheduling* so that the query data are refreshed on the schedule you determined when you built the query (e.g., once a day). Finally, click *Refresh Data* to return data for the first time so that you can start interacting with the data returned from your query. Return to your superProxy application's Admin page, where you will be able to manage your query and locate the public end point needed to create a chart visualization.

USING THE GOOGLE VISUALIZATION API
TO VISUALIZE GOOGLE ANALYTICS DATA

Included with the superProxy .zip file downloaded to your computer from the GitHub repository is a sample .html page located under /samples/superproxy-demo.html. This file contains sample JavaScript code that uses the Google Charts and the Google Charts API to generate two pie charts from data returned from superProxy queries. Google Charts is a service that can ingest raw data (such as JSON arrays that are returned by the superProxy) and generate visual charts and graphs (Google 2015b). You will need to save superproxy-demo.html onto a web server or onto your computer's localhost development environment to generate a visualization that can be viewed in a browser.[4] You can save this file on any web server by itself; it does not require the rest of the GitHub superProxy code to function. Instead of generating a pie chart, the code can be modified to generate a bar chart (see figure 9 in the photospread). The bar chart will use the data from the *Users by Browser* query saved in your superProxy app. Open superproxy-demo.html and locate this section of code:

```
var browserWrapper = new google.visualization.ChartWrapper({
// Example Browser Share Query
"containerId": "browser",
// Example URL: http://your-application-id.appspot.com/
query?id=QUERY_ID&format=data-table-response
"dataSourceUrl": "REPLACE WITH Google Analytics superProxy
PUBLIC URL, DATA TABLE RESPONSE FORMAT",
"refreshInterval": REPLACE_WITH_A_TIME_INTERVAL,
"chartType": "PieChart",
"options": {
"showRowNumber" : true,
"width": 630,
"height": 440,
"is3D": true,
"title": "REPLACE WITH TITLE"
}
});
```

Three values need to be modified to create a pie chart visualization:

dataSourceUrl. This value is the public end point of the superProxy query you have created. To get this value, navigate to your superProxy admin page and click *Manage Query* on the *Users by Browser* query you have created. On this page, right click the *DataTable (JSON Response)* link and copy the URL (figure 4.6). Paste the copied URL into superproxy-demo.html, replacing the text *REPLACE WITH Google Analytics superProxy PUBLIC URL, DATA TABLE FORMAT*. Leave quotes around the pasted URL.

Figure 4.6. Using the DataTable (JSON Response) link to copy a URL to your clipboard.

refreshInterval. This can be the same refresh interval of your superProxy query (in seconds, e.g., 86,400).

chartType. Change this value to BarChart to display the data as a bar chart instead of the default pie chart. You can change the chartType value to any type supported by the Google Charts API that makes sense with your data.[5]

title. This is the title that will appear above your chart.

Save the modified superproxy-demo.html file to your server or localhost environment, and load the saved page in a browser. You should see a bar chart that shows the types of browsers used by your website's visitors, similar to figure 4.1, shown at the beginning of this chapter.

CONCLUSION

Configuring the superProxy to return Google Analytics data requires an initial upfront investment in time and effort. However, once your superProxy application has been set up you can create multiple queries and reference the data in multiple visualizations that load on any web page. The ability to visualize and share usage trends can support decision making throughout a library's organization, and the superProxy is flexible enough to adapt to the changing data needs of your library's environment. As libraries are increasingly data-driven organizations required to demonstrate accountability and effectiveness to a variety of stakeholders, using Google Analytics data to illustrate the usage of your library's web resources can be one method of meeting that goal.

NOTES

1. Python 2.7 is freely available from https://www.python.org/download/releases/2.7/.

2. Available from https://developers.google.com/appengine/downloads - Google_App_Engine_SDK_for_Python.

3. https://github.com/googleanalytics/google-analytics-super-proxy.

4. A localhost development environment can be installed on Windows using free XAMPP software (available from https://www.apachefriends.org/index.html) or on Mac OS X with MAMP (available from http://www.mamp.info/en/downloads/).

5. A gallery of available chart types, as well as sample code, is available in the Google Charts Chart Gallery (https://developers.google.com/chart/interactive/docs/gallery?hl=en).

REFERENCES

Google. 2015a. *Google Analytics superProxy*. Accessed October 31, 2015.
   https://github.com/googleanalytics/google-analytics-super-proxy.
Google. 2015b. *Google Visualization API Reference*. Accessed October 31, 2015.
   https://developers.google.com/chart/interactive/docs/reference.
Google. 2015c. *Set up Analytics tracking*. Accessed October 31, 2015.
   https://support.google.com/analytics/answer/1008080?hl=en.
Google. 2015d. *User permissions*. Accessed October 31, 2015.
   https://support.google.com/analytics/answer/2884495?hl=en.
Google. 2015e. *What Is The Core Reporting API - Overview*. Accessed October 31, 2015.
   https://developers.google.com/analytics/devguides/reporting/core/v3/.

5

Minding the Gap

Utilizing Data Visualizations for Library Collection Development

Roger S. Taylor and Emily Mitchell

A large proportion of library data centers on our collections and their use. Each title that comes into the collection receives metadata through cataloging and then has further data associated with it as the library tracks its use. Even small libraries often contain several thousand titles, and the sheer numbers make it difficult for data novices to pull actionable information out of the massive spreadsheets that ILSs (integrated library systems) provide as usage reports.

This overwhelming flood of data, plus most librarians' lack of training on how to deal with it, may well explain why circulation data are rarely leveraged to the full extent they could be. Common advice to librarians taking over a new collection development area is to familiarize themselves with their collection by "browsing the book stacks, journals, and the reference section. . . . This type of assessment will provide information about the format, age, quality, scope . . . and physical condition of the collection" (Tucker and Torrence 2004).

Much less common is advice to spend time with circulation data. While browsing the stacks is indeed a useful means of getting a feel for a collection, it cannot hope to convey the same wealth of information that could be gleaned from well-visualized usage reports. As Tukey wrote in 1977, "The greatest value of a picture is when it forces us to notice what we never expected to see." Of course, this presupposes that the tools and skill set to create meaningful graphics are available.

In many libraries, it is extremely useful to have someone on staff with even a rudimentary idea of how to visualize all the data about the collection and make them more palatable to human beings. This point is well illustrated by a recent article in *Computers in Libraries* that focuses on using circulation data to improve collection development (Meyer 2015). The author used Microsoft Excel to create line graphs showing increases and decreases in circulation of particular library collections over time.

While this is a worthwhile first step toward using data visualizations to improve collection development, experts generally consider Excel to be a poor tool for processing data and creating visualizations (e.g., Panko 2008). There is a great deal more that can be done with circulation data than just creating line graphs in Excel! Better ways of visualizing the same data can help librarians learn more and different things about their collections. Using scripting rather than Excel reduces errors, increases the possibilities for how to visualize the data, and allows for better comparisons across time periods.

Collection development, reduced to its simplest form, is merely a matter of adding to the collection those items that can and should be added to the collection, and removing from the collection those items that can and should be removed from the collection. In practice, however, collection development requires a great deal more skill and knowledge than such a simplistic definition would imply. How can one know which items to select? How can one know which items to weed from the collection? A library's budget, goals, and policies all affect the answers to those questions—but so should data about the library's collections. This chapter will focus on the latter. Specifically, we will be looking at the following questions, which any collection development librarian would want answered:

1. Where is the collection mostly made up of old and possibly out-of-date materials?
2. Which parts of the collection see the most circulation?

Answering these questions can be difficult when all there is to look at is a spreadsheet containing data about thousands of titles. With visualizations, however, the task becomes much easier. This allows collection development librarians to make informed decisions based on the realities of their existing collections rather than basing their selections on anecdotal evidence from the reference desk or inaccurate impressions from walking through the stacks.

DATA VISUALIZATION SOLUTION

Data visualizations are a powerful technique to help solve this problem. However, this is rarely straightforward and frequently requires first "cleaning" messy, raw data, so in this chapter we'll first provide a guide on how to perform this process.

Of course, one first needs to obtain the relevant data. In our example we have one year of circulation data from our college library. The data were exported from the ILS in CSV (comma separated value) format. In the CSV format commas are inserted to distinguish both variable names and data values. The CSV format is a simple text file, which is advantageous because it is easy to read (it can be opened by any text editor), minimizes the chances of data corruption, and can be imported into virtually all visualization and statistical analysis software packages. For example, the beginning of the raw circulation data that we'll be using in this chapter follows:

```
"Bib Num","OCLC Num","Title","Author","Imprint","Year","Call
Num","# of Transactions"
```

```
"000014741","(OCoLC)10925248^","""Surely you're joking, Mr.
Feynman!" : adventures of a curious character / Richard P.
Feynman as tol","Feynman, Richard Phillips.","New York :
W.W. Norton, c1985.","1985","QC16.F49 A37 1985 Circulating
Collection, 3rd Floor","1",
"000365152","(OCoLC)53192156","""The willing servant" :
a history of the steam locomotive / David Ross.","Ross,
David.","Stroud : Tempus, 2004.","2004","TJ603 .R67 2004
Circulating Collection, 3rd Floor","1", Collection, 3rd
Floor","1",
```

Depending on the degree of the "messiness" of the data they might need to be processed before they can be loaded into analysis and visualization software. In our case, the data obtained from the ILS were relatively tidy (Wickham 2014). Namely, each variable was saved in its own column and each observation was saved in its own row. In addition, the column headers contained the variable names.

In our example the raw data required a moderate amount of cleaning before it could be processed using the R programming language. To solve this problem we used spreadsheet software for this first step of data cleaning. There are a variety of spreadsheet programs that can be used to open and process CSV files (e.g., Microsoft Excel, Apple Numbers). However, continuing with our goal of using accessible tools we used the free and open source LibreOffice (v. 4.4) Calc Spreadsheet (downloadable here https://www.libreoffice.org).

We opened (imported) the CSV file we named "circulation_data.txt" (see figure 5.1). Note the checkmark for the "Comma" separator options. The bottom of the window

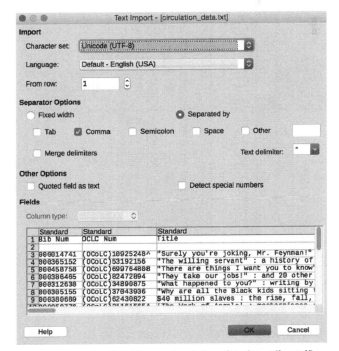

Figure 5.1. Importing library circulation data into LibreOffice.

provides a preview of how the data will be structured when opened in the spreadsheet. Many times the initial "raw" data set will include irrelevant variables, which one may want to remove at this point. In our case, we removed the first column (Bibliography Number), second column (OCLC Number), and fifth column (Imprint data).

The next step was to replace the variable names on the first row to make them easier to read for machines and humans. We eliminated all nonnumber and non-letter characters, with the exception of the underscore ("_"), which was used to replace blank spaces. In our specific case the variable "Call Num" was changed to "Call_Number" and the variable "# of Transactions" was changed to "Transactions." We were left with five variables, shown below in table 5.1 and figure 5.2.

Table 5.1. Variable names (R code variable names and the data to which they refer)

Variable Name	Data
Title	Title of the book
Author	Author of the book
Year	Year of publication
Call_Number	Call number code
Transactions	Number of transactions

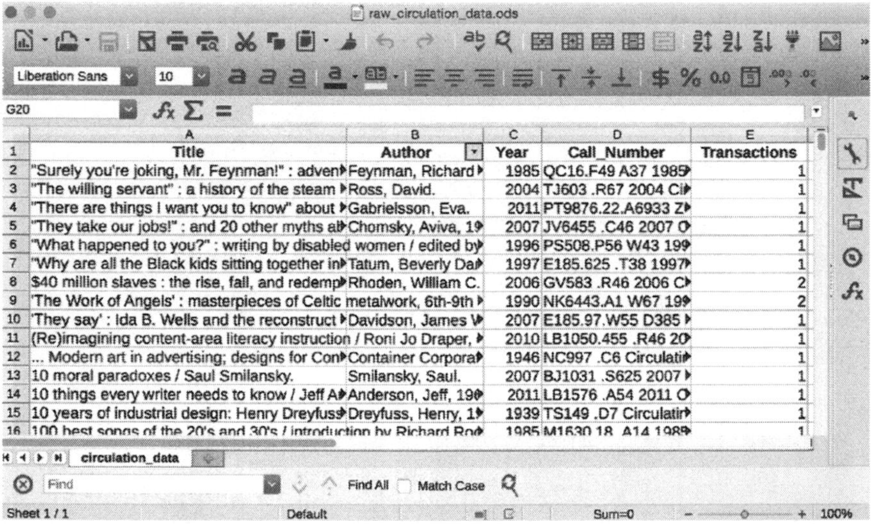

Figure 5.2. Cleaned and formatted spreadsheet view of CSV data file in LibreOffice.

After the variable names (column headers) had been fixed, we next examined the specific values (individual cells) for each variable. To do this we used the spreadsheet filter function to determine whether the variable values were appropriate (e.g., only numerical values in the year variable). For instance, there was an instance in which text ("New York . . .") was incorrectly entered in the year variable (see figure 5.3).

Figure 5.3. Filter function allowing a scan for nonviable values (e.g., nonnumerical years).

Another common problem is missing values—instances in which a variable value is empty (i.e., no data in a spreadsheet cell). We solved this problem by first using the spreadsheet's filter tool to display instances (rows) of a variable that were empty (i.e., missing). For instance, figure 5.4 shows how we selected the instances in which the author information was missing.

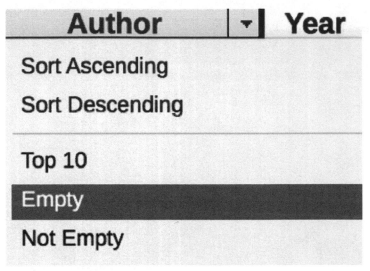

Figure 5.4.   Filter function allowing selection of all instances (rows) of a variable.

The next step was to fill in the missing values. However, there were many instances in which this was not possible. For those cases, we deleted the instances (rows) that could not be repaired. After deleting these cases, one must remember to *turn off* the filter to be able to view the main data set, which will no longer include the rows that had empty variables. After this initial cleaning, the data were tidy enough to be loaded into our data manipulation and visualization software, which we describe in the next section.

R SOFTWARE: DEDUCER

R is an open source programming language used for data manipulation, statistical analyses, and visualizations (R Core Team 2014). R is extremely powerful, but it has a steep learning curve, which limits its use for people without a programming background. To help overcome this problem we choose to use Deducer—a user-friendly graphical user interface (GUI) for R. More detailed information is available in Fellows's excellent 2012 *Journal of Statistical Software* Deducer article or at the software website: http://www.deducer.org. One especially valuable Deducer feature is that the software converts the GUI selections into R code, which appears in the Console window (see figure 5.5), which can be copied and reused or modified. The Data Viewer window has two tabs that can be selected: Data View and Variable View. The Data View tab, shown below in figure 5.6, shows the information as it would appear in a spreadsheet.

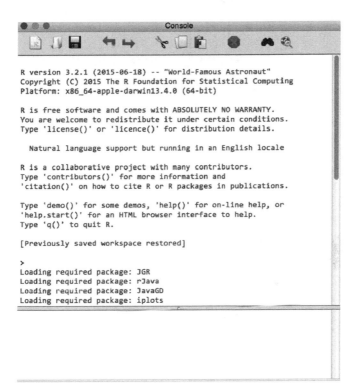

Figure 5.5.   Deducer software Console window.

	Title	Author	Year	Call_Number	Transactions
1	"Surely you're joking, Mr. Feynman!" :...	Feynman, Richard...	1985	QC16.F49 A37 1...	1
2	"The willing servant" : a history of the...	Ross, David....	2004	TJ603 .R67 2004...	1
3	"There are things I want you to know"...	Gabrielsson, Eva....	2011	PT9876.22.A693...	1
4	"They take our jobs!" : and 20 other...	Chomsky, Aviva, 1...	2007	JV6455 .C46 200...	1
5	"What happened to you?" : writing by,...	NA	1996	PS508.P56 W43...	1
6	"Why are all the Black kids sitting toget...	Tatum, Beverly Dan...	1997	E185.625 .T38 1...	1
7	$40 million slaves : the rise, fall, and...	Rhoden, William C....	2006	GV583 .R46 200...	2
8	'The Work of Angels' : masterpieces of...		1990	NK6443.A1 W67...	2
9	'They say' : Ida B. Wells and the recon...	Davidson, James W...	2007	E185.97.W55 D3...	1
10	(Re)imagining content-area literacy ins...		2010	LB1050.455 .R46...	1
11	... Modern art in advertising; designs f...	Container Corporati...	1946	NC997 .C6...	1
12	10 moral paradoxes / Saul Smilansky....	Smilansky, Saul....	2007	BJ1031 .S625 20...	1
13	10 things every writer needs to know...	Anderson, Jeff, 19...	2011	LB1576 .A54 201...	1
14	10 years of industrial design: Henry D...	Dreyfuss, Henry, 1...	1939	TS149 .D7...	1
15	100 best songs of the 20's and 30's /...	NA	1985	M1630.18 .A14...	1
16	100 butterflies and moths : portraits f...	Miller, J. C. (Jeff C.)...	2007	QL554.C8 M55 2...	1
17	100 dresses : the Costume Institute, t...	NA	2010	GT2060 .A15 20...	1
18	100 edible mushrooms / Michael Kuo...	Kuo, Michael, 1963...	2007	QK617 .K85 200...	1
19	100 great artists : a visual journey fro...	Gerlings, Charlotte,...	2013	N40 .G47 2006...	2
20	1000 chairs / Charlotte & Peter Fiell ;...	Fiell, Charlotte....	2005	NK2715 .F47 20...	1

Figure 5.6.   Deducer software Data Viewer window, Data View tab.

The Variable View tab (see figure 5.7) shows the data's variable names and type (categories). There are many different data types, but here we'll focus on just those directly relevant to our case study. The most straightforward is Integer, which means the data comprise only whole numbers. In our case there can't be fractional transactions, so these data are stored as integers. The second type is Character, in which R categorizes the data as a mere collection of letters, numbers, and symbols. In our case this would include the book titles, authors, and call numbers. The third data type is Factor, which is somewhat more complicated than the other two. Factor variables are used to distinguish groups that will be compared. In our case, we'll compare different call number subcategories (i.e., Architecture books versus Sculpture books). Factors represent what would be called levels of a variable in statistics. The ordering of the factors can influence the format of some data visualizations. Deducer automatically puts the factors in alphabetical order. The easiest way to change the ordering is from within the Data Viewer window Variable View tab. Simply click on the variable Factor Levels cell and a pop-up window will appear (see figure 5.8). Then use the arrow keys to change the ordering of the factor levels.

Depending on the structure of one's data and R settings, it might be necessary to adjust the category type of the imported variables. In our case, we need to change the Title, Author, and Call_Number variables from Factor type to Character type. This can be done in the Data Viewer Variable View tab by right clicking (Control-click on a Mac) on the word "Factor" and selecting "Character" instead. This will result in the corresponding R code appearing in the Output area of the Console Window (e.g., `circulation_data[,1]<-as.character(circulation_data[,1])`).

As we've seen earlier in this chapter, the Deducer GUI outputs the specific commands for every action taken. These are extremely valuable because they precisely

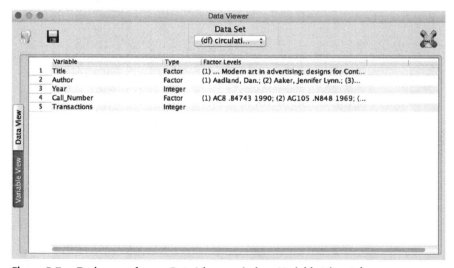

Figure 5.7. Deducer software Data Viewer window, Variable View tab.

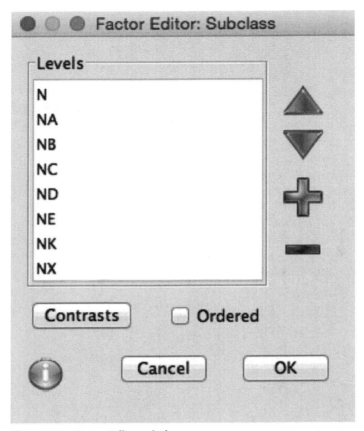

Figure 5.8. Factor Editor window.

record all actions taken. This output of specific commands allows one to document steps that one has taken, which helps to reveal errors and make it possible to easily rerun analyses at a later time. It also allows data and analyses to be shared with others, a critical aspect of *reproducible research* (e.g., LeVeque, Mitchell, and Stodden 2012; Peng 2011; Sandve, Nekrutenko, Taylor, Hovig, and Bourne 2013). Deducer has a built-in editor that can be used for this purpose (see figure 5.9). So in addition to saving the data and results, one should save the commands used.

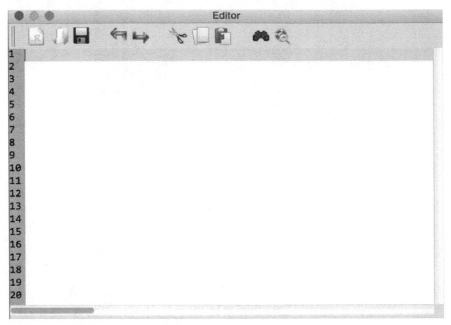

Figure 5.9. Deducer syntax editor.

R PACKAGES

As mentioned earlier, R is extremely powerful and allows several ways to accomplish the same result. Another advantage of R is the constant development of supplementary modules called *packages* that can be downloaded from the Internet and installed to provide the user with additional functionality. In this chapter we'll demonstrate how to install and use several such packages. For data manipulation we used "stringi," "dplyr," and "stringr," which we'll describe in detail below.

The *stringi* package was designed to provide users with a powerful way to manipulate their text data (Gagolewski and Tartanus 2015). The code box below shows how to install the *stringi* package and load it into R. The next three code blocks used the call number variable data to create three new variables: Class, Subclass, and Subclass number. These three new variables will be used in the subsequent data visualizations. Lines of code that begin with # are ignored by R and serve only to make the code more readable to humans.

```
install.packages("stringi")
library(stringi)
# Class. Matchs (extracts) first Letter.
circulation_data<- transform(circulation_data, Class =
as.character(stri_match_first(circulation_data$Call_Number,
regex = "[:alpha:]")))
```

```
# Subclass. Matches (extracts) first set of letters.
circulation_data<- transform(circulation_data, Subclass =
as.character(stri_extract_first(circulation_data$Call_Number,
regex = "[:alpha:]{1,}")))
# Subclass_Number. Matches (extracts) first set of digits.
circulation_data<- transform(circulation_data, Subclass_Number
= as.integer(stri_extract_first(circulation_data$Call_Number,
regex = "\\d{1,}")))
```

	Title	Author	Year	Call_Number	Transactions	Class	Subclass	Subclass_Number
1	"Surely you're joking, Mr. Feynman!"...	Feynman,...	1985	QC16.F49 A37...	1	Q	QC	16
2	"The willing servant" : a history of th...	Ross, Davi...	2004	TJ603 .R67 20...	1	T	TJ	603
3	"There are things I want you to know...	Gabrielss...	2011	PT9876.22.A6...	1	P	PT	9876
4	"They take our jobs!" : and 20 other...	Chomsky,...	2007	JV6455 .C46 2...	1	J	JV	6455
5	"Why are all the Black kids sitting tog...	Tatum, Be...	1997	E185.625 .T38...	1	E	E	185
6	$40 million slaves : the rise, fall, an...	Rhoden,...	2006	GV583 .R46 20...	2	G	GV	583
7	"They say" : Ida B. Wells and the rec...	Davidson,...	2007	E185.97.W55 D...	1	E	E	185
8	... Modern art in advertising; design...	Container...	1946	NC997 .C6 Circ...	1	N	NC	997
9	10 moral paradoxes / Saul Smilansk...	Smilansky,...	2007	BJ1031 .S625 2...	1	B	BJ	1031
10	10 things every writer needs to kno...	Anderson,...	2011	LB1576 .A54 2...	1	L	LB	1576
11	10 years of industrial design: Henry...	Dreyfuss,...	1939	TS149 .D7 Circ...	1	T	TS	149
12	100 butterflies and moths : portrait...	Miller, J. C...	2007	QL554.C8 M55...	1	Q	QL	554
13	100 edible mushrooms / Michael Ku...	Kuo, Mich...	2007	QK617 .K85 20...	1	Q	QK	617
14	100 great artists : a visual journey f...	Gerlings,...	2013	N40 .G47 2006...	2	N	N	40
15	1000 chairs / Charlotte & Peter Fiell...	Fiell, Charl...	2005	NK2715 .F47 2...	1	N	NK	2715
16	101 things to learn in art school / Ki...	White, Kit,...	2011	N325 .W49 20...	2	N	N	325
17	1014 GRE practice questions / Neill...	Seltzer, N...	2009	LB2367.4 .S44...	1	L	LB	2367
18	1066 : the year of the conquest / D...	Howarth,...	1978	DA195 .H69 19...	1	D	DA	195
19	11/22/63 : a novel / Stephen King...	King, Step...	2011	PS3561.I483 A...	2	P	PS	3561
20	12 million black voices; a folk histor...	Wright, Ri...	1941	E185.6 .W9 Cir...	1	E	E	185

Figure 5.10. Transformed data with call number extracted for new variables.

The *dplyr* package was designed to provide users with a powerful and easy way to manipulate their data (Wickham and Francois 2015).

In our example we decided to look at just the art books (Class N). A single line of code, shown below, shows how to create this subset. The new data frame will not automatically appear in the Data Viewer window. To view these new data click on the pull-down menu and select the data frame called "art_data":

```
install.packages("dplyr")
library(dplyr)
# Create subset of Art books (call numbers that begin with N)
art_data <- filter(circulation_data, Class == "N")
```

It's easy to forget the specific library subclass codes (i.e., NB for sculpture, etc.), so we decided to add a new variable, "Subclass_Names," to help with this problem. From the Deducer Console Window click on "Data" in the menu bar and select "Recode Variables" (make sure that "art_data" is selected; see figure 5.11).

After selecting "Subclass" and clicking the triangle to move it to the window on the right, select "Subclass -> Subclass" in the middle window and then click on the "Target" button on the right. This will open a new input window; type in "Subclass_Names" and press the "okay" button. Now click on the "Define Recode" button. In

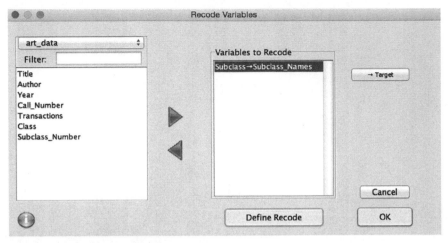

Figure 5.11. Recode Variables window.

the "Set Variable Codings" window specify how each variable gets recoded (e.g., N into Visual Arts, NA into Architecture, etc.; see figure 5.12).

```
art_data[c("Subclass_Names")] <- recode.variables(art_
data[c("Subclass")] , "'N' -> 'Visual Arts';NA ->
'Architeture';'NB' -> 'Sculpture';'NC' -> 'Drawing/Design/
Illustration';'ND' -> 'Painting';'NE' -> 'Print Media';'NK' ->
'Decorative Arts';'NX' -> 'General Arts';")
```

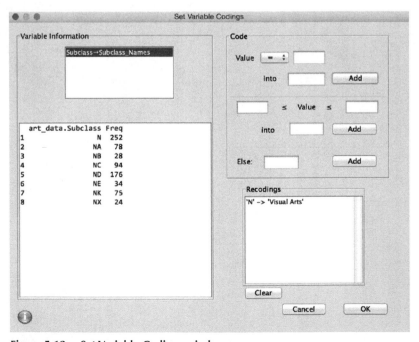

Figure 5.12. Set Variable Codings window.

Since the data have already been cleaned, they are now ready to be used to create the data visualizations. However, before proceeding we need to set the Working Directory, using the GUI command located under "File" in the Console Window pull-down menu. Then we save the data using the GUI command located under "File" in the Console Window pull-down menu. The example syntax for both is shown below.

```
setwd("/Users/rtaylor2/Documents/R_Folder/LDV_R")
save(circulation_data,file='/Users/rtaylor2/Documents/R_Folder/
LDV_R/circulation_data.rda'
```

DATA VISUALIZATION PRINCIPLES

Tempting as it may be, there are no "best" visualizations that we can recommend. Rather, data visualizations fall along a continuum of being more or less effective depending on the structure of the underlying data and the goals of the author.

A first step when considering the type of data visualization to use is to determine a variable's scale of measurement (Stevens 1946). The most basic category is called *nominal*, with specific values serving to "name" individual cases. For instance, athletes frequently wear numbered jerseys, but the numbers do not indicate attributes of the players (e.g., player #10 isn't twice as skilled as player #5). Nominal variables can also indicate membership in a category (e.g., offense or defense, home or away). In our case a book's subclass letter represents categories of library books and does not imply an order or ranking.

A second category is called *ordinal*, with specific values that do serve to measure the order or ranking of individual cases. For instance, we might know the order in which athletes finished a race (e.g., first/second/third, gold/silver/bronze) but not know their specific times. In the library world, we might see primary, secondary, and tertiary sources. Even if we don't know exact publication dates, the primary source definitely came before the secondary source, which in turn was before the tertiary source.

A third category is called *interval* (or ratio), which is the most accurate measurement category, with precise values along a variable. For instance, we might know the exact times in which all the athletes finished a race. In our case a book's year of publication and number of transactions are interval variables. The measurement scale of the data will help determine the appropriate visualizations to be employed.

Jacques Bertin's *Semiology of Graphics* (1983) provided one of the first systematic approaches to visual representations and will serve as the foundation for our discussion of data visualization principles. Bertin conceptualized visualizations as categories of "marks" on paper in which one could draw points, lines, or areas (or "zones"). This information was positional and placed on a two-dimensional (*xy*) plane. He then pointed out that one could encode additional variable "dimensions" by using other visual attributes such as size, shape, and color. We'll revisit these distinctions later in the chapter when we discuss our examples of library visualizations.

There is an enormous range of ways to represent data (e.g., Heer, Bostock, and Ogievetsky 2010). Thankfully, research has provided us with some guidelines. We've learned that our perceptual systems are most accurate with visualizations that utilize spatial position on a two-dimensional surface and the relative length of lines. In addition, color, size, and shape can be used to represent data, but these things have lower perceptual accuracy (Cleveland and McGill 1985). This research helped to inform our choice of the two types of data visualizations we recommend for library collection development: waffle charts and scatterplots.

DATA VISUALIZATION: WAFFLE CHART

One of the most frequently used (and misused) data visualization types is the ubiquitous pie chart (Spence 2005). Edward Tufte (1983) was particularly adamant about avoiding the use of pie charts:

> The only thing worse than a pie chart is several of them, for then the viewer is asked to compare quantities located in spatial disarray both within and between pies, as in the heavily encoded example from an atlas. Given their low data-density and failure to order numbers along a visual dimension, pie charts should never be used.

Perhaps the main reason for the popularity of pie charts is that under very specific circumstances, they can provide an intuitive understanding of part-whole relationships. This requires that the individual slices be mutually exclusive and add up to a meaningful whole. The main difficulty with pie charts is that people are not good at estimating the angles of the slices. A better alternative is the waffle chart, also called a "square pie chart" (Kosara and Ziemkiewicz 2010). The waffle chart eliminates the problem of angle estimation and allows the reader to easily compare the individual parts of the whole. Furthermore, if desired, one could count the number of squares to get more precise measurements. For instance, in the waffle chart (see figure 10 in the photospread) of library transactions per Fine Arts subclass, we can quickly count and see that General Art (shown in orange) had twenty transactions.

```
install.packages(c("waffle"))
library(waffle)
art_transactions <- c('Visual Arts (N)'=342,
    'Architecture (NA)'=82,
    'Sculpture (NB)'= 30,
    'Drawing.Design.Illustration (NC)'=116,
    'Painting (ND)'=187,
    'Print Media (NE)'=38,
    'Decorative Arts (NK)'=87,
    'General Arts (NX)'=36)
waffle(art_transactions, rows=20, size=.5,
```

```
colors=c("#E16D5E", "#D3709A", "#9289C0", "#2A9CB8", "#0BA287",
"#699D4D", "#A88D32", "#D3784E"),
   title="Transactions per Fine Arts Subclass",
   xlab="1 square == 1 Transaction during past year")
```

The waffle chart is good with a relatively small number of categories but is limited to a single dimension of data that can be expressed. In our case we would like to be able to see the book class/subclass, year of publication, and number of transactions. Scatterplots can provide us with the capability.

DATA VISUALIZATION: SCATTERPLOT

As discussed earlier, people are highly accurate when making judgments based on data represented on a two-dimensional plane. This is one reason for the ubiquity of scatterplots in both academic and nonacademic publications. It also allows one to add in the dimensions of color, size, and shape to represent other variables.

In our example, we followed the convention of representing time along the *x*-axis. The subclass categories were represented by both the *y*-axis and color (see figure 11 in the photospread). Because of the importance of this variable we represented it by two attributes to make interpretation easier for the reader. Lastly, the number of transactions was represented by the size of the individual data points ("marks"). Size was chosen because of the intuitive belief that the relative size of the data points corresponds to the relative size of the variable. A sign of good design is that the choices should seem "obvious" to the viewer.

```
ggplot() + geom_point(aes(x = Class,y = Transactions, colour
= Class),data = circulation_data, size = 3, alpha = 0.7,
position = position_jitter(width=.4))
ggsave("Transactions x Class - Scatterplot.png", units = "cm",
width=40, height=20, dpi=150)
```

SUMMARY AND FUTURE DIRECTIONS

Using these visualizations, it is possible to tell nearly at a glance which call number ranges are seeing the most use and how important currency of content is in driving usage of materials. Of course, even with these graphics to aid in understanding how materials are being used, collection development librarians still need to interrogate the information before them. *Why* is it that books in the call range NE (print media) are used less often than books in the call range ND (painting)? Is it because the library's patrons are just more interested in painting than in print media? Is it that the library's collection in print media isn't meeting patrons' needs so that they're turning elsewhere for information? Or might it be the simple fact that the library has fewer materials classified in the NEs than in the NDs?

The answers to these and other "why" questions can and should determine a collection development librarian's purchasing and deselection decisions. However, more information is needed to answer them than can be pulled from an ILS; institutional knowledge is necessary to know how to interpret them. By turning a list of materials and their usage into an appropriate and well-designed visualization, it becomes much easier for a librarian to hold enough of the relevant information in his or her mind at once to make informed decisions.

As more librarians become increasingly skilled at turning library data into visualizations, we should look for ways to integrate other data sources into our visualizations for collection development. The potential is there to integrate data from the collections budget or from interlibrary loan. Academic libraries might decide to find a way to integrate data about how many students/faculty members there are in a given subject area; public libraries might do something similar, but with age groups or other populations within their community. In all of these cases, the extra time spent learning a language like R and/or software like Deducer will pay rich dividends to any interested librarian.

REFERENCES

Bertin, Jacques. 1983. *Semiology of Graphics*. Madison: University of Wisconsin Press.

Cleveland, W. S., and McGill, R. 1985. "Graphical Perception and Graphical Methods for Analyzing Scientific Data." *Science* 229(4716): 828–833.

Fellows, Ian. 2012. "Deducer: A Data Analysis GUI for R." *Journal of Statistical Software* 49: 1–15.

Gagolewski, Marek, and Bartek Tartanus. 2015. *R Package Stringi: Character String Processing Facilities*. http://stringi.rexamine.com/. doi:10.5281/zenodo.19071.

Heer, Jeffrey, Michael Bostock, and Vadim Ogievetsky. 2010. "A Tour Through the Visualization Zoo." *Communications of the ACM* 53(6): 59–67.

Kosara, Robert, and Caroline Ziemkiewicz. 2010. "Do Mechanical Turks Dream of Square Pie Charts?" *Proceedings of the 3rd BELIV'10 Workshop*. 63–70.

LeVeque, Randall J., Ian M. Mitchell, and Victoria Stodden. 2012. "Reproducible Research for Scientific Computing: Tools and Strategies for Changing the Culture." *Computing in Science & Engineering*. 14(4): 13–17.

Meyer, J. 2015. "Monitoring the Pulse: Data-driven Collection Management." *Computers in Libraries* 6: 16.

Panko, Raymond R. 2008. *What We Know About Spreadsheet Errors*. Accessed November 10, 2015. http://panko.shidler.hawaii.edu/SSR/Mypapers/whatknow.htm.

Peng, Roger D. 2011. "Reproducible Research in Computational Science." *Science* 334(6060): 1226–1227.

R Core Team. 2014. *R: A Language and Environment for Statistical Computing*. R Foundation for Statistical Computing, Vienna, Austria. Accessed November 10, 2015. http://www.R-project.org/.

Rudis, Bob. 2015. *Waffle: Create Waffle Chart Visualizations in R*. R package version 0.3.1. Accessed November 10, 2015. http://CRAN.R-project.org/package=waffle.

Sandve, Geir Kjetil, Anton Nekrutenko, James Taylor, Eivind Hovig, and Philip E. Bourne. 2013. "Ten Simple Rules for Reproducible Computational Research." *PLoS Computational Biology* 9(10). http://doi.org/10.1371/journal.pcbi.1003285.

Spence, Ian. 2005. "No Humble Pie: The Origins and Usage of a Statistical Chart." *Journal of Educational and Behavioral Statistics* 30(4): 353–368. doi:10.3102/10769986030004353.

Stevens, S. S. 1946. "On the Theory of Scales of Measurement." *Science* 103(2684): 677–680.

Tucker, James Cory, and Matt Torrence. 2004. "Collection Development for New Librarians: Advice from the Trenches." *Library Collections, Acquisitions and Technical Services* 28(4): 397–409.

Tufte, Edward R. 1983. *The Visual Display of Quantitative Information.* Cheshire, CT: Graphics Press.

Tukey, John W. 1977. *Exploratory Data Analysis.* Reading, MA: Addison-Wesley.

Wickham, Hadley. 2009. *ggplot2: Elegant Graphics for Data Analysis.* New York: Springer.

Wickham, Hadley. 2014. "Tidy Data." *Journal of Statistical Software* 59(10): 1–23.

Wickham, Hadley, and Romain Francois. 2015. *dplyr: A Grammar of Data Manipulation.* R package version 0.4.2. Accessed November 10, 2015. http://CRAN.R-project.org/package=dplyr.

6

A Picture Is Worth a Thousand Books

OBILLSK, Data Visualization, and Interlibrary Loan

Ryan Litsey, Kenny Ketner, and Scott Luker

"A picture is worth a thousand words." This commonly spoken phrase captures the power an image can have, especially when we think about how we can represent large amounts of data in ways that can be better understood by decision makers and managers. The representation of large-scale data lies at the heart of data visualization. One of the biggest large-scale data sets in libraries exists in the transactions between institutions via Interlibrary Loan (ILL). The Online Based Inter-Library Loan Statistical Kit, or OBILLSK for short, can help both to report and direct decisions of librarians within a consortium. OBILLSK can also better represent visually the large amount of data that is contained within an ILL transaction. Being able to accurately and clearly represent a large data set of a workflow or process can serve as a tremendous guideline for better understanding the behavior of a system. Nowhere else is this more a necessary component than in today's modern academic libraries.

Academic libraries are very good at collecting data. We collect data on the circulation of books, eDatabase usage, patrons in the building, ILL statistics, and so on. All this data tracking, however, is a futile exercise unless we can accurately represent that data in models that can help inform decision making. One of the best areas in which we can utilize data visualization in decision making is in ILL. ILL, or resource sharing, as it has become more recently known, is the sharing of items owned by a library with another library that may not have access to that item. This is a process that at its core is a fundamental part of any library. However, in the academic library, it is of critical importance. Since not every library can be expected to own everything, resource sharing becomes an important part of the functioning of the academic library. This means that any large-scale academic library will have an ILL department that processes tens of thousands of these types of transactions every year. For example, last year the Texas Tech University Libraries handled over 90,000 transactions of either Texas Tech sending an item to another university, known in

ILL as lending, or another university sending Texas Tech something it owned, which is known as borrowing. These processes generate a mountain of data, depending on what the citation information for the item is, where it is going, the shipping address, when it is due back, and the overall current status of the request. At Texas Tech, this type of data is usually recorded in an SQL database that is utilized by the dominant ILL software ILLiad.

Atlas Systems's ILLiad is the software many academic libraries use to manage the exchanges between institutions in the ILL process. The software is very good at tracking the different statuses of the each request as well as the myriad potential outcomes of the request. There is one area though that the system is unable to process: what happens in between libraries. In an era of shrinking budgets, many libraries have entered into partnerships with other libraries to provide resources at little or no cost. In the ILL world, these partnerships are called consortiums. A library often will be a member of many consortiums to meet the resource needs of its patrons. While ILLiad does a good job of presenting in-house statistics, it does not provide much insight into the statistical data of the consortium as a whole. Essentially, how long does it take for a request to be sent from one library, received by another, and sent back? And what are the reasons for why each step takes the amount of time that it does?

Data about these kinds of transaction details are lacking in the world of ILL. The development of OBILLSK and the data it visualizes can rise to the challenge of filling that gap. Before we can illustrate what type of data is being visualized, it is important to understand the background behind the design, the architecture of how OBILLSK was built, the software involved, and problem it is solving of presenting the ILL metrics for all ILL transactions between the libraries of the Greater Western Library Alliance (GWLA). GWLA is a large academic consortium made up of the large research institutions of the American Southwest and Pacific Northwest. To see how we got to where we are today with OBILLSK, it is important first to examine how we as human beings come to need visualized data and how those data can help inform decision making in libraries, especially in the logistically complex arena of ILL.

BACKGROUND

To begin to understand the importance of data visualization, we must first engage in a bit of visualization ourselves. Imagine a river or stream flowing into a mountain lake. Now instead of water, think of data as the water flowing through a river and emptying into a big "data" lake. Traditional methods of "big data" analysis would argue that to get a picture of what is happening in the environment, we should sample the data in the lake. To sample the lake, we would dip our toes in and pull out a specific fact, maybe even casting in a line with a certain question like bait on a hook to elicit a response from the lake. We may even get lucky and catch a fish. The problem with this type of analysis is that it does not tell you anything about the composition of the data lake or how the data came to coalesce in that area. So to understand the formation of the data lake, we must examine the data as they are flowing in the river.

Of course, rivers do not stand still; they move in real time. To examine the data in real time, we must use visualization to accurately represent the different elements so that the researcher or analyst can get an accurate snapshot quickly, on demand. This simple description of data is emblematic of a larger point about the cognitive nature of human thinking. As Larkin and Simon argue,

> When they are solving problems, human beings use both internal representations, stored in their brains, and external representations, recorded on a paper, on a blackboard, or on some other medium. (Larkin and Simon 1987, 66)

Larkin and Simon touch on an ongoing debate about how we as people come to formulate ideas within our minds. Their paper illustrates how a diagram can serve as a better model for understanding than merely words, because data described by words in written sentences can relate to each other only laterally. In other words, a single word in a sentence can relate only to the word before it and the word after it. In contrast, data elements in a diagram can relate to a number of adjacent variables. This leads to the conclusion (Larkin and Simon 1987, 98) that a diagram is a superior method of communicating information for the following reasons:

- Diagrams can group together all information that is used together, thus avoiding large amounts of search for the elements needed to make a problem-solving inference.
- Diagrams typically use location to group information about a single element, avoiding the need to match symbolic labels.
- Diagrams automatically support a large number of perceptual inferences, which are extremely easy for humans to understand.

Understanding visualization in the form of a diagram can be a key component in the design of a software system that seeks to aid in understanding ILL between institutions. Thinking of the ILL transactions as mere lines of words and numbers in a spreadsheet would cause difficulty in conceptualization, but if we were to represent that data as a diagram, we could go a long way in better representing the large volume of over 600,000 ILL transactions each year between the libraries of the GWLA consortium.

The real-world value of this data visualization cannot be understated. The GWLA has always held as one of its core principles that all members of the Resource Sharing section are accountable to all of the other members to provide prompt service for all ILL transactions. To measure service promptness, the GWLA has historically run a semiannual data analysis of the ILL transactions to determine which libraries are meeting the benchmarks set for service. These benchmarks are a set of standards agreed on by the members:

- Eighty percent of all loans shipped from one GWLA school to another must be received within five days of receipt of request.
- Eighty percent of all articles must be received within seventy-two hours of receipt of the request from the borrowing institution.

This set of benchmarks has distinguished the GWLA consortium from other consortiums in that the member institutions are accountable for a standard of service to each other. These benchmarks are also known in ILL terminology as the turnaround time for processing items. They are a good indicator of the efficiency and effectiveness of the local institution's ILL operation.

The regular requirement to examine the GWLA metrics means that a member institution would need to volunteer to do the data analysis. Historically, it has been the responsibility of a single person to perform the data analysis; therefore the GWLA member institutions were limited to handmade reports based on semiannual sample sets of data. From a workflow perspective, this method required that each member of the consortium download a set of data from our ILL systems for the months of February through April and September through December of each year and then send them to the University of Kansas ILL department for analysis. This process is cumbersome and time consuming. There is also a high chance for error since the process relies on thirty-three people (the ILL librarians of the GWLA member institutions) to access their ILL data and send them to the analyst. So together the programmers at Texas Tech University Libraries brainstormed a way that we could make this process better.

CASE STUDY: OBILLSK AND ILL DATA SETS

In the summer of 2014 the work for OBILLSK began. During our initial few meetings, we discussed the nature of the problem. How can we build a system that can provide near real-time data analysis for thirty-three academic institutions with little impact on the ILL staff and generate near perfect data? Providing real-time data was a critical component for us, because we believe that having or analyzing the data from the river of data as it flows can help the decision makers at these institutions make better-informed decisions rather than visiting the metaphorical lake of data twice a year. To accomplish this list of objectives, we had to develop a set of workflow processes that would accomplish this task. Our first challenge was determining how to get the data from the schools without the ILL librarians being too inconvenienced by the system during their daily work. We made the decision to design a Windows executable file that would reside on the desktop of the ILL librarian. The librarian would activate this file once a week to run a series of processes that we will describe later. By having the system on the librarian's desktop, we were able to design an interface that librarians were comfortable with and used to using: the simple method of double clicking the file. Also, directly accessing the data at another institution created a second set of concerns, which we will discuss in a later section.

Once we had the icon on the desktop of the ILL librarian at each institution, the next step was to think of a way we could access the ILL data at each institution. That decision was rather easy. All of the GWLA libraries use ILLiad to run their ILL operations. ILLiad is a vendor-provided software that offers a local dashboard to clients and is supported by an SQL server. The SQL server is where all of the data about the ILL transactions at those institutions are stored. There are log-in credentials that the ILLiad dashboard uses to access the SQL. With the OBILLSK system, we used those same credentials to access the SQL data and run our data analysis. The software then sends the data to the OBILLSK server for analysis.

A Windows executable program written in C# was distributed to all participating institutions. The purpose of this executable program is to gather the local ILLiad data, package them, and upload them to the OBILLSK server at Texas Tech University. Users at each institution may review the data before uploading to Texas Tech so they can be confident that no personal patron information is being shared. The structure and layout of this program were kept as simple as possible for ease of use. A streamlined set of steps walk the user through each part of the process; the program enforces the order of these steps as well. In figures 6.1 and 6.2, the user can see how the program utilizes a minimal design using familiar interface elements.

The initial screen of the program is a minimal text input form requesting the location and log-in credentials for the institution's ILLiad SQL database (figure 6.1). On successful connection to the database, the next screen displays two buttons

Figure 6.1. The OBILLSK software log-in screen.

Figure 6.2. The OBILLSK software after the log-in screen.

(figure 6.2). The first button executes a query, populates a CSV file, and opens a save file dialogue window allowing the user to save the file to a location of choice. The second button facilitates the file upload process by linking directly to an upload page contained in the web application. In the final step, the user selects the CSV file generated by the program and uploads the file to the OBILLSK server. The data we are collecting are key to understanding how we negotiate the turnaround times.

The data collected consist of information from two ILLiad database tables: transactions and tracking. The data from the transactions table contain the ILL number, which serves as the system-level unique identifier, and citation information utilized in detailed lists within the web application. The data from the tracking table include timestamps and transactional status changes. These status changes are critical in analyzing the data and calculating borrowing and lending turnaround times. All data collected by the executable program are imported into the OBILLSK database. To achieve a high level of data integrity, this cumulative data set is referenced by only SQL queries and stored procedures, which create secondary data tables while leaving the source data pristine and intact. Once the data are collected the steps necessary to display them in a visually appealing way are very important.

Using ILL SQL data, we are able to gather around 100,000 records per institution at a time and upload them to the TTU servers. Such a large amount of data is not useful unless we can design and interface and present the data in a visually appealing and useful way. That is where the web application coding for OBILLSK takes center stage.

The OBILLSK system is a Microsoft ASP.NET web application written in C#. Visual Studio 2013 is the primary development environment. To remain consistent with the Microsoft technological stack selected for the user interface, Microsoft SQL Server 2012 powers the database and stored procedures behind the application. These Microsoft technologies provide simplification of complex processes and are institutionally supported at Texas Tech University.

On top of this .NET web application foundation, other contemporary website user interface technologies are implemented to make the data as visually appealing as possible. The OBILLSK site is designed with a responsive design using Bootstrap, a popular cascading style sheets (CSS) and JavaScript library for rendering websites mobile first, appropriately formatted for any size device. For example, larger menus automatically collapse into a single drop-down menu represented by a three-line icon commonly known as a hamburger button. Other buttons that open various reports on the screen will line up vertically for cell phone users and in a wide rectangle for tablet and PC users. Reports and charts resize automatically for changing screen resolutions, such as turning a mobile phone or tablet from a vertical to a horizontal orientation. Responsive design is a key element to the web pages because as decision makers access the site, they may not always be near a desktop computer. Because of this we needed to incorporate a design that allowed for ease of use on any device.

Charts, graphs, and reports are rendered through a third-party commercial tool called Shield UI, which was selected because the charts can be implemented easily and are visually appealing. For example, a few lines of code are all that is required to generate a line chart of historical data such as total loans by day over a five-day period. The Shield UI controls appear on the page as simple HTML div tags.

Additionally, the jVectorMap library is used to display a map of the United States with dots at each of the participating institutions. Users can hover over the dots to see a quick snapshot of total articles and loans sent to each institution. The map can be zoomed with the mouse scroll wheel as well, and the map view is clear at all levels of magnification due to its vector nature. The jVectorMap library is simple, lightweight, and highly customizable; these are the reasons for its use over more complex options such as Google Maps, Apple Maps, or Bing Maps. Each of those other options provides unnecessary functionality, which slows down the web application, and they are all harder to customize. Selecting the proper tool for simple geographic visualization will help users understand where their ILL materials are going. By incorporating a map in the center frame we are able to draw the users' attention away from the side buttons and to the center, which is where we placed our more pertinent and easy-to-access information. Since it is a dynamic map, it is not intended merely for graphic reference; it is able to reproduce where and how many items have gone to the different universities represented. This accomplishes two goals: (1) it gives perspective for how large the consortia is, and (2) it can tell the users where a majority of their items are going, which can influence shipping decisions.

Data analysis, calculations, and anomaly detection are primarily performed by a series of stored procedures. Stored procedures are subroutines contained within a database that consist of extensive SQL statements. This modular approach was chosen to isolate the complex logic required for statistical calculations from the web application to increase overall performance and efficiency. Another set of stored procedures monitors the database for any anomalies that may have occurred during the collection, analysis, or calculation processes. Scheduled tasks, a common server technology, are used to execute the stored procedures automatically requiring no human intervention.

What this complex set of stored procedures, web application code, and data provided by ILL librarians at each institution provides is a very user-friendly and visually appealing data presentation. As you can see in figure 6.3, there is a wealth of data being presented. Since our main focus was to graphically represent the ILL turnaround times for all of the GWLA institutions, we made that the central focus of the page when the users first log in. What they see is a main menu with a variety of easy-to-access informational options. In the center frame we have the quick-access buttons and the map.

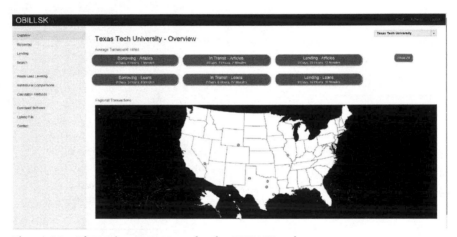

Figure 6.3.   The main menu screen for the OBILLSK web page.

As you can see in figure 6.3, we have divided the turnaround times into six unique categories. We followed a similar categorization already in existence with ILL processes. Those categories are the distinction between articles and loans and the division between borrowing, lending, and in transit. All of this terminology was chosen to correspond with the existing terminology of ILL. This allows users to be able to adopt the system faster because there is no barrier in understanding the wording of the different options. As Marlin Brown (1988) writes in his book on user interface design, "reduce the amount of mental manipulation of data required of the user. Present data, messages, and prompts in clear and directly useable form" (7). With this in mind we made sure to present the pertinent data the system was designed for front and center with terms that were comfortable to users. In addition to the dashboard we wanted a customizable log-in. To accomplish that we needed to create a user authentication system so we could control what the specific users see when they log in.

After authentication, the OBILLSK system begins with a dashboard screen that features average turnaround time summaries for six categories as well as the jVector-Map of the United States with dots for each institution. The average turnaround time summary reports presented on the dashboard include Borrowing Articles, In Transit Articles, Lending Articles, Borrowing Loans, In Transit Loans, and Lending Loans. These average times are presented in a format of days, hours, and minutes. The ability to categorize each of these times, especially the in-transit times, is new in the ILL world and is possible only because data from each institution are collected. Daily processing of that data guarantees up-to-date information presented to the users.

We have built within the center frame another subset of controls that can provide users with more detailed information should they require it. Each of the turnaround boxes is selectable and will display a graphical representation of the numbers of requests of the current calendar year. The decision was made here to provide a brief graph as a way of helping users draw a better idea of the trends within the current year of their ILL departments. From the central frame, where we choose to prioritize the most important data, we move to the left navigational menu.

The web page follows an F-pattern design. F-pattern design is a widely researched paradigm that illustrates that web users typically read a page in an F-shaped pattern, starting from the left and moving to the end of a line and then returning to the next line. With that in mind, we have a left navigational menu section that can help users navigate to the main overview, which displays the data above. However, we also give users the option to drill down to a more microlevel of detail in understanding the ILL transactions between institutions. In the left navigational menu, users can access the details of all the completed ILLs by looking at one of the options listed.

Borrowing and lending requests are further divided into lists of articles and lists of loans, for a total of four levels of analysis. When the user clicks on one of the options (for example the borrowing requests) the center frame will change and display an ordered list of all of the transactions for that function with additional details. Each row in each list displays basic identifying information about the request, including unique request number, borrowing institution, lending institution, and the turnaround and in-transit times for that request. Again, here we are trying to design a system that can present a lot of information in a visually easy-to-understand system. With that in mind, we kept all of the actions focused on the center frame. So when users first select an option on the left, the center frame changes as described above. If this information is not sufficient users can still take the analysis to a further level by clicking on the button shown in figure 6.4. Each row also has a button that can be clicked to display a modal pop-up window that presents the full citation information for that item. These historical lists of requests are also searchable.

One of the main benefits of viewing these request details in OBILLSK instead of in the native ILL interface (ILLiad) is the easy juxtaposition of the citation detail

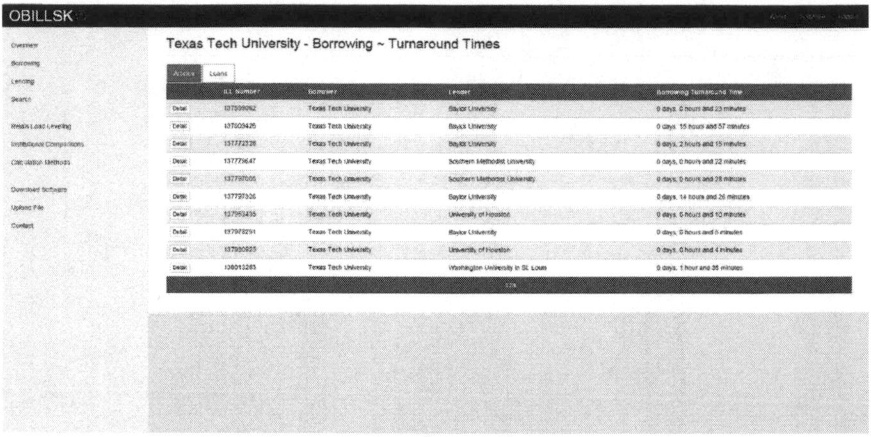

Figure 6.4.   An example of the transaction-level detail that OBILLSK can provide.

along with turnaround and in-transit times. It is in this microlevel of detail that the power of the system really begins to show through. If we travel with users from first log-in, we can see how as they move through the system they get better and better detail. This is very helpful in meeting the needs of a large audience. For example, upper administrators may be more interested in the global view of things. They may want to see what they are sending, where they are sending it, and how long it is taking to get there. This type of global overview is what we present first. Daily practitioners may be more concerned with what they are sending, which is where the tools on the left come into play. The left navigational menu also includes an option for institutional comparisons.

Institutional comparisons within the consortium are provided by OBILLSK. Two versions of this report are available: one for articles and one for loans. For articles, the report counts each institution's total articles lent—articles lent in 72 hours or less, articles lent in under 96 hours, articles lent in under 120 hours, and articles lent in 120 hours or more—and its compliance percentage within the rules of the consortium. For loans, the report counts each institution's total loans—items lent in under 5 days, items lent in under 6 days, items lent in under 7 days, and items lent in 7 days or longer—and its compliance percentage within the rules of the consortium. Institutional comparison gives users another avenue to understand how their libraries may compare to the other libraries in the consortium. The data here are presented in a grid pattern. This makes it easy to compare the fill rates of one library to those of another library. Users are able to see their institutions and compare them with other institutions. We have also incorporated an existing consortium-level chart generated outside of OBILLSK in this web page to centralize all of the services we offer into a single spot.

The final chart we added is an existing account of ILL statistics that we have been tracking. The OBILLSK system also hosts the Relais D2D load-leveling statistics within the GWLA as a courtesy to GWLA members. The Relais system is an additional service offered by the consortium that allows for real-time availability and building of lending strings. Although Relais provides interesting information on its own, the consortium wanted to get more complete detail about which universities were receiving requests and how many. This information was helpful to understand whether the load-leveling algorithms offered by the Relais service are functioning correctly. To accomplish this detective work, Texas Tech Libraries wrote a series of queries that interrogate the Relais D2D system and return a numerical value for requests received by that institution. We then divided the result into days and archived them by month so users could return to the chart and access the historical load-leveling statistics going all the way back to the implementation of the system.

The final options on the left navigational menu were designed to give users the ability to manage their accounts and to upload the data that are generated by the Windows executable file. This is the place where the data files are loaded into the server. Users are also able to contact us if they have any questions about the system or to download the executable file should they lose the copy, which can occur when their computers are replaced or re-imaged by their IT staff. The entire web page visualization scheme functions in the center frame. By isolating the actions of the different functions on the center frame, users are presented with a visually consistent set of actions and reactions. This overall design presents a consistent experience so that users can be comfortable with using the system and asking questions.

Taking into account the whole system, it is easy to see the amount of data collected. To collect transaction-level detail of all ILL transactions at a given institution is daunting enough, but to then make the comparisons to other institutions within a certain group makes it easy to see how the presentation of that type of data needed to be visual in nature. By presenting the data as graphs and charts users can easily get an "at a glance" understanding of what is happening in the ILL transactions within the consortium. By providing visual feedback of the options, selected in the form of the buttons changing color, we are able to guide users through the different displays on information presented. All of this design was deliberate to correspond to existing web presentation styles and user experiences. A consistent user experience is something we strive for in our design.

DISCUSSION AND ANALYSIS

User Experience

The design of the OBILLSK system is very comprehensive. It was our hope that we could construct a system that could take a large amount of very complex data and present them to users in a visually productive way. To accomplish that, we needed to grasp the many different distinctions that are in the ILL world. We had to decide what data were important and what data were not. We needed to assess how the data were to be presented so that users could make reasonable judgments about what was going on in the ILL departments of large research institutions and be able to criti-cally assess what was happening at their home institutions. To do that, we needed to have a series of discussions about the importance of visualization of data and data security. One of these discussions was the development of the left navigational menu tool bar. To organize those data in a meaningful way, we needed to organize navigation so that users could reasonably understand how to navigate the data. That is where the understanding of the magical number seven is important.

The magical number seven is a theory about the amount of information the immediate memory of the brain can handle at any given moment. In 1994, a psy-chologist from Harvard University wrote a paper about the human memory response when it was provided a series of stimuli. He writes,

> The span of absolute judgment and the span of immediate memory impose severe limitations on the amount of information that we are able to receive, process, and remember. By organizing the stimulus input simultaneously into several dimensions and successively into a sequence of chunks, we manage to break (or at least stretch) this informational bottleneck. (Miller 1994, 12)

What Miller is describing is the idea that the human mind can store in immediate memory only seven objects at any given moment. Further, if you would like to store more, then the object needs to be broken up into more than seven categories or chunks. Two designers at Microsoft echo this idea, writing this:

> In essence, G. Miller's findings that people are only able to make quick, accurate deci-sions with a small handful of objects at a time has had wide support across studies, and may provide useful guidance in the design of web hyperlinks across pages. (Larson and Czerwinski 1998, 26)

All three of these authors are illustrating one of the key components to the visual design for OBILLSK. Examining figures 6.1 and 6.2, you will see that much of what we have done follows this principle. The left navigational menu has only ten total options, which is close to the seven plus or minus two idea. What we have done, however, is make sure that the navigational menu is divided into distinct parts. That allows the immediate memory to grapple with the number of choices in a categorized way, thus allowing for more information to be fed to users. We also ensure that the center frame that dynamically changes had only seven options at log-in. Those op-tions are the six turnaround time metrics and the map. This total number of seven keeps users in a comfortable space for making decisions with the information. As users continue to drill down into the microlevel detail of the requests, they continue to be presented with seven options. Each of the microlevel analyses of the borrowing requests and lending requests, while having a long list of transactions, has between five and six headings for each column. This allows users to process the list in a more comfortable way by categorizing the information into discrete packets that can be assessed one at a time. You can also see that the dynamic between loans and articles is at work throughout the web page functionality. This leads to another important discussion point: the consistent user experience.

A consistent user experience is also a key component to the discussion of the visualization of the data. Even though we can categorize data into discrete packets and ensure that we organize them in a certain way to help users make assessments from what they are seeing, if we do not have a similar experience across categories, then we will lose users rather quickly. With that in mind, we incorporated a few elements to make the user experience seem consistent across the web page and software.

The first user experience element employed in the system, the color palette, is consistent with the branding of the software and occurs across both the executable file and the web pages. This gives users a sense of identification and familiarity that this is in fact an OBILLSK system. We also stuck with a more appealing palette of whites and blues.

The second element that helps with a consistent user experience is the feedback the page gives when an option is selected. We used green to highlight when a page is active. This is illustrated when you click on one of the turnaround metrics and the button highlights green to show that it is active. We also carried that over into the microlevel analysis. When you choose article or loan on the tabs above, the tab color changes to green, which lets users know that the tab is active. Using color to provide feedback across the platform allows users to have a consistent understanding of what is happening when things are active. Essentially, users can come to understand that the color green, which is already associated with action in our daily lives, also means action on the web page.

DATA SECURITY, FILE SIZE, AND ACCESSIBILITY

One of the biggest issues we encountered when we were first designing the system was determining how we could transmit large amounts of data from each institution to the server that performs the calculations. How could we send it using an executable file that satisfies the security requirements at each institution, while at the same time providing us access to the data we need? That is why we designed the executable file to run on the local machine at the discretion of the ILL librarian rather than as an add-on or persistent service with direct access to the local server. The potential to access confidential patron data by directly accessing a server without human oversight raises security and privacy concerns. To make sure users are comfortable, we make it abundantly clear what data we collect and where they go. We accomplish this by providing a "calculation methods" section on the left navigational menu of the main web page and by providing users the ability to examine their files before they are sent to the server. These precautions ensure that the local institutions understand and are comfortable with the data they are sharing with OBILLSK.

Secure online access to the OBILLSK web system completes our data security portfolio. Each user, one per institution, is required to log in to the system with a username and password. Upon successful log-in, a session variable is created and verified on each subsequent page load. The website utilizes secure sockets layer (SSL) security technology for encrypting all data transmitted between the web server and browser. HTTPS traffic is enforced at the server level; regular HTTP requests are automatically rejected. Additionally, to prevent malicious activity such as SQL injection and cross-site scripting, defensive coding practices are used throughout the website. These specific practices include form validation, input sanitization, and parameterized queries. Industry standard website security practices such as these provide OBILLSK users high confidence about the security of their data.

The large file size of the uploaded data from each institution also presents a design issue. The amount of data we request is typically too big to email so we needed to develop a secure way of uploading the data to the server. We therefore added an option to the Windows executable file that allows an institution to upload the file directly to the server. This method allows us to handle or generate a much larger data file, potentially millions of records from just a single institution. We gather as much information as we can so that our calculations are as accurate as they can be. With the data upload problem solved and security concerns addressed, we turned our attention to accessibility.

The visualization of ILL data is a major feature of OBILLSK, and we dedicated a tremendous amount of thought into how best to present it. However, if OBILLSK data visualization is not accessible to everyone, there is little reason to tout the impressive nature of the design. With that in mind, we ran multiple accessibility tests on the OBILLSK website to ensure that we were meeting accessibility standards. The OBILLSK web application was designed to meet web accessibility standards outlined by the W3C Web Accessibility Initiative and U.S. Section 508 standards. The website was evaluated using two industry-leading web accessibility compliance tools: the WebAIM WAVE Accessibility tool and Cryptzone Cynthia Says Portal. Based on the reports generated by the tools, the website was modified to meet web accessibility standards. Examples of accessibility modifications include invisible navigation and summary information for screen readers, adding alternate text description of visual elements, and presenting each web page in a consistent, logically organized manner.

CONCLUSION

The field of ILL is essentially a logistics management discipline. That means that librarians in this discipline, rather than viewing the books as resources of information, need to come to understand them as UPS or FedEx would understand a package. This leads to a few fundamental questions, the chief among them being "How do we get item A from here to there in the most efficient and effective way possible?" Viewing ILL in this manner can help increase the access to information that all users of the library need and deserve. However, to construct an efficient system, libraries must come to rely on visualized data that can tell a story not only of what is happening at their institutions but also what is happening across a more global system. Librarians in essence need to be able to see the entire supply chain to make accurate assessments. This goal, to give ILL librarians easy access to the ILL data across an entire consortium, is the core motivating idea behind the development of OBILLSK. Decision makers and practitioners of ILL should be able to make accurate assessments of what is happening on a broad scale and in near real time. To accomplish the display of so much varied detail, it is necessary to develop a cohesive, accessible system that follows consistent design principles so that the end users of the product can transition from the Windows executable file to the web page with little to no change in user experience. The OBILLSK system does a very good job of presenting this large-scale information with varied complexity in a simple and easy-to-use interface. As we go forward, it will be interesting to see how the influence of large-scale logistical management systems like OBILLSK can help create a more efficient ILL system and thus continue to help library patrons get the resources they want when they want them.

REFERENCES

Brown, C. Marlin. 1988. *Human-Computer Interface Design Guidelines*. Norwood, NJ: Ablex Publishing.

Larkin, Jill H., and Herbert A. Simon. 1987. "Why a Diagram Is (Sometimes) Worth Ten Thousand Words." *Cognitive Science* 11(1): 65–100.

Larson, Kevin, and Mary Czerwinski. 1998. "Web Page Design: Implications of Memory, Structure and Scent for Information Retrieval." *CHI '98 Proceedings of the SIGCHI Conference on Human Factors in Computing Systems*, 25–32.

Miller, George. 1994. "The Magical Number Seven, Plus or Minus Two: Some Limits on Our Capacity for Processing Information." *Psychological Review* 101(2): 343–352.

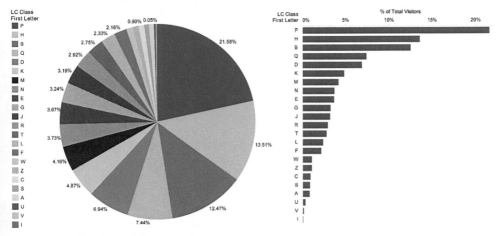

1. Two visualizations of the same data.

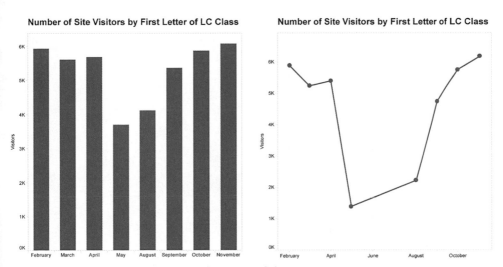

2. The problem with using bar charts for temporal data.

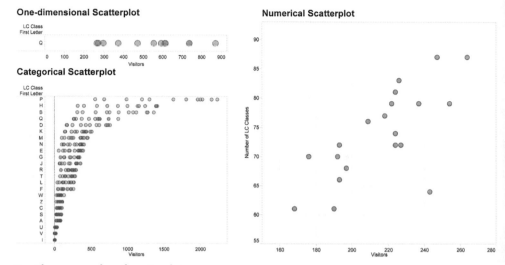

3. Three examples of scatterplots.

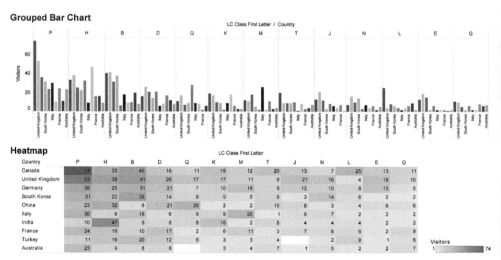

4. Using a grouped bar chart yields a chart with redundant labels and wasted space.

Choropleth Map with Rainbow Color Scale

Avg. Daily High (in F)

37.61 - 41.09
41.10 - 44.86
44.87 - 48.95
48.96 - 52.23
52.24 - 55.64
55.65 - 59.18
59.19 - 62.47
62.48 - 65.44
65.45 - 68.92
68.93 - 72.40
72.41 - 76.39
76.40 - 80.50
80.51 - 84.30
84.31 - 90.00

Choropleth Map with Continuous Color Scale

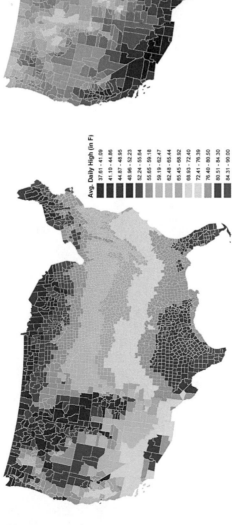

Avg. Daily High (in F)

37.61 - 41.09
41.10 - 44.86
44.87 - 48.95
48.96 - 52.23
52.24 - 55.64
55.65 - 59.18
59.19 - 62.47
62.48 - 65.44
65.45 - 68.92
68.93 - 72.40
72.41 - 76.39
76.40 - 80.50
80.51 - 84.30
84.31 - 90.00

5. Two choropleth maps of the counties of the contiguous United States.

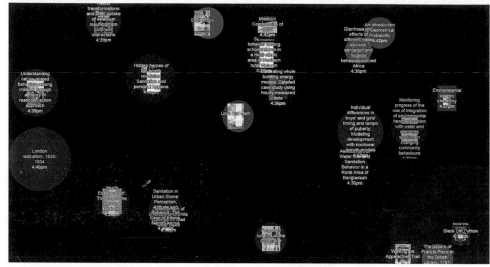

6. Listen to Summon.

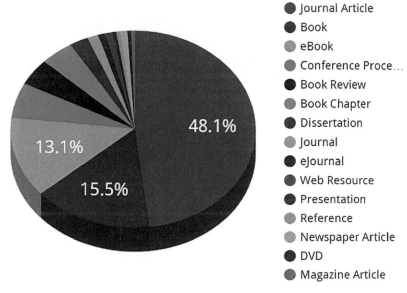

7. A pie chart displaying the content types of the last 100 items.

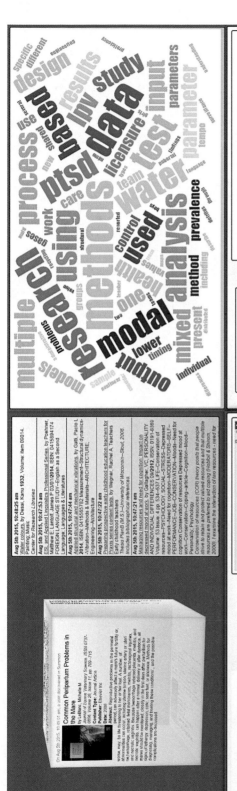

8. Prototype of the 2 × 2 display mounted in the Newman Library entrance.

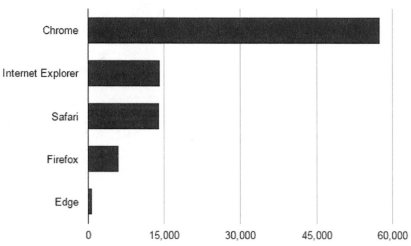

Top Browsers by User (Last 30 Days)

9. A sample bar chart showing the proportion of users using particular browsers.

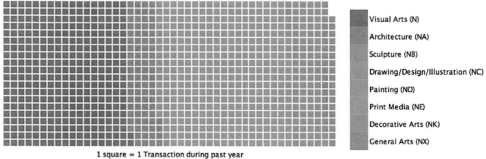

Transactions per Fine Arts Subclass

Visual Arts (N)
Architecture (NA)
Sculpture (NB)
Drawing/Design/Illustration (NC)
Painting (ND)
Print Media (NE)
Decorative Arts (NK)
General Arts (NX)

1 square = 1 Transaction during past year

10. Waffle chart visualization.

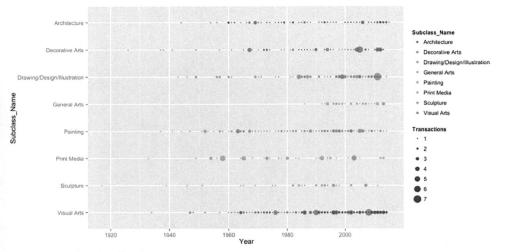

11. Scatterplot visualization.

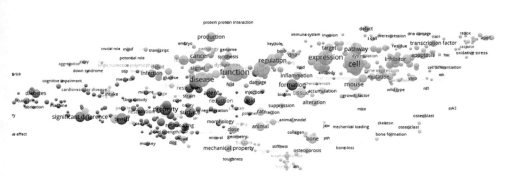

12. Science-related terms with clustering resolution of 1.5.

13. ScholarWorks term map with six term clusters.

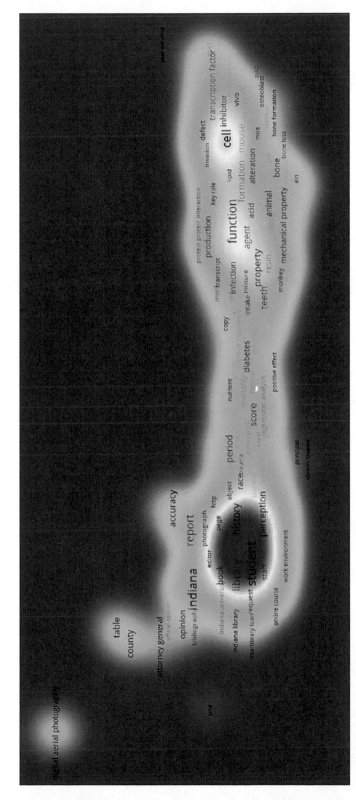

14. ScholarWorks term map in Density Visualization view.

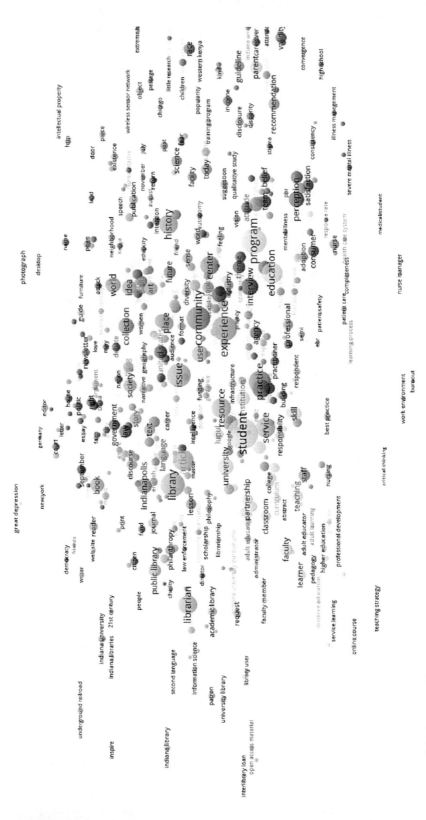

15. Social science and humanities terms at 1.00 cluster resolution.

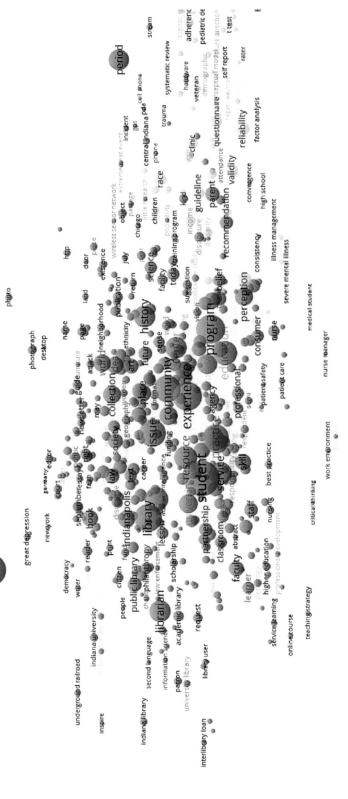

16. Social science and humanities terms at 2.00 cluster resolution.

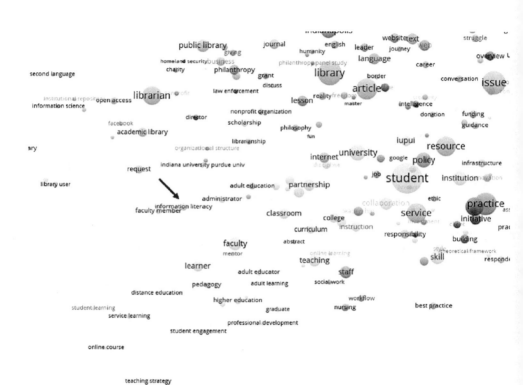

17. Information literacy term appears at the boundary between education-related research and library-related research.

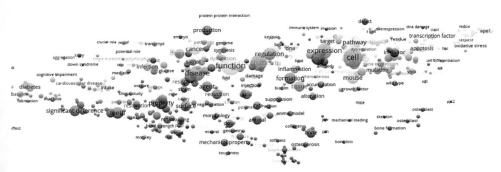

18. Science-related terms with clustering resolution of 2.0.

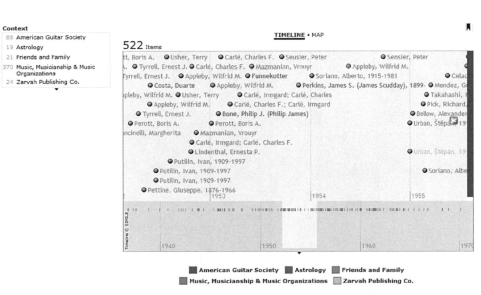

19. Visual timeline of a correspondence collection.

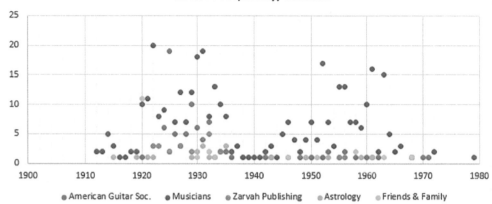

20. Scatterplot timeline of a correspondence collection displaying peaks and types of activity.

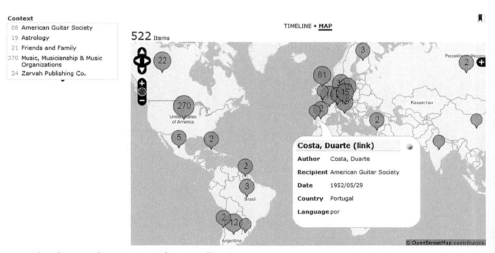

21. Visual map of a correspondence collection.

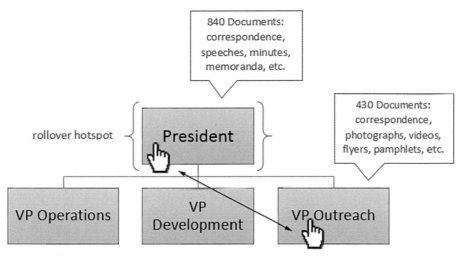

840 Documents: correspondence, speeches, minutes, memoranda, etc.

430 Documents: correspondence, photographs, videos, flyers, pamphlets, etc.

rollover hotspot

President

VP Operations

VP Development

VP Outreach

22. An org chart as a navigational interface.

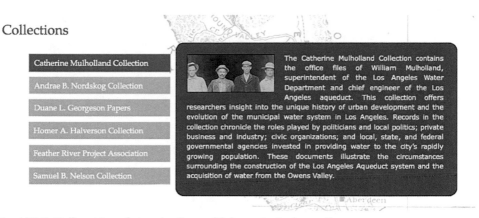

Collections

Catherine Mulholland Collection

Andrae B. Nordskog Collection

Duane L. Georgeson Papers

Homer A. Halverson Collection

Feather River Project Association

Samuel B. Nelson Collection

The Catherine Mulholland Collection contains the office files of William Mulholland, superintendent of the Los Angeles Water Department and chief engineer of the Los Angeles aqueduct. This collection offers researchers insight into the unique history of urban development and the evolution of the municipal water system in Los Angeles. Records in the collection chronicle the roles played by politicians and local politics; private business and industry; civic organizations; and local, state, and federal governmental agencies invested in providing water to the city's rapidly growing population. These documents illustrate the circumstances surrounding the construction of the Los Angeles Aqueduct system and the acquisition of water from the Owens Valley.

23. HTML Gallery Menu for navigating multiple contextual narratives.

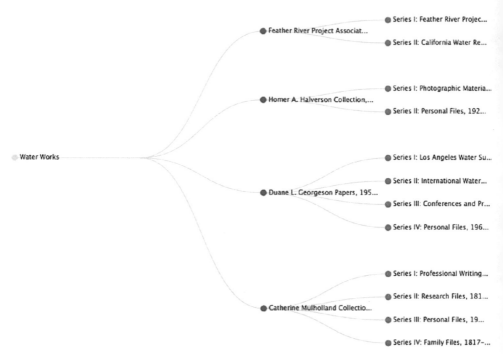

Water Works
- Feather River Project Associat...
  - Series I: Feather River Projec...
  - Series II: California Water Re...
- Homer A. Halverson Collection,...
  - Series I: Photographic Materia...
  - Series II: Personal Files, 192...
- Duane L. Georgeson Papers, 195...
  - Series I: Los Angeles Water Su...
  - Series II: International Water...
  - Series III: Conferences and Pr...
  - Series IV: Personal Files, 196...
- Catherine Mulholland Collectio...
  - Series I: Professional Writing...
  - Series II: Research Files, 181...
  - Series III: Personal Files, 19...
  - Series IV: Family Files, 1817–...

24.   Tree chart demonstrating archival arrangement of multiple collections.

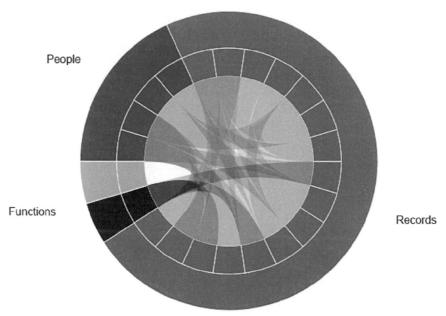

People

Functions

Records

25.   A radial chart that displays relationships between records, creators, and functions.

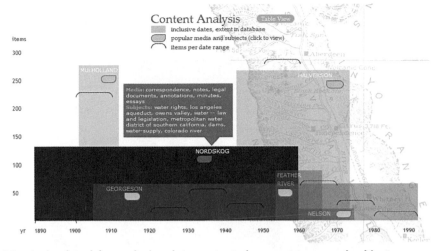

26. A visual tool for analyzing dates, extent, document types, and subjects across multiple collections.

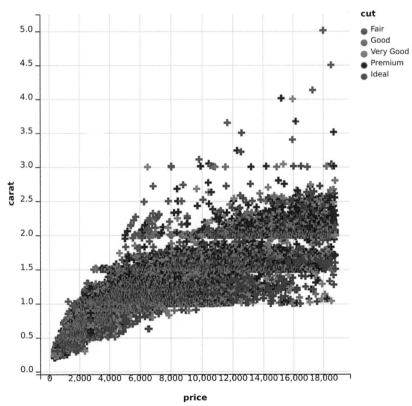

27. A ggvis-generated scatterplot created from the diamonds data set showing carat weight by price. The color of each data point represents the quality of the cut of each diamond.

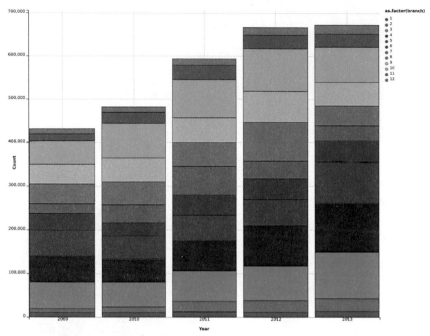

28. Using the same data as figure 9.4, color has been added using the fill property to enable differentiation of branch data.

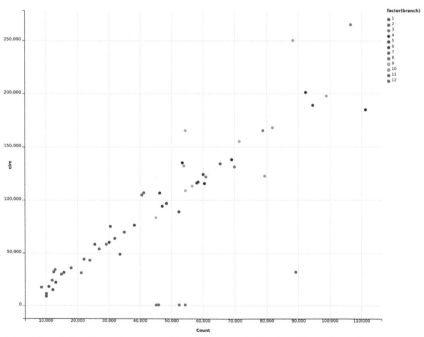

29. Circulation by gate count with a fill color indicating library branch.

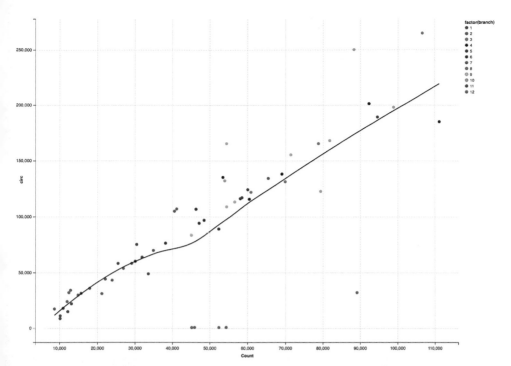

30. A scatterplot using the same data as figure 9.7, with the addition of a smooth model curve to highlight the data trend, which shows a positive relationship between gate count and circulation.

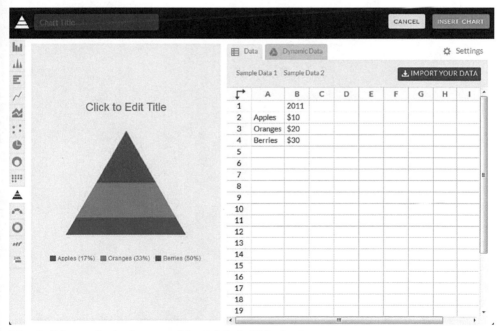

31. Building a chart using spreadsheet data in Piktochart.

Lorem Ipsum

Lorem ipsum dolor sit amet, consectetur adipiscing elit.

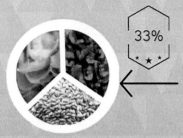

33%

Lorem ipsum dolor sit amet, consectetur adipiscing elit. Fusce eget elit vitae felis lacinia facilisis quis vitae elit. Nullam nec nibh ac massa molestie mattis vitae et lacus. Fusce venenatis vel dolor et fermentum. In facilisis tortor eu felis molestie euismod. Ut at nunc id ligula laoreet rhoncus. Duis mollis, leo et pharetra ornare, lacus metus sagittis dolor, at malesuada magna augue eget sapien. Donec eu risus purus. Nunc hendrerit, quam in tincidunt viverra, urna metus semper lacus, non bibendum justo ante at erat. Maecenas eu semper mauris. Suspendisse eget tortor ac purus consequat semper eget ut elit. Vivamus ut orci hendrerit, laoreet mi at, porta eros. Donec eget vulputate enim. Maecenas eu nibh libero. Phasellus tempor sem sed maximus vulputate

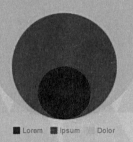

■ Lorem ■ Ipsum □ Dolor

Pros
- Lorem ipsum dolor sit amet
- consectetur adipiscing elit.
- Fusce eget elit vitae felis lacinia
- quis vitae elit. Nullam nec nibh

Cons
-ac massa molestie mattis vitae et
-lacus. Fusce venenatis vel dolor et
-fermentum. In facilisis tortor eu

SOLD

1 in 5 Lorem ipsum dolor sit amet consectetur adipiscing elit.

Last Name, First Name. Title. City of Publication. Publisher. Format.

powered by
Piktochart
make information beautiful

32. A sample of a generic Piktochart infographic with all elements required by the in-class assignment.

7

Visualizing the Topical Coverage of an Institutional Repository with VOSviewer

David E. Polley

Using text mining and visualization to identify, display, and analyze the topical coverage of large text corpora is increasingly common in a number of academic disciplines. This process, sometimes called bibliometric mapping, is fairly common in the field of library and information science. While its practical application in academic libraries is fairly new, it is conceivable that librarians could use these methods for a variety of purposes. This chapter will demonstrate the potential use of term co-occurrence maps, visualizations that demonstrate the relationships between highly occurring terms in a set of documents, as a means to understanding the scholarship archived in a library-run institutional repository. In these maps, terms are placed in a two-dimensional space so that terms that appear more often in combination with other terms are placed closer together. This process causes these frequently co-occurring terms to cluster together, and these clusters are interpreted as representing research areas present in this body of text. It is important to note that the computer simply recognizes rates of occurrence and co-occurrence, clustering terms together. It is incumbent on the person viewing the map to assign the meaning to these clusters. Nonetheless, these data visualization techniques provide a useful way to explore a set of documents, uncover latent patterns, and pose new questions to further analyze using additional methods.

As the push for open access to scholarship continues, libraries invest significant resources in setting up and maintaining institutional repositories. Term co-occurrence maps provide an opportunity to evaluate these services beyond traditional metrics such as download counts. Generating these maps from the titles and abstracts of items in a repository visually demonstrates how research clusters around specific areas across the sciences, social sciences, and humanities. This kind of analysis can help librarians determine whether a repository's content accurately represents the research output of an institution as a whole or whether it is lacking in some key area. For example, a librarian might know that his or her institution is highly regarded for its active research in sociology, but upon analyzing the library's repository this librarian could find an absence of terms that indicate the presence of sociological research. It should be noted that the analysis of these maps is difficult and often requires consultation with subject-matter experts (Peters and van Raan 1993). However, this data-driven approach can complement what librarians already know about their repositories and combined with the input from subject-matter experts provide insight into the way research happens at their institutions. Armed with knowledge of the institutional research landscape, librarians can better perform outreach to faculty and communicate the value of institutional repositories as a key research service.

This chapter will outline the process for generating term co-occurrence maps from the titles and abstracts of items in ScholarWorks, the institutional repository at Indiana University-Purdue University Indianapolis (IUPUI). Term co-occurrence maps are created using VOSviewer, a freely available tool for generating bibliometric maps (van Eck and Waltman 2010). The resulting visualizations show clustering of relevant terms, representing the major research areas present in the repository's scholarship. An overview of how to export the necessary metadata from the repository and clean and prepare the data, and a step-by-step guide to the visualization workflow are provided. The chapter will conclude with some discussion on interpreting term maps and specific ways librarians can use these maps to understand the research environment of their institutions. The raw data used in this project, the R script used in cleaning and preparing the data, and the graph modeling language (GML) files for the resulting maps are all available on IUPUI DataWorks.[1]

BACKGROUND

Term co-occurrence maps (sometimes referred to as co-word maps or term maps) have a rich history in bibliometrics, a subfield of library and information science that uses various methods to quantitatively analyze scholarly literature. Most often this analysis focuses on a specific domain to understand both its current state and evolution over time. Term co-occurrence maps attempt to show the dominant themes in a set of documents by connecting terms that occur together in a single document. A document can be a paragraph, an abstract, a title, or the full text of an article. Term co-occurrences in a body of text are organized into a matrix, which is interpreted as a network where terms are nodes connected by links based on their co-occurrence in a document. These maps are typically displayed in two dimensions using a variety of techniques. Term maps date back to the early 1980s with Callon et al.'s (1983) landmark study involving a co-word analysis of keywords from 172 scientific articles on dietary fibers. When mapped, terms are placed in a vertical fashion with more frequently occurring terms appearing at the top and co-occurrence represented by links connecting terms. Not all co-occurrences are represented in the map. To simplify the maps and reduce term density, a term must appear at least three times in association with one other term in the data to meet the threshold for inclusion in the map (Callon et al. 1983).

Subsequent term maps emphasized the strength of co-occurrence by using weighted links to connect the terms. The more frequently two terms co-occur, the thicker the link connecting the terms appears in the map. In their article, Rip and Courtial (1984) show the connections between keywords from articles published over a ten-year period in *Biotechnology and Bioengineering*, a core journal in biotechnology. Both circular and vertical maps are used to visualize the data. Similarity between terms is measured using the Jaccard Index and shown through weighted links (Rip and Courtial 1984). The circular maps used facilitate interpretation by placing the most highly occurring terns at the center of the map.

One of the major drawbacks of early term co-occurrence maps is the lack of objectivity regarding term placement on the map. Terms are situated in two-dimensional space in an ad hoc manner simply to facilitate ease of reading (Rip and Courtial 1984). The arguably intuitive assumption that distance between terms in the map corresponds to the terms' similarity does not hold true. To address this shortcoming, multidimensional scaling (MDS), a method from spatial-data analysis, was introduced as a method for creating term maps. Using this approach, maps are generated where terms are automatically placed using computer software so that the distance between terms reflects the rate of co-occurrence, resulting in highly co-occurring terms being placed in close proximity, forming clusters of similar terms (Tijssen and Van Raan 1989). Ultimately this approach yields maps that are more intuitive than previous term co-occurrence maps. However, map readability, especially for larger term maps, still proves challenging due to overlapping term labels and link density.

More recently, computer programs such as VOSviewer enable the analysis of much larger bodies of text and increase map readability simultaneously through improvements in term placement. At the heart of the tool is a mapping technique referred to as visualization of similarities (VOS), which differs from prior methods for term placement. The VOS method improves on multidimensional scaling by locating terms closer to their ideal coordinates on the map and by giving weight to indirect similarities (van Eck and Waltman 2007). Additionally, previous tools for visualizing term co-occurrence maps, such as SPSS or Pajek, suffer from problems of labels overlapping and a lack of ways to explore small portions of the map in any detail (van Eck and Waltman 2010). The VOSviewer program is highly flexible. The tool can read data directly from Web of Science or Scopus, allowing users to generate term maps from article abstracts, or from text files, allowing for the creation of term maps from any text. Users can employ the VOS mapping method to create maps from a data set in the tool itself or view maps created using multidimensional scaling in other programs such as SPSS (van Eck and Waltman 2010). Once maps are created, either natively or in another tool, VOSviewer provides two ways to visualize the data: the network visualization view or the density visualization view. In the network visualization view terms are presented by labels on top of circles. The size of the label and circle corresponds to the overall frequency in the data set. The color of the circle corresponds to the cluster to which the term has been assigned. In the density view, terms are represented by labels, which again correspond to frequency in the data set. The color in the density view ranges from blue (lowest density) to red (highest density). These color values are determined by the number of nearest terms in the area around a point and the weight, or relative frequency, in the case of term co-occurrence maps, in the data set (van Eck and Waltman 2015). Each view offers users a unique way to uncover patterns in the data. Additionally, users can view small portions of the map by using a zoom and scroll functionality. Finally, the tool also offers the ability to take screenshots of maps and to save both image and map files in a variety of formats.

While VOSviewer was initially designed to create bibliometric maps such as journal citation maps, it performs well as a text-mining tool for creating term co-occurrence maps, easily ingesting large amounts of text. Creating a term co-occurrence map in VOSviewer involves four steps. In the first step, the tool identifies noun phrases, which are word sequences consisting of only nouns and adjectives, via part-of-speech tagging using the Apache OpenNLP tool kit (van Eck and Waltman 2011). In the second step, VOSviewer identifies relevant terms, a process that ultimately reduces clutter in the resulting map. To determine a term's relevance, the tool filters out more general noun phrases by comparing certain noun phrases that co-occur with only a limited set of other noun phrases versus those noun phrases that co-occur with many different noun phrases (Waltman, van Raan, and Smart 2014). The third step involves mapping and clustering the terms using the VOS mapping technique combined with a modified modularity based clustering approach (Waltman, van Eck, and Noyons 2010). Finally, the map is displayed in both the network visualization view and the density visualization view.

VOSviewer has recently gained popularity for its ease of use, the intuitive maps it generates, and its scalability. The tool has been used to study the evolution of scholarship in academic domains as diverse as land use and urban planning (Gobster 2014) to computer and information ethics (Heersmink et al. 2011). The tool is also adept at illuminating connections between research areas in highly interdisciplinary fields, such as the interface between engineering and physical sciences with health and life sciences (Waltman, van Raan, and Smart 2014). Due to VOSviewer's easy-to-use interface, ability to ingest large volumes of text, and utility in showing connections in highly interdisciplinary areas, it is a good tool for analyzing the topical coverage of an institutional repository.

AN EXAMPLE OF A PROJECT

Background

This project began in early 2015 as a way to understand the current state of IUPUI's institutional repository, ScholarWorks. The first item was deposited in the repository, which at the time was named IDeA (IUPUI Digital Archive), in August 2003 (Odell

Table 7.1. ScholarWorks communities and number of items

ScholarWorks Community	Number of Items
Theses, Dissertations, and Doctoral Papers	1,255
School of Medicine	1,136
Faculty Articles	858
University Library	772
School of Liberal Arts	467
Office of the Vice Chancellor for Research	286
School of Informatics and Computing	241
Robert H. McKinney School of Law	214
Lilly Family School of Philanthropy	175
School of Education	142
School of Public and Environmental Affairs	78
School of Science	70
Herron School of Art and Design	64
School of Engineering and Technology	55
School of Dentistry	49
Richard M. Fairbanks School of Public Health	41
Moi University/IUPUI Partnership	38
School of Nursing	37
Kelly School of Business–Indianapolis	26
Indiana University-Purdue University Columbus	23
Center for Service Learning	17
School of Rehabilitation Sciences	12
School of Physical Education & Tourism Management	11
School of Social Work	8
Alumni Works	5

2014). The first instance of IUPUI's repository ran on the first version of DSpace, which was released the year before. Early adopters on campus included the School of Medicine, University Library, and Herron School of Art and Design (Staum and Halverson 2004). Over the years the repository has grown and been organized into different communities, with some of the original communities subsumed as collections into larger communities. At the time of this study, ScholarWorks archives over 4,000 unique items and hosts twenty-five communities, spanning the sciences, social sciences, and humanities (see table 7.1).

Initially the project was undertaken as a proof of concept, but it was also done with an eye toward the future. One of the goals of this project is to serve as a baseline against which to assess the evolution and growth of ScholarWorks as a repository. This study proves timely due to the recent passing of a campus-level open access policy. In October 2014, the IUPUI Faculty Council passed an open access policy, encouraging faculty and researchers to make their scholarship as openly available as possible ("Open Access Policy" 2015). While self-archiving is not mandated by the policy (researchers are able to opt out on an article-by-article basis), a significant component of the work involved in implementing the policy centers on an aggressive outreach program aimed at helping faculty and researchers self-archive their journal articles in ScholarWorks. Due to an increase in this work, the number of submissions to the repository is expected to expand its coverage significantly in the coming years. Thus, studying the dominant research themes of items archived in the repository at this point is an important first step in assessing future expansion of repository coverage.

Obtaining and Cleaning the Data

This project analyzes the abstracts and titles of items in the repository. Each title and abstract are considered to be distinct documents in this corpus. Using titles and abstracts as the units of analysis is preferable to using keywords or subject terms due to the higher prevalence of titles and abstracts in the data. Submitting an item to the repository involves filling out a series of web forms, which populate Dublin Core metadata fields on the repository back end. To allow for flexibility in the submission process the only metadata requirements are the provision of a date and a title. Additionally, records cannot be created in the repository without a file. The flexibility in the submission process is useful but results in incomplete metadata for many items. However, the fact that item title is a required field in the submission process ensures that at least some text will be associated with each item in the repository. Ultimately, using titles and abstracts for topical analysis results in a more complete data set than using keywords or subject terms.

In ScholarWorks, metadata files are available for export at the community level to users with administrative privileges. A comma separated value (CSV) file for each of ScholarWorks' twenty-five communities is exported. Each community CSV file contains the standard Dublin Core elements, using various properties, to describe community content. Obviously, the abstract and title are needed for this analysis, but the item ID is also used for de-duplication, as an item's membership in a ScholarWorks community is not mutually exclusive (more on the de-duplication process later). Each CSV file is opened in Microsoft Excel to check data integrity. It is immediately apparent that the level of specificity used to describe an item varied greatly both within and across communities. This variation stems from the submission process where users have lists of options for describing an item via drop-down menus. For example, when selecting the language for an item, users can select *English* or *English (US)*. Ultimately, these differences result in varying levels of consistency in metadata both across and within repository communities, resulting in the element dc.description.abstract[en] being used to describe one item, while dc.description. abstract[en_US] is used to describe another. A similar problem occurs with the titles for items. To address this inconsistency, the Excel concatenate function is used to combine the columns, across which abstracts and titles are spread into a new column in each file titled *abstract.combined* and *title.combined*. After combing abstracts and titles into one column, each file is saved as a separate CSV file.

The next stage in preprocessing involves loading the data into R for further cleanup. Using a simple R script is seen as preferable to performing the rest of the cleanup in Excel due to the size of some of the files and the fact that scripting the cumbersome cleanup process reduces the chance for human error. Using the script, each CSV file is loaded into R. Then the IDs, combined abstracts, and combined titles are extracted from each file and saved as vectors. These vectors are then combined into subsets of the original files. Each subset is then combined into one data frame containing the IDs, abstracts, and titles from all twenty-five CSV files. The item ID is used to de-duplicate the data set, and the unique titles and abstracts are saved as character vectors. Finally, the character vectors are written to two separate text files, one containing unique abstracts and the other containing unique titles. These files are then manually checked and combined into one file using a text editor. At this stage the file is ready for visualization using VOSviewer. The next section provides a step-by-step overview of the visualization process.

The Visualization Workflow

Creating term maps in VOSviewer is a relatively easy process. The first step is to download and install the tool, which is freely available from http://www.vosviewer.com/.

1. Launch the program and select *create* from the action panel menu on the left of the tool. A pop-up will appear; select *Create a map based on a text corpus*.
2. Choose the text file with the abstracts and titles. Load that file as a *VOSviewer corpus file*. It is not necessary to use a *VOSviewer scores file*.
3. Set counting method to *binary*. This is preferred over full counting, especially for larger bodies of text. Full counting uses every instance of a term in a document to assess its similarity to others, while binary counting uses only the presence of the term. This prevents the maps from being skewed by a single term's appearing frequently within one document.
4. Ignore the *thesaurus file*. This file will eliminate certain noun phrases from the final map. Terms can always be deselected at a later stage, but supplying a thesaurus at this step can be helpful in eliminating potentially nonmeaningful terms, such as *results* or *methodology*, from the resulting map.
5. Set the *minimum occurrence threshold*. By default, VOSviewer uses a threshold of ten, which works well for fairly large data sets. The total number of terms in the ScholarWorks data set is 75,134 terms. Using a minimum occurrence threshold of ten, the data set is pared down to 1,801 terms.
6. VOSviewer assigns relevance scores to each term. The distribution of second-order co-occurrences of a single noun phrase over all noun phrases is compared with the overall distribution of noun phrases over all noun phrases; the greater the difference between these two distributions, the more relevant the term is considered to be (van Eck and Waltman 2011). This significantly reduces the

number of terms to 60 percent of the terms above the selected threshold. For the ScholarWorks data, reducing the terms to the most relevant 60 percent results in 1,081 terms.

7. Verify selected terms and deselect any nonmeaningful terms outside the scope of analysis. Clicking on the column heading for *Occurrences* or *Relevance* allows for the sorting of these terms in either ascending or descending order. Sorting by the most frequently occurring terms facilitates the removal of nonmeaningful terms from the map. For example, frequently occurring terms such as *article* could be removed from the analysis. This ultimately makes the map easier to read and highlights meaningful relationships between the terms. Generally, term deselection is done in an ad hoc fashion and will vary depending on the data and goals of the project. For the initial exploratory analysis of the ScholarWorks data, no terms were deselected.

8. Click *finish* and VOSviewer performs mapping and clustering. Term co-occurrence maps created from text files are available to view in either *Network Visualization* or *Density View*. To change between views, click on the tabs at the top of the main panel in the center of the tool.

9. Changing the *clustering resolution* increases or decreases the number of clusters in the map, which can help uncover patterns in the data. To change this parameter, click on the *Map* tab in the action panel on the left of the tool. By default, the clustering resolution is set to 1.0. Increasing this number produces more clusters in the map, and decreasing reduces the number of clusters.

Results

The initial map shows six clusters of terms in the *Network Visualization* view (see figure 13 in the photospread). The red cluster to the left of the map includes terms associated with social sciences and humanities disciplines, the green and blue clusters to the right include science-related terms, and the yellow cluster that connects the two areas has many public health–related terms (see table 7.2). These four clusters will be examined in detail later. However, it is worth analyzing the remaining two clusters. The purple-colored cluster in the upper left of the map contains terms that could not easily be assigned to one of the other clusters. This occurs for two reasons. First, general terms, such as *period*, appear in many titles and abstracts but do not co-occur frequently enough with any other specific terms to be assigned to either of the other clusters. Second, terms in this cluster such as *attorney general*, and *opinion* are highly specific to a set of items within the repository. In the case of *attorney general, opinion,* and *official opinion*, these terms refer to a historical set of digitized opinions from the Indiana attorney general. Other terms such as *digital aerial photography, county, accuracy,* and *report* are all associated with a set of county horizontal accuracy reports, which provide aerial photographs of Indiana counties. Due to the uniformity of the titles and lack of additional text that might associate them with their respective disciplines, law and geography, these items are clustered together.

Table 7.2.   Top five most frequently occurring terms from each cluster

Term	Occurrences	Cluster	Color
student	568	Social Sciences & Humanities	Red
cell	441	Molecular Biology & Genetics	Green
function	412	Molecular Biology & Genetics	Green
experience	376	Social Sciences & Humanities	Red
program	371	Social Sciences & Humanities	Red
library	353	Social Sciences & Humanities	Red
community	334	Social Sciences & Humanities	Red
mechanism	329	Molecular Biology & Genetics	Green
protein	327	Molecular Biology & Genetics	Green
expression	292	Molecular Biology & Genetics	Green
property	198	Other Sciences & Dentistry	Blue
concentration	169	Other Sciences & Dentistry	Blue
teeth	166	Other Sciences & Dentistry	Blue
score	165	Public Health	Yellow
agent	144	Other Sciences & Dentistry	Blue
surface	143	Other Sciences & Dentistry	Blue
diabetes	99	Public Health	Yellow
predictor	92	Public Health	Yellow
reliability	89	Public Health	Yellow
item	86	Public Health	Yellow

The light blue cluster consisting of two terms, *una* and *cultura*, represents a small number of Spanish language items in the repository, all of which are found in the Theses, Dissertations, and Doctoral Papers community. VOSviewer is designed for data in English and cannot perform part-of-speech tagging on other languages, which is why the article *una* made it through to the map and was not excluded during stopword removal. However, the presence and clustering of these terms suggest some possibility for a basic language-based map for multilingual repositories. Due to the limited number of foreign-language materials in ScholarWorks, this type of analysis is beyond the scope of this study.

The largest cluster is the humanities and social sciences cluster at the left of the map, including 478 terms (see figure 13 in the photospread). Upon initial review, the terms that stand out the most include *student, program, experience,* and *library*. It is not really surprising that library-related terms figure so prominently in this cluster. The University Library community is the fourth largest in ScholarWorks, which is likely due to the fact that librarians are more aware of this service and are often advocates for open access. However, it is interesting that despite its relatively small size, especially when compared to the School of Medicine and Theses, Dissertations, and Doctoral Papers communities (see table 7.1), that terms from this community dominate the map. This suggests the presence of a large amount of library-related research in the repository or that these items use similar language to describe the research.

Switching to the density visualization view provides more information on the overall structure of the map (see figure 14 in the photospread). It is immediately apparent that the highest term density occurs at the center of the social sciences and humanities cluster. The highest density area centers on the term *student*, which makes sense given that it is the most frequently occurring term in the data set. The next two highest areas of term density occur in the science clusters, centered on the terms *cell* and *function*. The area connecting the science clusters with the social sciences and humanities clusters, containing public health terms, has a relatively low term density compared to the rest of the map.

To examine the social sciences and humanities cluster more closely, the clustering resolution is increased in VOSviewer to provide a more granular view. The default clustering resolution of 1.0 does not provide much detail (see figure 15 in the photospread). However, changing this parameter to 2.0 yields a map with sufficient granularity to see different research areas (see figure 16 in the photospread).

There are now four prominent subclusters present. The largest of these subclusters is the arts and humanities (green) and is spread across the upper portion of the map. Within this subcluster, the most frequently occurring terms are *experience*, *history*, *place*, *world*, and *idea*. It is important to note that while the terms *experience* and *history* appear in this subcluster, they are centrally located on the map, suggesting their use as terms in a variety of items across the social sciences and humanities and providing an example of how VOSviewer handles indirect similarities. The next largest subcluster includes terms that are related to the scholarship of education (yellow) in the lower left of the social sciences and humanities cluster. The most frequently occurring terms in this cluster include *student, program, education, opportunity,* and *university.* It is interesting to note the overlap between this subcluster and the adjacent library research subcluster (gold), above the scholarship of education subcluster. In fact, the term *information literacy*, which is too small to appear in figure 16 in the photospread but can be seen in figure 17 in the photospread, spans the boundary between these two subclusters. The library research cluster is dominated by terms that include *article, resource,* and *service.* The last subcluster within the social sciences and humanities cluster is *government, public policy,* and *law*, which can be seen in purple at the top of the social sciences and humanities cluster. The most frequently occurring terms in this cluster include *United States, law, opinion, government,* and *right.*

The right side of the term map (figure 13 in the photospread) is dominated by the two science clusters, which include the biophysics and dentistry cluster (blue) and the molecular biology and genetics cluster (green). Examining the structure of the two clusters yields nothing unexpected. For example, the term *mechanical property* appears toward the bottom of the biophysics and dentistry cluster, far away from terms such as *protein protein interaction*, which occurs at the top of the molecular biology and genetics cluster due to a high level of dissimilarity (see figure 12 in the photospread). Conversely, highly similar terms such as *disease* and *resistance* occur at the boundary between these two clusters. To identify further patterns, the clustering resolution is changed. Increasing the clustering resolution parameter to just 1.5 results in a clearer distinction between the dentistry-related terms (purple) and biophysics terms (light blue) to their right, which include mostly bone-related research (see figure 12 in the photospread). To confirm the relative large amount of bone-related research, a quick keyword search is done in ScholarWorks for the term *bone*, returning 761 results.

Even at this level of clustering, all the molecular biology and genetics terms appear clustered together, represented by the green-colored terms (see figure 12 in the photospread). Increasing the clustering resolution to 2.0 produces higher granularity, but without validation by a subject-matter expert it is difficult to identify any meaningful subclusters or patterns in the data (see figure 18 in the photospread). However, even with expert input, this research area could still lack any easily identifiable clusters of terms because of either the relatively small amount of data or the diversity of research in this area.

Perhaps the most interesting feature of the map is the cluster that connects the three clusters of social sciences and humanities, biophysics and dentistry, and molecular biology and genetics. The yellow cluster that bridges the sciences with the social sciences and humanities contains many public health–related research terms. This cluster is the most widely dispersed in the map, with terms scattered among the social sciences and humanities cluster, and the two sciences clusters. In total, the public health cluster contains 145 terms, which include frequently occurring terms such as *diabetes, predictor, mortality, depression,* and *race.* There are also a number of terms that indicate the heavy use of surveys as a data collection method, such as *score, item,* and *questionnaire.*

Probably the most interesting feature of the public health cluster is where it intersects with the other clusters on the map. As an interdisciplinary field, there is much overlap between public health and other areas. At the intersection of the public health cluster with the social sciences and humanities cluster, terms that indicate health economics research such as *consumer, patient care,* and *health care system* are found. Additionally, terms such as *race, income,* and *disparity* are found at the edge of the public health cluster and the social sciences cluster, indicating the presence of sociological and public policy health-related research. On the opposite side of the public health cluster, terms that are more often associated with health-related research in the sciences are found. Terms such as *smoking, cardiovascular disease,* and *infection* intermingle with the terms in the two science clusters.

Discussion

The distribution of term densities across the map is interesting and somewhat unexpected. The relative high density of terms in the social sciences and humanities cluster was surprising, given that the majority of research at IUPUI is happening in medicine and health sciences. When the two science clusters are combined, they total 442 terms, which is roughly similar in size to the social sciences and humanities cluster, with 478 terms. However, the density of terms appears far greater in the social sciences and humanities cluster. This raises interesting questions about the research that is archived in these areas. Perhaps research in the social sciences and humanities has a more limited set of terms with which to describe the research being done. Or perhaps the research archived in ScholarWorks in the social sciences and humanities is more on similar topics such as student engagement. Whatever the case, it appears that the research in the sciences that is archived in ScholarWorks is more diverse than the research in the social sciences and humanities, at least based on the terms used to describe this research. This difference represents an area where ScholarWorks may not accurately reflect the research landscape of the institution and is something to which librarians should give consideration. Those librarians serving faculty in the social sciences and humanities should take steps if possible to ensure that the full range of research happening in their departments is accurately reflected.

The overall structure of the map provides further insight into the connections between major research areas. As mentioned earlier, IUPUI is a campus with a strong emphasis on the health sciences, and as such it is not surprising to see so many health-related terms scattered throughout the map. In this way, the term map serves as an apt metaphor for campus, with researchers focusing on health-related issues physically spread across campus in various departments. Furthermore, it is interesting to see how distinctly the public health cluster bridges the gap between the social sciences and humanities cluster with the two science clusters, providing evidence for the highly interdisciplinary nature of public health research. However, one of the major challenges in this project reveals itself in the structure of the map. The small collections of specific items, usually with uniform titles such as the Opinions of the Attorney General of Indiana collection in the Robert H. McKinney School of Law community, create separate clusters not connected to the rest of the map that make interpreting the map difficult. If viewers are unaware of these collections and their uniform titles that increase the frequency of certain words, they might lend too much weight to the importance of these clusters. While these clusters do provide important insight into the contents of the repository, they distract from the more interesting relationships between the research areas that are depicted in the rest of the map. Therefore, librarians engaged in creating these types of term maps should have some basic level of familiarity with the contents of their repositories and, as should always be the case, approach the resulting maps with a critical eye. Another challenge related to the structure of the map and cluster formation pertains to the way bodies of text containing many different research areas do not always form coherent clusters. While VOSviewer can show the connections between interdisciplinary areas of research, it relies on sufficient high-quality data. The ScholarWorks data set needs to be larger to more accurately delineate the relationship the research areas present.

Despite the relatively small amount of data, there are many groups of terms in the clusters that point to easily identifiable research areas. Some of the more prominent terms provide clues about institutional values, or at least the values of those actively engaged in supporting the repository. For example, terms related to student engagement and educational research figure prominently in the social sciences and humanities cluster. Much of this research is archived in the Center for Service Learning community. However, it is interesting to compare the prevalence of these terms with the relatively small size of the community, suggesting that these terms are used throughout the social sciences and humanities cluster. This pattern meshes well with many of IUPUI's institutional values, which prize student engagement and student learning as key values. Similarly, the health-related research across the disciplines and not just in the health sciences is strongly indicative of IUPUI's culture. Programs such as Medical Humanities & Health Studies[2] and new degrees such as the PhD in Health Communication[3] mean that health research terms show up in unexpected places, as evidenced by the many health-related terms at the bottom left of the social sciences and humanities cluster. However, these terms do not form into any easily identifiable clusters, due in equal parts to the small number of items in these research areas and the difficulty in clustering interdisciplinary research. One of the limitations of using term co-occurrence maps to draw conclusions about the nature of research archived in an institutional repository is how susceptible they are to individual researchers with many items on the same topic. For example, much of the bone-related research in the biophysics subcluster (see figure 18 in the photospread) is attributable to one researcher at the university. The "repeat customer" phenomenon can make it seem as though a lot of research is being done institutionally in a particular area when in reality there are ten articles from one researcher on a single topic. Again, accurate interpretation of these maps relies heavily on a knowledge of the repository's contents.

There are a number of areas noticeably absent from the ScholarWorks term map. Given the strong presence of an engineering program on campus, it is surprising to see the lack of an engineering cluster or at least a significant number of engineering-related terms. Another gap in the map is in the area of physics. These gaps are confirmed by consulting the repository. Only one item is archived in the Physics collection within the School of Science community, and the School of Engineering and Technology community has only fifty-five items. Further gaps include math, chemistry, and chemical biology. The lack of chemistry-related research is not surprising due to issues around research-related patents and trepidation toward open access. Despite the lack of some areas in the map, there are small clusters of terms that suggest emerging areas in the repository. Identifying a potential emerging area requires a general knowledge of the institution and its research. One potential emerging area at IUPUI is in Philanthropy, with the recent founding of the Philanthropic Studies program in the Lilly School of Philanthropy. Terms related to this emerging area appear in the social sciences and humanities cluster, just above the library-related terms, and include *philanthropy, giving, grant, fund,* and *nonprofit organization.*

CONCLUSION

This chapter demonstrates how librarians can visually represent the research archived in library-run institutional repositories using term co-occurrence maps. Specifically, these maps demonstrate different research clusters around themes in the sciences, social sciences, and humanities. Somewhat unexpectedly, the highest density of terms appears in the social sciences and humanities, followed by the sciences. These two sections of the map are connected by public health. This map serves as a valuable resource to subject librarians in two primary ways. First, the map charts the research landscape of the institution, showing connections that while obvious to some, are new to others. For example, some librarians may be unaware of just how pervasive health-related research is on IUPUI's campus, showing up in social sciences and humanities research as well as in the sciences. Second, the map identifies gaps in the repository's coverage. One prominent example is the relatively small amount of scientific research outside of the health sciences. Many of these gaps are evident when looking directly at the numbers of items in the collections that make up the ScholarWorks communities, but visualizing the entire repository as one term map brings these gaps into context.

The two biggest limitations of these term maps are the relatively small data set and the necessary reliance on subject-matter expert input for interpretation. These maps are made with the titles and abstracts from 4,346 items, which is a relatively small amount of data for this type of large-scale textual analysis. Furthermore, the relatively small amount of data makes these term maps susceptible to being skewed by small special collections with uniform titles, such as the Opinions of the Indiana Attorney General, and single researchers who have a number of articles on the same topic. However, as the repository expands in size it will be less vulnerable to being skewed and will more accurately reflect the institution's research landscape. Additionally, input from subject-matter experts will result in a more comprehensive analysis. Many librarians lack the specialized knowledge to connect clusters of terms with the research areas these terms potentially represent. For the ScholarWorks term map, this is especially true in the sciences, where a lack of expert knowledge allows for only the general classification of clusters as dentistry, biophysics, and molecular biology and genetics.

Future iterations of this project will need to include an interpretation and validation phase that involves input from faculty or other subject-matter experts on cluster identification. This input will facilitate librarians' understanding of the map and improve everyone's understanding of the research landscape at IUPUI. Furthermore, a much larger high-quality data set will improve the resulting map. As more time passes since the implementation of the campus-level open access policy and librarians work to mediate submissions of faculty research, the amount of text in the repository for analyzing will only continue to grow. Replicating these term maps in a year or two years will yield a much fuller picture of the research landscape and potentially provide insight into new and emerging research areas on campus. Despite the drawbacks of the ScholarWorks term maps, they are still useful for librarians planning outreach around the open access policy. With these term maps in mind, librarians should focus on increasing the diversity of social sciences research beyond library and education research and increase the repository's holdings in scientific research beyond the health sciences. Lastly, these maps have the potential for helping librarians, particularly those new to campus, to begin to chart the research and intellectual landscape at their institutions.

NOTES

1. Visualizing the topical coverage of an institutional repository using VOSviewer. http://hdl.handle.net/11243/9.
2. Medical Humanities & Health Studies. http://liberalarts.iupui.edu/mhhs/.
3. Communication Studies. http://liberalarts.iupui.edu/comm/.

REFERENCES

Callon, Michel, Jean-Pierre Courtial, William A. Turner, and Serge Bauin. 1983. "From Translations to Problematic Networks: An Introduction to Co-Word Analysis." *Social Science Information* 22(2): 191–235. doi:10.1177/053901883022002003.

Gobster, Paul H. 2014. "(Text) Mining the LANDscape: Themes and Trends over 40 Years of Landscape and Urban Planning." *Landscape and Urban Planning* 126 (June): 21–30. doi:10.1016/j.landurbplan.2014.02.025.

Heersmink, Richard, Jeroen van den Hoven, Nees Jan van Eck, and Jan van den Berg. 2011. "Bibliometric Mapping of Computer and Information Ethics." *Ethics and Information Technology* 13(3): 241–249. doi:http://dx.doi.org/10.1007/s10676-011-9273-7.

Odell, Jere. 2014. "Building, Growing and Maintaining Institutional Repositories." Presented at the Michiana Scholarly Communication Librarianship Conference, IUSB, South Bend, IN, October 20.

"Open Access Policy, IUPUI Faculty Council (October 7, 2014) | Open Access @ IUPUI." 2015. Accessed May 20. https://openaccess.iupui.edu/policy.

Peters, H. P. F., and A. F. J. van Raan. 1993. "Co-Word-Based Science Maps of Chemical Engineering. Part I: Representations by Direct Multidimensional Scaling." *Research Policy* 22(1): 23–45. doi:10.1016/0048-7333(93)90031-C.

Rip, Arie, and J. Courtial. 1984. "Co-Word Maps of Biotechnology: An Example of Cognitive Scientometrics." *Scientometrics* 6(6): 381–400.

Staum, Sonja, and Randall Halverson. 2004. "IDEA: Sharing Scholarly Digital Resources." IUPUI, Indianapolis, IN, February 27.

Tijssen, R., and A. Van Raan. 1989. "Mapping Co-Word Structures: A Comparison of Multidimensional Scaling and LEXIMAPPE." *Scientometrics* 15(3-4): 283–295.

van Eck, Nees Jan, and Ludo Waltman. 2007. "VOS: A New Method for Visualizing Similarities Between Objects." In *Advances in Data Analysis*, edited by Reinhold Decker and Hans-J. Lenz, 299–306. Studies in Classification, Data Analysis, and Knowledge Organization. Springer Berlin Heidelberg. http://dx.doi.org/10.1007/978-3-540-70981-7_34.

———. 2010. "Software Survey: VOSviewer, a Computer Program for Bibliometric Mapping." *Scientometrics* 84(2): 523–538. doi:10.1007/s11192-009-0146-3.

———. 2011. "Text Mining and Visualization Using VOSviewer." *arXiv:1109.2058 [cs]*, September. http://arxiv.org/abs/1109.2058.

———. 2015. "VOSviewer Manual (Version 1.6.0)."

Waltman, Ludo, Nees Jan van Eck, and Ed C. M. Noyons. 2010. "A Unified Approach to Mapping and Clustering of Bibliometric Networks." *Journal of Informetrics* 4(4): 629–635. doi:10.1016/j.joi.2010.07.002.

Waltman, Ludo, Anthony F. J. van Raan, and Sue Smart. 2014. "Exploring the Relationship between the Engineering and Physical Sciences and the Health and Life Sciences by Advanced Bibliometric Methods." *PLoS ONE* 9(10): e111530. doi:10.1371/journal.pone.0111530.

8

Visualizing Archival Context and Content for Digital Collections

Stephen Kutay

Digitization projects have expanded access to locally embedded historical and primary sources that were once beyond the reach of many would-be researchers. As digital collections continue to appear online, the need to aggregate access through multiple search engines and portals has helped streamline research through protocols for sharing metadata[1] across the growing landscape of collections around the globe. Recent years have ushered in "big digital heritage"[2] in the wakes of the Digital Public Library of America (DPLA 2015) and Europeana (2015). These massive digital libraries provide access to archival materials from heritage organizations throughout the United States and Europe and are made possible through partner institutions that act as hubs to host and/or organize digitization of resources that can extend deep into remote communities. Since the first wave of digitization projects decades ago, digital collections are now an important and growing extension of archives and heritage institutions everywhere.

Though digital surrogates are derived from, and therefore related to, their archival counterparts, some tensions exist regarding their fundamental modes of engagement that question whether source and surrogate are indeed the same. On the one hand, virtual archival materials remove barriers to access but, on the other, are extracted from their embedded positions within a collection of records that contain interdependent relationships that help inform their meaning through the contexts of their creation and use. Digital surrogates cannot reveal all traces associated with these material qualities any more than physical sources can possess the digital traces of the surrogate. It is argued that due to the transformative nature of surrogates, they possess archival value of their own as mobile and mutable reproductions (Conway 2014, 52). To contend with this disjuncture, digital collections traditionally offer introductory text to help ground the documents in a contextual narrative. Data visualizations, however, offer users another effective tool to convey context and provide access to these materials with respect to their origination.

This chapter focuses on applying metadata visualizations to communicate context and content of digital collections, which is critical to understanding the source archival materials from which digital collections are populated. Those with advanced knowledge of archives will find the section headed Visual Techniques and Metaphors for Archival Context/Content most useful. Those with less experience will gain insight into some of the challenges regarding the use of archival materials online, as well as review some of the fundamental archival principles that inform the objectives and design of these online tools. Whether used to supplement existing textual collection descriptions or as a stand-alone graphic or interface, visualizations will assist users in obtaining a broad understanding of the topics, documents, dates, names, and circumstances represented in digital collections. First, we examine how context as a fundamental aspect of archival records is hidden when using online surrogates. Then we will look at where to locate and how to apply context and content descriptions as data that populate a visualization. Finally, we will analyze ways to visualize contexts and contents of digital collections and archival metadata.

A NOTE ON TERMINOLOGY

To provide clarity, definitions for the following terms are provided as they pertain to the subject of this chapter. Digital collections are not restricted to primary sources; however, *digital collections* are referenced here as collections of *digital surrogates* (or *digital objects*) derived from documents that make up physical and/or digital archival collections. *Source collection* refers to the archival collections from which a digital collection is, at least in part, derived. *Record* refers to the original (or archival) source document from which a digital surrogate (or object) is derived. *Agent* refers to the creator of a record. *Digital heritage* is referenced here to broadly describe the publication and promotion of surrogates of archival materials online.

THE PROBLEM OF ONLINE ARCHIVES

Much has been gained by technological advancements that enable the discovery and utility of archival sources online. Archival surrogates, however, possess their own histories as educational assets, marketing resources, or in some cases as objects that are refigured, repurposed, or otherwise appropriated for new social or consumer *milieu* (Appadurai 1988, 14–16). With so much to gain, however, there is also much to lose. As reproductions of records, users of surrogates bring with them their own ways of understanding or knowing them within their own contextual frames (Duff, Monks-Leeson, and Galey 2012, 80–81). Well-established means for searching collections through finding aids help reinforce essential context associated with records that cannot be easily communicated through digital asset management systems. With growing emphasis on primary source literacy and critical thinking, users of digital collections have become more diverse, but finding concrete ways with which to inform users of a collection's original context are not a typical function of the database discovery process. Such systems are designed to deliver resources as discrete, self-contained objects and so may obscure archival sources from their overall function (context) and placement (original order) within a records group of a corporate body, person, or family (provenance). Surrogate records do not naturally express contextual traces of the larger collection (or records group) at only the item level from which users typically engage with these sources online.

Our understanding of a collection of records lies within the names, dates, places, and circumstances of their origination. Some of these elements are indeed captured within item-level metadata; however, the logic of the database inevitably privileges some elements over others unless consciously acted on by users. Descriptions serve many purposes for access and vary widely from collection to collection and institution to institution, thus limiting the consistent communication of context from metadata alone. Context, as found within finding aids, provides a historical narrative critical to users of archives. Furthermore, understanding the *archival bond* that demonstrates relationships between documents is an essential by-product of using archives in person but is lost in databases designed to accommodate a vast array of information queries and ordered lists. Unless extraordinary care is taken when assigning metadata, most digital collections are ill-equipped to reproduce such interdocumentary relationships. As mentioned previously, a high-level view of archival context is generally mediated through generous textual descriptions at the level of the collection. However, it can also be effectively represented by visualizations that not only utilize metadata from digital collections, finding aids, linked data, or other reliable sources of contextual information but also be programmed to mediate direct access as interfaces through which context and content provide the access points. Such access points may be useful to less-experienced users, who may struggle with controlled terminologies when querying subjects or document types. Moreover, visualized content is an effective tool to define the general parameters of a digital collection's document types, subjects, and temporal range while providing meaningful access points to a collection.

As archival surrogates, digital collections are unique with respect to the types of documents they contain, as well as their extents, subjects, and histories that imbue them with meaning. This uniqueness requires information specialists to be thoughtful when considering what types of visualizations and metadata to highlight. This also means that there is no correct way to apply visualizations for digital collections. Creativity and a strong knowledge of the collection will ultimately guide the selection and design of visual discovery tools. Though specific technologies and services are mentioned, the focus of the chapter is reserved to highlight some of the numerous ways in which user experience of digital collections is enhanced through visualizing archival context and content. To exacerbate this, communicating archival context is especially difficult with digital collections containing items from multiple archival collections that commonly feature a broad theme or narrative (e.g., an online exhibit or historical overview).

ARCHIVAL CONTEXT

To clarify the meaning of the term as it is applied here, *A Glossary of Archival and Records Terminology* defines "context" as:

> 1. The organizational, functional, and operational circumstances surrounding materials' creation, receipt, storage, or use, and its relationship to other materials. 2. The circumstances that a user may bring to a document that influences that user's understanding of the document. (Pearce-Moses 2005, 90)

In one sense, context is fixed in time, based on the circumstances surrounding a record's creation. In another sense, context may evolve based on how a record is subsequently managed or used. Context is also described as one of three fundamental aspects of a record to include the "content" and "structure" (Pearce-Moses 2005, 91). As a fundamental aspect, context is an important factor in understanding the historical (or secondary) value (Ham 1993, 7) records contain as evidence.

Unlike many resources located through library catalogs and article databases, archival records are understood as an intrinsic part of a larger organizational entity, the collection. Other than finding-aid descriptions, record contexts are preserved in part by the arrangement of the physical collection, which may include series and subseries that reflect the functions and activities of a person, family, or organization. Whenever possible, collections maintain the original order of the materials (i.e., the order with which documents were organized and kept by the records' creator(s) or custodian(s). This preserves the contexts of their use as well as the bonds between documents that demonstrate their interrelatedness. This "archival bond" is defined as:

> The relationship that links each record, incrementally, to the previous and subsequent ones and to all those which participate in the same activity. It is originary (i.e., it comes into existence when a record is made or received and set aside), necessary (i.e., it exists for every record), and determined (i.e., it is characterized by the purpose of the record). (University of British Columbia 2002, 1)

When visualizations are interactive, they provide additional access points that help to restore arrangement, for example, results in original order or a list of all surrogates in a specific record series in addition to ordered lists of objects according to place, date of creation, or document genre.

Locating Context

Context for archival collections (and by extension digital collections) resides in multiple locations. Precisely what constitutes context may vary depending on the perspective of the user/researcher. Descriptive metadata that may logically pertain to content could under some conditions provide context depending on the nature of one's research inquiry. For example, a box list inventory in a finding aid used to order and describe the content of an archival collection could also help demonstrate the frequency with which an agent was engaged in some kind of activity; thereby the number of records supporting (or not supporting) such activity provides the *context* for a researcher's argument or assertion. Therefore, context is relational, elusive, and target dependent (Lee 2011, 96). Contexts shift and emerge according to new needs, and the line between context and content is not always clear. Add to this the emergence of *digital humanities* that facilitate computational analyses of digitized works and corpora, and it becomes unreasonable to predict *how* and *why* a researcher is interested in a collection or a record or its digital surrogate. However, locating original context can be mediated for the benefit of students and researchers alike. Some of the most useful sources for locating context for digital collections include finding-aid metadata, individual records, digital collection–level metadata, annotations, publications, related collections, and encoded archival context (EAC).

Finding-Aid Metadata

Finding aids place archival materials in their original context (Pearce-Moses 2005, 168) by supplying a biographical or historical narrative regarding the person, family, or organization responsible for creating the collection. A section devoted to the scope and contents of the collection reveals the extent and media that make up each record series that together illustrate the arrangement of the records in a collection according to the activities of the agent(s). Finding aids are critical sources for locating original context that help inform the description of a digital collection. The rules for creating finding-aid metadata are provided by *Describing Archives: A Content Standard (DACS)*, which designates the elements and formatting of values for archival description in finding aids. Elements that are especially rich with context are noted below and paraphrased from DACS.

Identity Elements (see DACS 2.0)

Names of Corporate Bodies, Persons, or Families (CPF) describes the agent(s) responsible for the creation, assembly, accumulation, and/or maintenance of records in a collection (DACS 2013, 31). This reveals the provenance (or origination) of the described material.

    Administrative/Biographical History provides a historical narrative that may include the contexts in which an agent(s) created, assembled, accumulated, or maintained a collection of records (DACS 2013, 34).

    Dates (bulk or inclusive) describe the dates relating to the creation, assembly, accumulation, and/or maintenance of the described material (DACS 2013, 24).

Content and Structure Elements (see DACS 3.0)

Scope and Content is an especially rich source of context. This element describes "the function(s), activity(ies), transaction(s) and process(es)" involved in the creation of records. It may also describe documentary forms (minutes, diaries, letters, etc.), dates, geographic locations, and subjects (DACS 2013, 45).

System of Arrangement describes the various relationships between aggregated materials that share a common function or activity. The arrangement is often represented by series (and in some cases subseries) of materials in which such relationships are apparent (DACS 2013, 49).

* * *

Just as authorized terms enable sorting and filtering of database search results, archival authorities are also effective as access points to digital collection content and context when integrated into data visualizations. Archival authorities are provided by the "International Standard Archival Authority Record for Corporate Bodies, Persons and Families."[3] These authorities are listed below along with the sections in which they are commonly referenced in DACS.

Names: Title, Creator, Administrative/Biographical History Note, Scope & Content, Custodial History, Acquisition (DACS 2013, 17, 31, 34, 45, 63–64)

Places: Title, Creator, Admin/Bio History Note, Scope & Content (DACS 2013, 17, 31, 34, 45)

Subjects: Title, Admin/Bio History Note, Scope & Content (DACS 2013, 17, 34, 45)

Documentary forms: Title, Extent, Scope & Content (DACS 2013, 17, 28, 45)

Occupations (agent): Admin/Bio History Note, Scope & Content (DACS 2013, 31, 45)

Functions (records): Title, Admin/Bio History Note, Scope & Content (DACS 2013, 17, 31, 45)

Individual Records

Some individual records within archival collections are especially rich with context. Articles of incorporation, mission statements, mandates, diaries, correspondence, or other documents help supply evidence to support the administrative and biographical narratives that are commonly found in finding aids and digital collections. Graphic hierarchies and networks communicate relationships, structures, and functions, thereby placing the records in context to the overall activities of the group. To leverage these relationships interactively, however, a corresponding metadata element must be assigned to describe each functional entity responsible for the creation of each document in a collection. For example, a department or other designated role can be assigned to each digital object by using *creator, contributor,* or *description* elements. In doing this, metadata serve to mediate access to the corpus of documents of each functional entity via the URL produced by searching the appropriate field in which the entity is described.

Digital Collection–Level Metadata

When taken collectively, digital collections metadata provide context through the vocabularies generated by numerous item-level descriptions of *names, dates, places,* and sometimes *subjects*. Free-text description fields are especially rich in context but generally as they pertain to the item being described; therefore are often less useful as a resource for describing the overarching context of a collection. Nonetheless, some documents are especially critical to the work of a person or organization and provide useful evidence captured in free-text descriptions that contribute to context at the collection level.

Annotations, Publications, and Related Collections

The amount of context available for archival description of a collection varies widely. Some collections have local significance, where little is known about the creators, and they are preserved for community posterity. Other collections are created by well-known agents for which much is known and written. Appending context of a given collection may require consulting outside sources that should be vetted and transparent to users. Deliberate documentation comprising community member annotations of archival or digital collections can provide important context to append to a collection of a lesser-known agent(s) or to comprehensively round out (or challenge) existing narratives. Annotations may be found directly on the archival record or posted online in relation to a surrogate. Publications such as books and newspapers can also help to supply context or corroborate what is already known about a collection. In some cases, collections of a single provenance are distributed across multiple institutions, through which published descriptions could be shared.

Encoded Archival Context: Corporate Bodies, Persons, and Families

Encoded archival context (EAC) is helping to provide an accessible, reliable, and universal store of linked contextual data regarding corporate bodies, persons, and families. Though still in its early stages, EAC has been mainly focused on the schema to encode contextual data, which enables the sharing of context associated with agents for which archives are held at institutions (Society of American Archivists 2015).

ARCHIVAL CONTENT

In contrast to context, content speaks to the "informational value" (Schellenberg 1984, 58) of a record beyond its significance as evidence and provides the "intellectual substance" (Pearce-Moses 2005, 89) often useful to researchers. It reflects what a record is and what it is about (as opposed to what it historically represents or demonstrates). With respect to aggregations of records, a collection's scope of documentary genres and subjects gives users of digital collections a comprehensive idea of a collection's content. As such, visualizing content enables users to understand the parameters of a digital collection according to its breadth and scope, while providing exceptional access points based on authorized terms used to describe the activities and types of documents created by them. Archival content is best reflected by archival and digital collection metadata elements such as *document type* or *genre, extent, subject* (as it pertains to what something is "about"), and archival *arrangement* (as it pertains to document types or genres produced). Note that *subject* and *arrangement* can represent both context *and* content depending on what is described or suggested in the descriptions. A user's exposure to the overall *content* of a digital collection is critical to understanding what a collection has to offer that user and subsequently provides a way for her or him to make informed choices regarding search queries.

VISUAL TECHNIQUES AND METAPHORS FOR ARCHIVAL CONTEXT/CONTENT

There are no rules that guide the decision to integrate data visualization into digital collections of archival materials, nor that guide what kind of visual metaphor is most appropriate to use. However, in the spirit of best practice, this section highlights several examples as techniques to visualization that utilize standard metadata descriptors, many of which use controlled vocabularies such as *Library of Congress Subject Headings, Library of Congress Name Authority File, Union List of Artist Names, Thesaurus for Graphic Materials, Art & Architecture Thesaurus*, and *Thesaurus of Geographic Names*, to name a few. These serve to efficiently expose and connect users to the contexts and contents of digital collections and other sources of related information.

The examples and techniques discussed here are not intended to provide a comprehensive treatment of the subject. Given the growth of visualization technologies and the innumerable possibilities for their application, examples are limited to demonstrating some strategies for selecting, creating, or implementing metadata visualizations. Visualized data can range from static and familiar representations (e.g., bar and line graphs) to the more elastic and abstract (e.g., interactive trees and radial charts). Ultimately, visualized context and content for digital collections must effectively convey information to many audiences that possess varying levels of information literacy. Therefore the examples presented here are practical and selected for their ability to represent archival materials through common contextual axes (e.g., provenance, time, and place) and content descriptions (e.g., genres, subjects, and extents). The examples presented here were created from simple spreadsheet renderings or free hosted services or customized in HTML. Others with more advanced coding knowledge or programming resources should investigate JavaScript libraries such as D3, Dygraphs, and Info-

Vis Toolkit.[4] Though not represented here, there are numerous paid visualization and infographic services that could be used for digital collections visualizations.

Note: When deploying a data visualization technology consider accessibility regarding its performance across device platforms, as well as how it will be rendered and interpreted by assistive technologies.

Selecting Metadata for Visual Display

Metadata visualizations, or "metadata-enhanced visual interfaces" (Shiri 2008, 764), utilize digital collections metadata or are supplemented by other sources such as finding aids. In some cases data are generated from the collection metadata and calculated to measure broader aspects of the entire collection. For example, using collection metadata, one could quantify the number of documents produced by a specific author per year to provide useful categories for researchers. The database can be used to perform a search of the author field, which is subsequently sorted by date to record the number of documents per year, per author. Alternatively, popular subject headings assigned to an author could be calculated using an online word-frequency calculator on the entire values copied from the subject field.

Selecting metadata to highlight in a visual representation can be challenging. Consider the elements that best reveal the context, content, and uniqueness of a collection, ensuring that the selected fields can be efficiently visualized or interactively manipulated within the chosen visual technique, metaphor, or technology. A contextual narrative is best visualized by adequate variation in the data. For instance, a map displaying the geographic distribution of a collection of photographs is visually effective if multiple locations are used. Conversely, a map of textual records of an organization is not useful if those records are created and used in a limited or confined location. In such a case, an alternative might be to create a timeline that historically plots activities and transactions as represented by the records in the collection. Another alternative might be to graphically represent the extents of individual series of archival records by way of a simple bar graph, pie chart, or other graphic element that groups or clusters information.

Table 8.1 is a sample spreadsheet of metadata edited and prepared for loading into a visualization application. Note that many essential elements that typically accompany a resource description have been removed, leaving only the elements to be utilized *in* the visualization. If seeking to provide access to digital objects from within the visual interface, URLs must be supplied for each of the digital objects or from premade (canned) searches to produce groups of objects such as items per author, place, or date. It is best to consider in advance of the production phase of a digital collection how metadata will be visualized. This will help inform what elements should be added to the element set that will be utilized in the visual interface. For instance, consider assigning an element for *Records Series* taken from the arrangement in a finding aid or *Broad Topic* to generally categorize objects into a manageable number of groupings for display.

Table 8.1. Example of metadata from a digital collection of correspondence, stripped of all fields except those required to populate a data visualization with context, content, and a means to access the resource (URL)

Letter (content)	Date (context)	Author (context)	Country (context)	Language (content)	Topic (context, content)	URL (access)
1	1912-12-06	Suydam, Lambert	United States	eng	Musicianship	http://digital-
2	1912-12-17	Bone, Philip J.	Great Britain	eng	Musicianship	http://digital-
3	1913-04-02	Laurie, Alexander	United States	eng	American Guitar Society	http://digital-

Visualizing Temporal Coverage

As a linear representation of history, *time* effectively places events (and the documents produced for and by them) within the context of the circumstances of their creation. Time can relate to people, events, objects, and ideas as a result of their shared occupation of a period in time. When taken collectively, periods of time demonstrate the arc of change, the trajectory of progress, or the ebb and flow of activity.

The timeline presented here was created via Viewshare from the Library of Congress.[5] This service is intended for use with library collections and offers numerous data visualizations ("views") that are hosted online but that can be embedded into local web pages or digital collection landing pages.

In this example using the *Vahdah Olcott-Bickford Correspondence* digital collection,[6] multiple time views are displayed concurrently with "years" occupying the larger, uppermost portion of the frame and "decades" occupying the bottom of the frame. Users view the correspondence placed on the timeline as a scrollable window of time, yet they can also see the letters written over decades as a trend in the broad timeline. Context is represented by the authors' names, the dates, and a filter to display letters specific to a broad topical focus (shown here as "Context"). Content is represented by the extent of letters assigned to each broad topic. For added value, the correspondents' names can be clicked to view additional information that includes a link directly to the digital resource, thus transforming the visualization into an interface for accessing the materials (see figure 19 in the photospread).

Specifications

> Type: Timeline
> Mode: Interactive
> Host technology: Viewshare (Library of Congress)
> Purpose: Communicate context and content through temporal distribution
> Recommended metadata: *Author, Date*
> Optional metadata: *Broad Topic, Place of origin,* URLs (to access digital objects)

Instructions

1. Create a new data set from a selected set of fields such as *author*, date, country of origin, and digital object URL.
2. Upload the data set into Viewshare.
3. Configure the Timeline view to publish and embed, if desired.

Visualizing Frequency and Context

In this variation of the same correspondence collection, the scatterplot provides a birds-eye view of the collection in its entirety. Context is represented by the topics (subjects) and dates. Content is represented by the frequency of plotted dots per topic. In this example, peak activity regarding correspondence with musicians covers roughly 1920 through 1935 and 1950 through 1964. Peak correspondence regarding the American Guitar Society, which Vahdah founded and served as president, covers 1923 through 1933. Potentially, researchers viewing this data will have some knowledge with which to guide their database search queries and a foundation for generating a hypothesis that addresses the peaks and lapses in correspondence (see figure 20 in the photospread).

Specifications

> Type: Scatterplot/timeline
> Mode: Static
> Host technology: Microsoft Excel or other spreadsheet application (alternative: Google Charts)[7]
> Purpose: Communicate context and content through temporal distribution
> Recommended metadata: *Date* (year), date frequency (calculated)
> Optional metadata: *Broad Topic*, *Subject*, or other desired element

Instructions

1. Custom format the *date* column of the collection metadata to display only *year* (yyyy).
2. Alphabetically sort the Broad Topic field (or *subject*).
3. Copy and analyze the frequency of years per Broad Topic. This can be achieved by (1) searching the database for both *author* and *topic* and then sorting by *year* or (2) using a word-frequency calculator.
4. Create a new data set and paste the year frequency data into columns each labeled by a Broad Topic.
5. Assign a scatterplot chart from the spreadsheet application (if charts are supported).

Visualizing Geographic Coverage

This example reinterprets the metadata from the first timeline according to geographic location. This visual interface conveys context through the scope of countries for which correspondence transpired and the ability to filter according to broad topical focus (shown here again as "Context"). Content is represented by the overall *extent* of the collection as well as the *extents* of each broad topic and country of origin. A link in the interactive pop-up bubble labeled "Link" launches the digital resource (see figure 21 in the photospread).

Specifications

> Type: Geolocation map (or geographic distribution)
> Mode: Interactive

Host technology: Library of Congress's Viewshare (alternative: Google Fusion Table)
Purpose: Communicate context and content through geographic distribution
Required metadata: *Author* (or *Title*), *Country* (or coordinates)
Optional metadata: *Date, Language, Broad Topic,* URLs (to access objects)

Instructions

1. Create a new data set from at least the following fields: author, date, country of origin, and digital object URL.
2. Upload the data set into Viewshare.
3. Configure the Timeline view to publish and embed, if desired.

Visualizing Archival Documents as Interfaces

Organization charts and family trees are useful for visually describing resources according to their origination. Though not a data visualization technology per se, these documents can be refigured as image files (or reconstructed) and programmed into web pages as visual interfaces. These highly contextual documents effectively communicate relationships, structure, and functions (or roles) within an organization or family. As HTML encoded images, documents created by specific people, offices, departments, or other subgroups can be accessed. The example below demonstrates how an organization chart visually conveys context in the form of a structural hierarchy and when coded into a web page delivers collection content information (e.g., *extent, document types, or subjects*) through rollover hotspots. Clicking the hotspots can be made to generate a database list of the digital objects associated with each organizational entity, role, or function (see figure 22 in the photospread).

Specifications

Type: Representational interface
Mode: Interactive (optional static display)
Host technology: HTML (alternative to HTML coding: *Adobe Muse* application)
Purpose: Communicate context and content through the transformative use of an archival document
Recommended metadata elements: *Creator, Genre, Subject, Extent*

Instructions

The interface is dependent on the type of document and its structure; therefore instructions are limited to aggregating the metadata that are desired and relevant to display over (or from) the chosen document. Knowledge of HTML coding is recommended, if not required.

Visualizing Narratives

Many digital collections are accompanied by introductory text that provides archival context in a narrative format. As previously mentioned, this effective method of grounding a collection to its archival counterpart becomes complicated or overwhelming when a digital collection incorporates materials from multiple archival collections. In thematic collections, the argument for communicating context is even greater. One solution is to treat the individual narratives as access points into the collection, thereby promoting use of the materials according to provenance.

In this example, six independent collections are used to populate a digital collection based on a history of water development in Los Angeles.[8] Rather than place the narratives together, forming a lengthy page of text, this visual element utilizes an HTML gallery menu to show/hide narrative text of each collection via rolling over the collection name. Users can generate all the digital objects within each archival collection by clicking the collection name (see figure 23 in the photospread).

Specifications

> Type: Navigational gallery menu
> Mode: Interactive
> Host technology: HTML
> Purpose: Independently communicate contexts across multiple collections
> Recommended metadata: *Source collection* and *Administrative/Biographical history* and/or *Scope and Contents* (from finding aid)

Instructions

> 1. Select or create a gallery menu.
> 2. Collect archival collection names, pictures (if desired), and associated text from finding aids or other sources.
> 3. Record URLs from canned searches of the *Source Collection* field and hyperlink from the collection names.
> 4. Populate the gallery menu with text, images, and linked URLs. Some HTML coding may be required.

Visualizing Archival Arrangement

In a database environment, the functions of the archival documents represented by the surrogates are obscured when searched and viewed independently. The physical arrangement of archives, in many cases, provides users with a fundamental understanding of the functions and types of materials as organized into a record series. A series provides users of digital collections with an effective access point to view related documents in their *original order*, which is more akin to how users of archives experience physical materials.

Tree charts, like org charts, demonstrate structure and relationships. Given the ability to nest information, they are one of a number of data visualization types (e.g., tree maps) that can be adapted to demonstrate clustered hierarchies such as provenance and records series and subseries and the documents that populate them. By clicking nodes, branches form to display the contents of the previous heading. This kind of interactivity provides both context and access points for viewing materials as a complete series. The example here was created using the Scalar[9] web development platform; however this popular type of visualization can be found in JavaScript libraries and other online sources. Users of Scalar for the presentation of digital heritage materials should consider utilizing the visualization functions for their ability to display context and content and for their ease of implementation inside the Scalar environment (see figure 24 in the photospread).

Specifications

Type: Tree chart
Mode: Interactive
Host technology: Scalar (alternatives: D3, JavaScript InfoVis Toolkit)
Purpose: Communicate context and content through a display of a collection's physical (series) arrangement. This is especially useful for digital collections of multiple archival collections.
Recommended metadata: *Source Collection* and *Arrangement* from "Scope and Contents" in the finding aid
Optional data: *Title*, URL (to access objects)

Instructions

1. In Scalar, set up one page for every collection, series, and subseries (if applicable).
2. Call up each page to edit and tag associated pages (and media, if applicable) and then save.
3. Click "Explore/Visualization" on the left toolbar menu.
4. Click "Paths" to display.

Visualizing Relationships

Records are associated with their creators and the functions they serve. *Radial charts* effectively communicate these relationships because of the differences in position each point occupies around the circle, which enables connections between all points. In this example, contexts are communicated through the visible association of records with its creator and function(s). Hovering over any record, function, or person (entity) highlights these relationships through the connections that appear in the chart. Like the tree chart, this example was created using the Scalar web development platform; however, this visualization type is available as part of JavaScript libraries (see figure 25 in the photospread).

Specifications

> Type: Radial chart
> Mode: Interactive
> Host technology: Scalar (alternative: D3)
> Purpose: Communicate context and content through a display of relationships or associations between records, their creators, and the functions they serve
> Recommended metadata: *Creator* or *Contributor, Title*
> Optional metadata: *Function* or *Functional Entity* (preferred from a repeated instance of *Description* or other dedicated element), URLs (to access objects)

Instructions

1. In Scalar, set up one page for every creator, record, and function (if applicable).
2. Call up each page to edit and tag associated pages (and media, if applicable) and then save.
3. Click "Explore/Visualization" on the left toolbar menu.
4. Click "Radial" to display.

Visualizing Layers of Provenance, Context, and Content

Many of the visualization tools discussed thus far provide some kind of prism with which to understand the context and content of a collection, such as those that highlight their temporal scope, geographic scope, organization, functions, and relationships. As with most digital collections comprising multiple archives, it can be difficult to apply a single visual tool that is effective for each, given their unique origins, histories, extents, scopes, document types, and subjects.

The following is a customized visual tool created in HTML that reveals layers of provenance, context, and content for multiple archival collections within a single digital collection.[10] Utilizing *x*- and *y*-axes, this tool describes fundamental aspects of six archival collections. The area created by plotting these axes defines each collection according to its *origin* and *extent* and *inclusive dates*. These areas serve as hotspots for highlighting the collections. Clicking one of these zones will generate a list of all the documents of the chosen archival collection (i.e., by *provenance*) within the database. To assist users with selecting a collection to view, a callout feature is added to each zone in which a button reveals the most popular document types and subjects that populate each archival collection.

A final layer presents additional access points for generating a list of all documents from all collections created within a specified decade. Clickable brackets are placed across each decade and vertically positioned along the *y*-axis to demonstrate the number of documents available for each decade. This visual approach indicates to users the time periods that are more or less represented within the digital collection. The view-by-decade function is intended to facilitate users seeking the subject matter from an overarching perspective and who wish to generate all available documents according to a specific window in time (see figure 26 in the photospread).

Specifications

    Type: Combo chart
    Mode: Interactive
    Host technology: HTML (alternative to HTML coding: *Adobe Muse* application)
    Purpose: Communicate provenance, contexts, and contents for digital collections comprising multiple archival collections.
    Recommended metadata (per archival collection): *Source Collection, Date, Extent, Document Genre* (or type), *Subject*
    Optional data: *Source Collection* URLs (from a database search in the *Source Collection* field), *Date* URLs (from a database search of the date range by decade)

Instructions

1. Via code/place *x*-axis (decades) and *y*-axis (number of documents).
2. Collect and consult metadata per source collection regarding the most popular document types and subjects.
3. Using date ranges and overall extents for each source collection, code or place rectangles of unique colors with *rollover* and *hyperlink* actions within the correct positions along the *x*- and *y*-axes; hyperlink each rectangle using the URL generated by searching the corresponding *Source Collection* field.
4. Label each rectangle with the name of the creator of the collection.
5. For each rectangle, embed a button action that launches a callout box containing a list of popular media and subjects relevant to each collection.
6. Create and place brackets within the correct positions along the *x*- and *y*-axes according to the number of documents per decade; then hyperlink using the URL generated by a date range search of the database.

LIMITATIONS AND DISCUSSION

Visualizations and interfaces presented here are offered as examples for visually communicating archival context and content. Though published research exists regarding data visualization, there is very little that addresses this subject with respect to reinforcing original context for digital collections. As a relatively unexplored niche, studies are required to measure the utility of these and other visualizations for communicating archival context and content from the user's perspective.

Like other online information systems, digital collections are accessed via some kind of interface that enables user queries, many of which implement search management tools such as limiters and filters. In this way, heritage databases are no different than other information resource databases. They are subject to any number of usability issues and user behaviors typically experienced on the web. In addition, information-seeking experience and cognitive search abilities vary between users of digital image collections (Matusiak 2006, 485). The effectiveness of a database supported by visual tools for information retrieval is a function of *user experience*, information architecture, and human-computer interaction. This places users in direct relation to both *web content* and *their own context*. That is, *user experience design* effectively mediates the discovery of content under the *context of the users' needs* (Morville 2015). It is the goal, therefore, that visualizations be selected and implemented based on their ability to facilitate user needs and communicate digital collection content and original contexts of archival sources.

Over the years, studies involving the assessment of visualizations for supporting information retrieval have produced mixed results (Koshman 2005, 825). To some extent, metadata visualizations and interfaces offer a way to help alleviate the *cognitive load* (i.e., memory, tasks, etc.)[11] encountered while searching for information (Bergström and Atkinson 2010, 384–385). However, *cognitive load* may actually increase based on higher levels of visual, data, and task complexity exhibited (or required) by a visualization (Huang, Eades, and Hong 2009, 146). This suggests that simpler visual representations may be most effective at reducing cognitive load. Studies regarding the types of effective visualization exist but vary according to their application or discipline.[12] The subject matter presented here will no doubt continue to benefit from research methods such as usability testing to provide future guidance in the development and implementation of visual tools for navigating collections of archival surrogates.

MOVING FORWARD

One important indicator of the future of digital collections is the coordination of many academic and heritage institutions, both large and small, that are invested in making archives discoverable from even the most remote locations. Massive digital libraries such as the DPLA have helped remove barriers to archives that otherwise lack the resources to place their materials online. Archives with digital collections programs have begun to share their metadata with the DPLA, OCLC, and other regional services to increase the discoverability and utility of their materials by reaching audiences far beyond the localities that their collections represent. Another indicator of digital collections growth is that granting agencies are providing more focus on the digitization, preservation, and availability of archival materials online,[13] not just the physical processing required to make them initially accessible to researchers.

With digital collections becoming more discoverable, there is little doubt that online archives will continue to gain momentum. Yet important questions must be considered. What kinds of purposes will future researchers have for "big digital heritage"? To what extent will heritage data become further removed from the contexts that embed them in their local communities and give them meaning? Can archival surrogates withstand their digital mobility and malleability as part of a menagerie of materials among online social and market spaces? Regardless of whether such concerns ever come to fruition, we are well served by investigating methods that help ground digital surrogates in original context should any future counterweight be needed to balance emerging ways of interacting with these sources that prompt new archival theorizing. It could be that metadata visualizations and interfaces for digital collections offer at least one helpful step toward that end as tools for mediating archival context and content.

NOTES

1. Metadata sharing from data providers that operate digital libraries is facilitated by the Open Archives Initiative (2015) Protocol for Metadata Harvesting (OAI-PMH), which maps all elements used to describe a resource to simple Dublin Core, where the metadata is ingested, indexed, and delivered to users by Internet service providers.

2. The DPLA and its European counterpart provide portals for searching digital heritage materials throughout the United States and Europe, respectively.

3. "International Standard Authority Record for Corporate Bodies, Persons and Families," International Council on Archives, April 1, 2004, http://www.icacds.org.uk/eng/ISAAR(CPF)2ed.pdf.

4. "D3 Data-Driven Documents," accessed August 14, 2015, http://d3js.org/. "Dygraphs," accessed August 14, 2015, http://dygraphs.com/. "InfoVis Toolkit," accessed August 14, 2015, https://philogb.github.io/jit/. These libraries consist of data visualization templates that utilize JavaScript programming language to populate sophisticated graphic renderings of data.

5. "Viewshare," Library of Congress, accessed August 14, 2015, http://viewshare.org/. Viewshare is a free service for creating and embedding or linking useful data visualizations for libraries. Visualizations include maps, timelines, scatterplots, bar and pie charts, tables, and galleries. Prospective users must request an account.

6. "Vahdah Olcott-Bickford Correspondence," Delmar T. Oviatt Library, California State University Northridge, accessed August 14, 2015, http://digital-library.csun.edu/cdm/landingpage/collection/VOBCorr.

7. "Google Charts," Google Developers, accessed August 14, 2015, https://developers.google.com/chart/?hl=en. Google charts provide a large set of JavaScript visualizations from which to choose.

8. "Water Works: Documenting Water History in Los Angeles," Delmar T. Oviatt Library, California State University Northridge, accessed August 14, 2015, http://digital-library.csun.edu/WaterWorks/.

9. "Scalar," The Alliance for Networking Visual Culture, accessed August 17, 2015, http://scalar.usc.edu/. Data visualizations in Scalar are created through tagging pages, digital media, and other elements used in presentations (or online exhibits) of media with text.

10. "Water Works."

11. As with Koshman's "Testing User Interaction," Bergström and Atkinson's study, "Augmenting Digital Libraries with Web-Based Visualizations," compared the effectiveness of visualizations used to reduce the mental activities and barriers required to locate relevant sources of academic information.

12. Some studies offering data or guidelines that address effective visualizations for specific disciplines are Gehlenborg and Wong, 2012, "Into the Third Dimension," 851; Gehlenborg and Wong, 2012, "Power of the Plane," 935; and Kelleher and Wagener, 2011, "Ten Guidelines for Effective Data Visualization in Scientific Publications," 822–827.

13. Funded by the Andrew W. Mellon Foundation, "Digitizing Hidden Special Collections and Archives" is a new program of the Council on Library and Information Resources (2014), which effectively replaces the program "Cataloging Hidden Special Collections and Archives."

REFERENCES

Appadurai, Arjun. 1988. "Introduction: Commodities and the Politics of Value." In *The Social Life of Things: Commodities in Cultural Perspective*, edited by Arjun Appadurai, 3–63. Cambridge, UK: Cambridge University Press.

Bergström, Peter, and Darren C. Atkinson. 2010. "Augmenting Digital Libraries with Web-Based Visualizations." *Journal of Digital Information Management* 8(6): 377–386. http://go.galegroup.com/ps/i.do?id=GALE|A250885768&v=2.1&u=csunorthridge&it=r&p=CDB&sw=w&asid=f9461a7badcc72732806acd9ff2c4c39

Conway, Paul. 2014. "Digital Transformations and the Archival Nature of Surrogates." *Archival Science* 15(1): 51–69. doi:10.1007/s10502-014-9219-z.

Council on Library and Information Resources. 2015. "Digitizing Hidden Special Collections and Archives." Council on Library and Information Resources. Accessed August 17, http://www.clir.org/hiddencollections.

Dey, Anind K. 2001. "Understanding and Using Context." *Personal and Ubiquitous Computing* 5(1): 4–7. doi:10.1007/s007790170019.

Digital Public Library of America. 2015. "Become a Hub." Accessed August 17, http://dp.la/info/hubs/become-a-hub/.

Duff, Wendy M., Emily Monks-Leeson, and Alan Galey. 2012. "Contexts Built and Found: A Pilot Study on the Process of Archival Meaning-Making." *Archival Science* 12(1): 69–92. doi:http://dx.doi.org.libproxy.csun.edu/10.1007/s10502-011-9145-2.

Europeana. 2015. "Why Become a Data Provider?" *Europeana Pro*. Accessed August 17, http://pro.europeana.eu/page/become-a-data-provider.

Gehlenborg, Nils, and Bang Wong. 2012. "Into the Third Dimension: Three-Dimensional Visualizations Are Effective for Spatial Data But Rarely for Other Data Types." *Nature Methods* 9(9): 851. http://go.galegroup.com/ps/i.do?id=GALE|A302298887&v=2.1&u=csunorthridge&it=r&p=HRCA&sw=w&asid=1354e6b6b2e3c36a85980c2781c1c4e6.

———. 2012. "Power of the Plane: Two-Dimensional Visualizations of Multivariate Data Are Most Effective When Combined." *Nature Methods* 9(10): 935. http://go.galegroup.com/ps/i.do?id=GALE|A304942671&v=2.1&u=csunorthridge&it=r&p=HRCA&sw=w&asid=e340ce3461b1fa6016092fe243066244.

Ham, F. G. 1993. *Selecting and Appraising: Archives and Manuscripts*. Chicago, IL: Society of American Archivists.

Huang, Weidong, Peter Eades, and Seok-Hee Hong. 2009. "Measuring Effectiveness of Graph Visualizations: A Cognitive Load Perspective." *Information Visualization* 8(3): 139–152. doi:http://dx.doi.org/10.1057/ivs.2009.10.

Kelleher, Christa, and Thorsten Wagener. 2011. "Ten Guidelines for Effective Data Visualization in Scientific Publications." *Environmental Modelling & Software* 26(6): 822–827. doi:10.1016/j.envsoft.2010.12.006.

Koshman, Sherry. 2005. "Testing User Interaction with a Prototype Visualization-Based Information Retrieval System." *Journal of the American Society for Information Science and Technology* 56(8): 824–833. doi:10.1002/asi.20175.

Lea, Martin, Tim O'Shea, and Pat Fung. 1995. "Constructing the Networked Organization: Content and Context in the Development of Electronic Communications." *Organization Science* 6(4): 462–478. http://www.jstor.org/stable/2634998.

Lee, Christopher A. 2011. "A Framework for Contextual Information in Digital Collections." *Journal of Documentation* 67: 95–143. doi:10.1108/00220411111105470.

Matusiak, Krystyna K. 2006. "Information Seeking Behavior in Digital Image Collections: A Cognitive Approach." *The Journal of Academic Librarianship* 32(5): 479–488. doi:10.1016/j.acalib.2006.05.009.

Morville, Peter. 2015. "User Experience Design." Semantic Studios. Accessed August 20, http://semanticstudios.com/user_experience_design/.

Pearce-Moses, Richard. 2005. *A Glossary of Archival and Records Terminology*. Chicago, IL: Society of American Archivists. Access August 15, 2015, http://www2.archivists.org/glossary.

Open Archives Initiative. 2015. "Open Archives Initiative Protocol for Metadata Harvesting." Accessed August 14, https://www.openarchives.org/pmh/.

Schellenberg, Theodore. 1984. "The Appraisal of Modern Public Records." In *A Modern Archives Reader: Basic Readings on Archival Theory and Practice*, edited by Maygene F. Daniels and Timothy Walch, 57–70. Washington, DC: National Archives and Records Service, U.S. General Services Administration.

Shiri, Ali. 2008. "Metadata-Enhanced Visual Interfaces to Digital Libraries." *Journal of Information Science* 34(6): 763–775. doi:10.1177/0165551507087711.

Society of American Archivists. 2015. "Encoded Archival Context - Corporate Bodies, Persons, and Families (EAC-CPF)." Accessed August 17, http://www2.archivists.org/groups/technical-subcommittee-on-eac-cpf/encoded-archival-context-corporate-bodies-persons-and-families-eac-cpf.

Thangaraj, M., and V. Gayatri. 2013. "An Effective Technique for Context-Based Digital Collection Search." *International Journal of Machine Learning and Computing* 3(4): 372–375. doi:10.7763/IJMLC.2013.V3.341.

University of British Columbia. 2002. "InterPARES Glossary: A Controlled Vocabulary of Terms Used in the InterPARES Project." Accessed August 14, 2015, http://www.interpares.org/documents/InterPARES Glossary 2002-1.pdf.

US Department of Health and Human Services. 2015. "User Experience Basics." Usability.gov. Accessed August 20, http://www.usability.gov/what-and-why/user-experience.html.

Weiler, Angela. 2005. "Information-Seeking Behavior in Generation Y Students: Motivation, Critical Thinking, and Learning Theory." *The Journal of Academic Librarianship* 31(1): 46–53. doi:10.1016/j.acalib.2004.09.009.

9

Using R and ggvis to Create Interactive Graphics for Exploratory Data Analysis

Tim Dennis

Creating interactive web graphics requires a heterogeneous set of technical skills that can include data cleaning, analysis, web development, and design. Data need to be acquired, munged, transformed, and then sent to a web application for rendering as a plot. This creates a barrier to entry for an analyst to effectively explore data and create interactive graphics using a single programming language in a flexible, iterative, and reproducible way. This chapter will cover how a new package for the R programming language, *ggvis* (Chang and Wickham 2015), enables librarians to explore data and communicate findings using interactive controls without the overhead of tinkering with web application frameworks. To make the data visualization workflow more coherent, ggvis brings together three concepts: (1) it is based on a grammar of graphics, a structure for defining the elements of a graphic; (2) it produces reactive and interactive plotting in a rendered web-based graphic; and (3) it provides support for creating data pipelines, making data manipulation and plotting code more readable.

I will start the chapter by going over the technology suite and dependencies needed to run ggvis. I'll also cover the data used in the chapter and where to obtain them. Once the computing and data sources are covered, I'll introduce how ggvis utilizes a grammar of graphics to break graphs into components made up of data, a coordinate system, a mark type, and properties. This modularity allows analysts to better understand graphical elements and swap out different components to make a multitude of different plots. Following the grammar of graphics, I'll start using ggvis to build simple static graphs with a built-in data set in R. While demonstrating how to create simple plots such as histograms, bar charts, and scatterplots, I will introduce how ggvis incorporates the R data pipelining syntax to improve code readability and maintenance. I will also show how to use ggvis in conjunction with features from the data manipulation package, *dplyr* (Wickham and Francois 2015), to filter, group, and summarize the data before graphing. After covering the basic features of ggvis, I will introduce interactivity by plotting library-related data sets (gate count data, circulation counts, and article-level metrics). Starting simply, I will add a slider to a scatterplot. I will then show how to create a histogram and density plot with interactive inputs. Still very young, ggvis is currently not recommended for production use. However, ggvis is under active development and coauthored by two important R developers with strong track records of delivering important R packages.

For a librarian with knowledge of R, ggvis opens the door to creating interactive graphics without knowing the intricacies of a JavaScript framework or data format transformations. Furthermore, through the grammar of graphics and data pipelines, ggvis makes graphing code understandable and more reproducible.

BACKGROUND

Used extensively in both business and academic settings, R is a statistical programming language. One of the major reasons for its popularity is that statisticians and developers have contributed over 7,000 packages that provide additional functionality to base R, including statistical techniques and data acquisition, visualization, and reporting tools. Developed by Winston Chang and Hadley Wickham, ggvis is an R package that employs a *grammar of graphics* in making data visualizations (Chang and Wickham 2015). The goal of the package is to make it easier for people to build dynamic interactive visualizations that can be embedded on the web or in a dynamic report.

Grammar of Graphics

Leland Wilkinson introduced the concept of a grammar of graphics in 1999 partly from a reaction to tools such as Excel that provided a selectable taxonomy of visual treatments that users then altered postselection (Wilkinson 2005). Breaking away from this canned approach to visualizations, he proposed decomposing graphics into their elemental parts such as scales, layers, and marks and developing a language for descriptively defining a plot in code. In 2005, Hadley Wickham implemented his take on Wilkinson's grammar of graphics in an R visualization package, *ggplot2*, which was intended to make it easier to create publication-quality static graphics in R (Wickham 2009). Typically among the top package downloads in the Comprehensive R Archive Network (CRAN), ggplot2 has been a very popular package in R. However, ggplot2 is primarily focused on providing R users with easier ways to string together different parts of a plot to create static graphics. With ggvis, Wickham also employed a grammar of graphics to organize and provide structure to the graphing syntax that outputs as web-based plots.

Interactive Data Visualization

Since the *New York Times* popularized the use of the D3 interactive visualization JavaScript framework, interactive visualizations with sliders and other user-facing controls are increasingly favored. In R, the development of the Shiny package (Chang et al. 2015) provides an interactive visualization framework that lets R users create client and server R code to handle plotting interactivity. However, this still requires technical savvy beyond what most typical data analysts might possess. They must understand how the Shiny client and server work together to effectively create an interactive plot. ggvis was created to allow analysts to use the analytic power of R and create interactive graphs that are "of the web" without having to think about client and server operations. In the background, ggvis uses Shiny to render its visualizations, but Shiny's main benefit is that analysts will not have to understand the technology stack that produces the client and server code. In R, they will declaratively code the type of visualization and interaction they want to create and then ggvis will prepare the data and the consuming JavaScript visualization on the fly. Programmatically, this adheres to a functional programming paradigm that creates a call-and-response type of interface. This design style tries to solve the issue of interactivity in a dynamic graphic, where the data will change. In R, the data are prepared for the interactive visualization and fed to a Shiny graphic. The reactivity occurs when a user triggers something through an interactive control that changes the data needed. The benefit for librarian analysts using ggvis is that they can concentrate on creating their analysis and visualizations in R without focusing on the technical details of how a web graphic or interactivity in a graphic is ultimately accomplished.

Literate Programming and Data Pipelining

> Let us change our traditional attitude to the construction of programs: Instead of imagining that our main task is to instruct a computer what to do, let us concentrate rather on explaining to human beings what we want a computer to do. (Knuth 1984)

In 1984 Donald Knuth conceptualized *literate programming*—the idea of embedding code in a text document that explains the code. Recent adaptations of this approach to improve reproducibility of analytic code and provide a way to create dynamic documents were developed in R with Rmarkdown and knitr (Allaire et al. 2015b; Xie 2015). This approach makes it easier for researchers or analysts to write reports and papers that contain runnable code that outputs inline plots and tables. It also improves the reproducibility of the report, and since code is interleaved inside the report, the code and its output are contextually more comprehensible.

Data pipelining is based on the Unix convention of building small programs that can be composed in such a way that each program's output can be an input into another program. In R, the utility package magrittr (Bache and Wickham 2014) provides the facility to do this using a forward pipe operator %>%. Packages implementing magrittr such as ggvis allow the use of %>% to pipe an object from the left of the operator to the function on the right. These functions can then be chained together in a way that, for example, cleans, filters, and then visualizes a data set in one interlinked code block. This makes the code simpler and easier to understand and maintain.

USING GGVIS

Setup

To use ggvis or run the code in this chapter, you must install a number of tools on your machine. You must have base R, RStudio, ggvis, *tidyr* (Wickham 2014c), and dplyr installed and available. These tools are all open source and freely download-able via the R repository. Follow the instructions below for more information on getting set up.

Install R

If you are on a Linux machine, R is most likely in the package manager for your distribution (e.g., apt-get install r-base). On Windows and Macs, go to http://www.r-project.org and follow the *download R* link on that page. R code and packages are mirrored all over the world via the CRAN, so choose the mirror nearest you (in my case it's http://cran.stat.ucla.edu/). Choose your operating system, select "base," and then download the latest R release (as of this writing it's R 3.2.2). Run the installer, and you should have R installed. You can confirm R is installed by opening a terminal in Mac or Linux and typing R. On Windows, click the RGui desktop icon that the install process created. Once started, you should see a note about the R version you are running and information about demos, citing R, and so on.

R belongs to a class of programming languages (Python, Julia, and Stata are others) that adopts an REPL (read-evaluation-print-loop) style of interactive coding. This simply means that you will often interact with a console to work out code to see how your code snippets work in the console and continually build up a runnable script in a text file. You can try this out by using the console as a calculator. Type 2 + 2 or 4 / 2 and observe the output. Familiarizing yourself with how the R console operates is a key step in becoming an efficient R data analyst. Before we explore further, let's install an integrated development environment for R. Type q() to quit R.

Install RStudio

There are many ways to create and edit R scripts and interact with the R language. For this chapter we are using RStudio because it makes presenting interactive ggvis plots seamless (RStudio Team 2012). Running R natively via the console will open ggvis plots in a browser, so you can do it that way, but RStudio provides a nice View panel for viewing graphics. It also provides a multipaneled interface with separate areas for script editing, the R help library, package installation, environment objects, command history, and a project management tool. The author highly recommends it to use with the code in this chapter. To install, go to https://www.rstudio.com/products/rstudio/download/ and select your operating system to download. Once installed you can open the application and familiarize yourself with the RStudio windows. With R and RStudio installed, you can work through any number of introductory free R courses on the web. One novel tutorial is Swirl,[1] an interactive R course built as an R package (Carchedi et al. 2015). This tutorial will also develop your familiarity with RStudio as you interact with the challenges.

Install ggvis and Other Packages

To install the latest release of ggvis you can use the RStudio Packages window or simply type the following in the Console window in RStudio:

```
install.packages("ggvis")
```

This will install R from CRAN, the R package manager. However, since ggvis is under active development, you can also install the development version available in GitHub. To do this you will need to install a package called *devtools* first. You can type the following in the console to get the development version of ggvis:

```
install.packages("devtools")
devtools::install_github("hadley/lazyeval", build_vignettes =
FALSE)
devtools::install_github("hadley/dplyr", build_vignettes =
FALSE)
devtools::install_github("rstudio/ggvis", build_vignettes =
FALSE)
```

After one of the versions is installed, you can tell R you are ready to use the package by typing `library("ggvis")` in the console.

In this chapter, we will also be using both the tidyr and dplyr packages (Wickham 2014c; Wickham and Francois 2015). Created by the same author of ggvis, Hadley Wickham, these packages provide a number of functions that are helpful in cleaning and manipulating untidy data. Also, both of them implement the magrittr forward pipe syntax, so you can use them to build up your data pipelines. If you installed the development version of ggvis above, you should have dplyr installed, so ignore the install dplyr statement below (it won't hurt to reinstall). To install tidyr and dplyr run the code below from the console. We are also installing ggplot2 because it provides the diamonds data set we will work with in this chapter.

```
install.packages('tidyr')
install.packages('dplyr')
install.packages("ggplot2")
```

Other Tools

When you installed RStudio, a number of helpful packages were installed in the background. *Rmarkdown* is a package that enables writing documents in a markdown markup syntax with interspersed R code chunks (Allaire et al. 2015a; Allaire et al. 2015b). *knitr* is a package that takes the Rmarkdown document and creates a target output format such as HTML, Word, or presentation slides. This chapter was initially written in Rmarkdown and converted to Word for further editing and publication. The Rmarkdown for this chapter can be found on the author's GitHub account: https://github.com/jt14den/rggvis-libdata. If you download the GitHub files, open the *ggvis-library-data.Rmd* file, and select *Knit HTML* at the top of the RStudio edit window, then knitr will transform the markdown into HTML and run the embedded R code. As discussed earlier in this chapter, this documentation style is called literate programming and is a powerful way to create clear and understandable code because the code is interleaved with markup text and the resulting document contains code, code output, and text. It is also an excellent way to create dynamic reports or documents because the analytic code and results are embedded with any expository text. Plots and figures will be embedded inline in the document as well.

A Note on the Data

The data and code used for this chapter can be found in the author's GitHub account.[2] The library gate count and circulation data are canned and for illustrative purposes only. The shape of the data is based on real data found on the web, but the numbers and names have been massaged. The article-level metrics data were generated using the R *alm* package (Chamberlain, Boettiger, and Ram 2015a), which pulls from the Lagotto Altmetrics Platform API[3] and is also stored as a CSV in the GitHub account.

Get Started with ggvis

Begin by starting RStudio and running the following code. We will use ggvis to create a plot with a built-in data set in R. Following is the code used to create the graph. See figure 9.1 to see the result.

```
library(ggvis)
diamonds %>%
  ggvis(x = ~carat, y = ~price) %>%
  layer_points()
```

Let's analyze the code. First, we must use the library() statement to load the ggvis into the current R session. Otherwise, even though we installed it on our file system earlier, R will not know the package is available. Explicitly loading packages that are installed will limit the cluttering of our session (and memory footprint). *dia-*

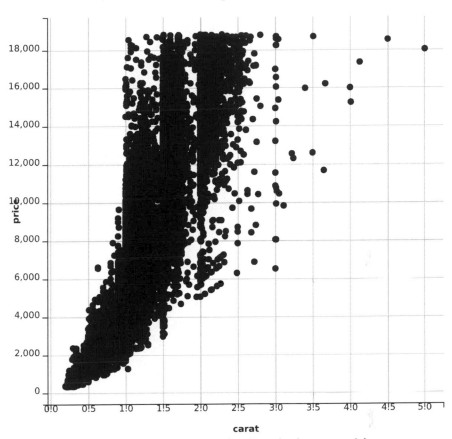

Figure 9.1.   A ggvis-generated scatterplot showing price by carat weight.

monds is the name of a data set containing prices, carat size, and other features of diamonds. It is installed as part of the ggplot2 package that we installed earlier. To find out more information about the data set, type `?diamonds` in the R console. Notice there are variables such as price, carat, and cut, among others. To create figure 9.1, we need to provide ggvis with a data set and map variables in the data set to some type of mark in the graph. We do this by mapping *x* to the weight variable (~carat) and *y* to the price variable (~price). We then select the ggvis points mark with `layer_points()`. This creates a scatterplot of points with the carat variable on the *x*-axis and price on the *y*-axis. These elements are composed this way using the pipe-forward symbol (%>%) and are intended to be read as a sequence, like so:

1. Access diamonds data.
2. Send diamonds data to the ggvis function with the *x*- and *y*-axes mapped to variables in the data set.

3. Send the resulting data from step 2 to a ggvis function layer_points(), which will arrange as points on *x*- and *y*-axes.

This pipe-forward (%>%) operator is a relatively new syntactical element in R provided by the package magrittr (Bache and Wickham 2014). Along with an increasing number of other useful data cleaning and manipulation packages, ggvis uses this piping operator so we can logically sequence data preparation, manipulation, and visualization in one code block. Without the piping operator in ggvis, to get the same effect, we would have to nest functions like this:

```
p <- layer_points(ggvis(diamonds, x = ~carat, y = ~price))
```

We will return to data piping later in this chapter, but note that piping is an important development in an effort to create logical, sequential, and readable code.

Grammar of Graphics

As we've seen in figure 9.1, to produce a graphic, ggvis needs, at its most elemental level, data and a variable mapping to a coordinate system. But this is just the starting point for how we can use ggvis functions to define our graph. To express a graphic output of visual elements, ggvis implements a grammar of graphics. In ggvis, this grammar of graphics is the ability to declaratively state components of a graphic. The components are composed of data, a coordinate system, a marking system, and properties.

Coordinate System

In this chapter, we are mainly concerned with Cartesian coordinates. Currently, ggvis doesn't support polar coordinates (pie charts), and the other coordinate systems supported are out of scope for this chapter.

Marks

We've already encountered a marking system by using layer_points() in the previous example. We can change this marking system by editing the previous code to pipe our data into layer_lines() instead. See figure 9.2 to see the result.

```
library(ggvis)
diamonds %>%
  ggvis(x = ~carat, y = ~price) %>%
  layer_lines()
```

Besides points and lines, other layers include layers_paths(), layers_ribbons(), layers_rects(), and layers_histogram(). Use the ?? help operator on each and try running

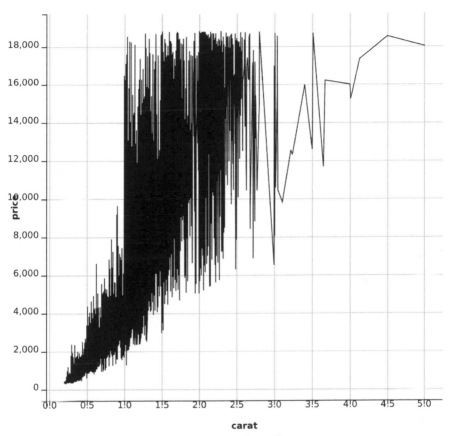

Figure 9.2. A ggvis-generated line chart using layer_lines().

it on the diamonds data. Some layers will require more mappings and some less. For instance, layer_histograms() can be run only on a single, continuous numeric variable because it visualizes the shape of a variable's frequency distribution. layer_paths(), in contrast, takes two variables and will draw a path between the points in the data, sequentially connecting points in the order in which they appear in a data set.

Properties

Layers have different properties that can be altered. Points can be set to specific colors, sizes, shapes, opacity, and stroke. Those attributes can also be mapped to values in the data set. Lines have similar properties like color and opacity but also have additional properties such as stroke, strokeDash, and strokeWidth. When working with properties, it is important to understand that you can map the property to values in a variable in your data set or you can manually set it to something arbitrary. A property mapped to values in the data will subsequently communicate another aspect about your data. To map variable values to a color we use the equal operator (=). However, to manually set properties, ggvis introduces a new operator of a colon followed by an equal sign (:=). To illustrate this let's play with the *diamonds* data in R. First, I want to add a color attribute to figure 9.2 that represents the *cut* variable (quality of the cut). We do this by adding `fill = ~cut` to the layer_points() function. Note that we could also add this argument to the ggvis() function, which would propagate down to the layer_points(), but mapping it in layer_points() will limit knock-on effects if we use other layers because other layers might not have a fill property. We will also change the point to the shape of a cross. For this, notice that I'm using the `(:=)` set operator and not the mapping operator because it will set the shape to a cross and not map it to a variable in the data (see figure 27 in the photospread).

```
library(ggvis)
diamonds %>%
  ggvis(x = ~price, y = ~carat) %>%
  layer_points(fill = ~cut, shape := "cross")
```

Data Pipelines

Let's return to the concept of data pipelining and demonstrate the power of this approach in data preparation. Hadley Wickham has characterized tidy data (data that are ready to be analyzed) as data with variables across the columns and observations in the rows (Wickham 2014b). The data we normally receive in the library world aren't in this tidy format. Often, data we receive will be in a spreadsheet format with values such as year across the columns or variables down the rows. We also may receive data in separate files that need to be merged before analysis or visualization. Hadley Wickham's tidyr package helps us get the data in the proper shape. In the past, to do these types of operations on data we often needed to nest function calls and save outputs of these processes as intermediary data frames. The problem of nesting these functions calls is sometimes called the "Dagwood sandwich problem" (Wickham 2014a, 237) and makes the code hard to parse or work with. Additionally, having to name and track intermediary data frames as we create steps to clean and prepare the data clutters up our code and makes it harder to understand and maintain. The piping operator provided by magrittr solves these problems by allowing us to forward our data through cleaning, manipulation, and visualization functions, making our code cleaner and easier to read (and comprehend).

As mentioned before, you might receive data such as that below that have been created for human consumption but aren't ready to visualize in a tool such as R.

```
gate <- read.csv('data/1-gate-count.csv', check.names=F,
sep=',')
gate <- tbl_df(gate)
head(gate)
```

```
## Source: local data frame [6 x 6]
##
##    branch  2009   2010   2011   2012    2013
##     (int) (int)  (int)  (int)  (int)   (int)
## 1      1  10238  10203  12223  11005   13172
## 2      2   8710  12950  23917  26936   29171
## 3      3  60946  56632  69950  78811  106627
## 4      4  60529  53500  69088  92319  111320
## 5      5  58549  52418  58113  60111   94568
## 6      6  38199  30085  46305  47137   48466
```

In this case, we see years are in the column headers and branches are in the rows. With the data frame in this form, there would be no way to plot branch by count and year in ggvis because neither count nor year is accessible as a variable. We need to use the package tidyr to reshape the data so the year and count variables are in their own columns. In tidyr, we do this by using the gather() function, which will take multiple columns and gather them into key value pairs. In this case, we want to gather the years and their counts and create two columns for each. Once we have a variable for each branch, year, and count in our data frame, we can then use the group_by() function provided by dplyr to group the data by branch. Only after these steps are finished can we plot our data.

Let us first look at how we would tidy the data as described above using tidyr and dplyr without pipes.

```
library(tidyr)
gate2 <- arrange(gather(gate, Year, Count, -branch), Year,
Count)
gate3 <- group_by(gate2,branch)
head(gate3)
## Source: local data frame [6 x 3]
## Groups: branch [6]
##
##    branch   Year Count
##     (int)  (fctr) (int)
## 1      2    2009  8710
## 2      1    2009 10238
## 3     12    2009 12044
## 4     11    2009 15715
## 5      7    2009 22107
## 6      6    2009 38199
```

Above we are nesting arrange() and gather() functions with the gate data and saving it to a gate2 temporary data frame. Following this, we use the group_by() function to group gate3 by branch. With data requiring multiple steps for cleaning, sorting, and summarization, the R code can quickly become nested or littered with temporary data objects. Let's clean this code up by using the pipe operator to set up a chained sequence and then saving it as a new data frame (gate2).

```
library(tidyr)
gate2 <- gate %>%
  gather(Year, Count, -branch) %>%
  group_by(branch) %>%
  arrange(Count)
head(gate2)
## Source: local data frame [6 x 3]
## Groups: branch [2]
##
## branch   Year Count
##   (int)  (fctr)  (int)
## 1       1    2010 10203
## 2       1    2009 10238
## 3       1    2012 11005
## 4       1    2011 12223
## 5       1    2013 13172
## 6       2    2009  8710
```

Now, both examples above produce the same data frame. But the second example is clear, and it is easy to see what operations are happening to the data frame. Plus, we neither have to name and keep track of temporary data objects in our code nor use hard-to-read nested function calls. We will now repeat our data-cleaning operations with the last chain plotting the data using the ggvis. See figure 9.3 to see the result.

```
gate %>%
  gather(Year, Count, -branch) %>%
  ggvis(x= ~Year,y= ~Count) %>%
  layer_bars()
```

Wouldn't it be better if we added some color and a stacked bar to differentiate the branches? This is easy to do in ggvis by adding a fill property assigned to our branch variable as an argument inside our ggvis() function. We also need to convert our branch to a factor (categorical variable) so ggvis can group these on the graph (see figure 28 in the photospread). The changes are made as follows:

```
gate %>%
  gather(Year, Count, -branch) %>%
  ggvis(x= ~Year,y= ~Count, fill = ~factor(branch)) %>%
  layer_bars()
```

Now we have color! ggvis will take the factor and automatically group and assign a color to represent each branch (there are ways to control the color, but that's beyond the scope of this chapter). Notice how the resulting code is easy to read and much more maintainable than nesting functions and keeping track of temporary data frames. We can also easily alter the layers and properties to create different plots. This is a powerful way to explore data in a succinct way and build up meaningful plots in an interactive process.

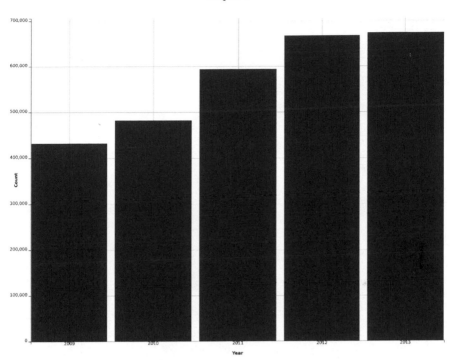

Figure 9.3. A ggvis-generated bar chart showing gate counts for each year.

Let's add another variable, circulation statistics, to our gate count example and look at a scatterplot. We will need to read in another CSV that contains our library branches, gate, and circulation counts by year. These data have already been cleaned and prepared for our use.

```
gcirc <- read.csv('data/2-gate-circ.csv', check.names=F,
sep=',')
gcirc <- tbl_df(gcirc)
head(gcirc)
## Source: local data frame [6 x 4]
##
##    branch  Year Count   circ
##     (int) (int) (int)  (int)
## 1       8  2009 45210    689
## 2       8  2010 52468    785
## 3       8  2013 45961    800
## 4       8  2011 54392    858
## 5       8  2012 89169  32105
## 6       1  2010 10203   8780
```

Returning to ggvis, we can create a scatterplot with this new data frame (figure 9.4).

```
gcirc %>%
  ggvis(x = ~Count, y= ~circ) %>%
  layer_points()
```

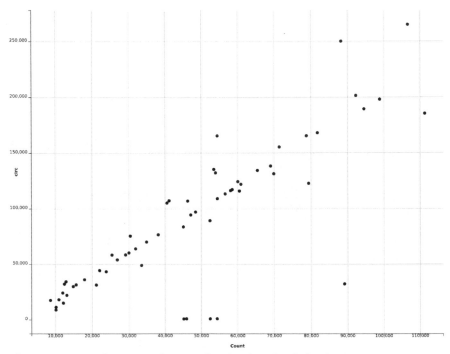

Figure 9.4. A ggvis-generated scatterplot showing circulation by gate count.

Nothing too surprising here. We expect there should be a relationship based on gate count and circulation. We notice a few outliers that might be branches that do not circulate as much or have restricted collections.

We can add a fill color to the graph for each branch. Once again, we need to convert our branch numbers to a factor; otherwise ggvis will treat them as a continuous spectrum of color instead of as groups (see figures 29 and 30 in the photospread).

```
gcirc %>%
  ggvis(x = ~Count, y= ~circ, fill = ~factor(branch)) %>%
  layer_points()
gcirc %>%
  ggvis(x = ~Count, y= ~circ, fill = ~factor(branch)) %>%
  layer_points() %>%
  layer_smooths()
```

Finally, we can draw a fitted curve between our two variables on the graph using the layer_smooths(). This is a prediction line that is added to the graph with a smooth model, which lets us know whether the two variables have a trend relationship to one another. In this case, increase in gate count has a relationship with circulation statistics. If we had noisier data, this fitted, curved line might highlight trends that were not readily apparent in the scatterplot.

Adding Interactivity

Now that we have used the grammar of graphics with ggvis and have created a number of plots, we can start to add interactivity to our plot. ggvis supports the following interactive controls that you can include in your plot:

input_slider(): a slider that produces a range control
input_checkbox(): an interactive checkbox
input_checkboxgroup(): a grouping of checkboxes
input_numeric(): a validator that allows only numbers to be imputed
input_radiobuttons(): selectable radio buttons, only one can be selected
input_select(): a drop-down textbox
input_text(): plain text input

Let's continue on from our previous example and alter it to add a point size operator to the graph. We do this by setting the size of layer_points() to an input_slider on a range from 100 to 1,000 (figure 9.5).

```
gcirc %>%
    ggvis(x = ~Count, y = ~circ) %>%
    layer_points(size := input_slider(100, 1000, value = 100))
%>%
    layer_smooths()
```

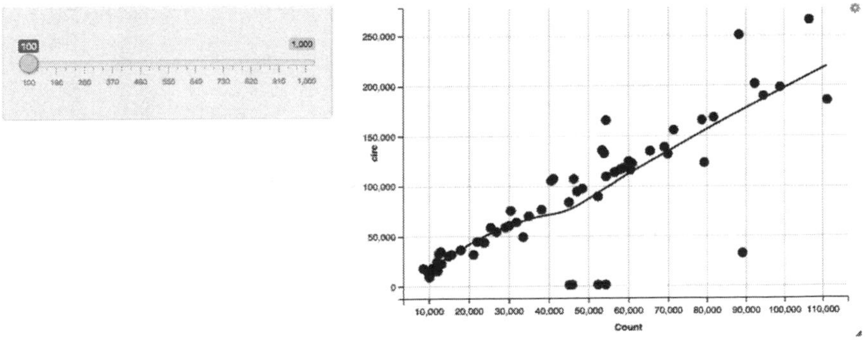

Figure 9.5. A scatterplot using the same data as those used in figure 9.8.

We can also add radio buttons that set the color of the points by adding a fill parameter set to input_radiobuttons(). For this example, we will see how the output looks in RStudio (figure 9.6).

```
gcirc %>%
  ggvis(x = ~Count, y = ~circ,
    fill := input_radiobuttons(label = "Choose color:",
    choices = c("blue", "red", "green"))) %>%
  layer_points(size = ~Count)
```

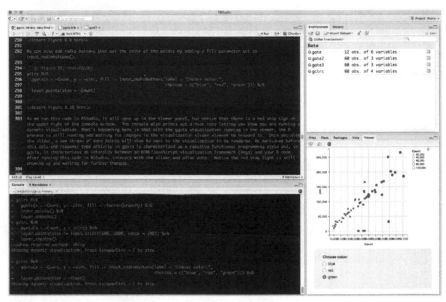

Figure 9.6.   The Viewer panel and console in RStudio.

As we run this code in RStudio, it will open up in the Viewer panel, but notice that there is a red stop sign on the upper right of the console window. The console also prints out a nice note letting us know we are running a dynamic visualization and how to stop it. What's happening here is that with the ggvis visualization running in the viewer, the R process is still running and waiting to respond to changes in the visualization radio button element. Once we select a different button, the plot will be rendered again with the changes to the plot. As mentioned before, this call-and-response type activity in ggvis is characterized as a reactive functional programming style, and in ggvis it characterizes an interplay between an HTML/JavaScript visualization framework (Shiny) and our R code. After running this code in RStudio, interact with the slider and alter data. Notice the red stop light is still showing up and waiting for further changes.

Examining Variable Distribution

I obtained the following data using both the PLOS API[4] and Lagotto Altmetrics Platform with the *rplos* and alm packages saved to the GitHub repository for this chapter. The code I used to obtain the data is also in the GitHub package, but the rplos package (Chamberlain, Boettiger, and Ram 2015b) makes it easy to query the

PLOS API by various criteria (subject, author, title). The resulting query will return DOIs that we can then feed to the alm package, which will query the Lagotto service for article-level metrics. Of note, other publishers (CrossRef, PKP, Pensoft) are using the Lagotto platform to serve up metrics on their journals. The data represent fifty article metrics by DOI and saved out as a CSV file as *data/3-alm.csv*. Each column represents metrics from various sources, including Counter, CrossRef, Scopus, and Twitter. First, let's read in the alm data that I saved as a CSV and look at the titles.

```
altmet <- read.csv('data/3-alm.csv', check.names=F, sep=',')
altmet <- tbl_df(altmet)
head(altmet$title)
## [1] Small-Group Learning in an Upper-Level University
Biology Class Enhances Academic Performance and Student
Attitudes Toward Group Work
## [2] Differential Extinction and the Contrasting Structure
of Polar Marine Faunas
## [3] Competitive Interactions between Invasive Nile Tilapia
and Native Fish: The Potential for Altered Trophic Exchange
and Modification of Food Webs
## [4] Eu-Social Science: The Role of Internet Social Networks
in the Collection of Bee Biodiversity Data
## [5] Does Collocation Inform the Impact of Collaboration?
## [6] A Reliability-Generalization Study of Journal Peer
Reviews: A Multilevel Meta-Analysis of Inter-Rater Reliability
and Its Determinants
## 50 Levels: "Positive" Results Increase Down the Hierarchy
of the Sciences . . .
```

To get a better sense of what is in the data we can use the glimpse() function provided by dplyr. For brevity, I have snipped the output by picking off columns of interest.

```
altmet <- altmet[,c(2,3,15,33,39,51,63,69,99)]
glimpse(altmet)
## Observations: 50
## Variables: 9
## $ id             (fctr) http://doi.org/10.1371/journal.
pone.0015821, h...
## $ title          (fctr) Small-Group Learning in an Upper-
Level Univers...
## $ crossref_total (int) 4, 10, 15, 10, 22, 19, 5, 39, 11,
12, 77, 5, 0,...
## $ scopus_total   (int) 6, 12, 20, 14, 29, 27, 7, 68, 17,
16, 90, 11, 0...
## $ counter_total  (int) 4434, 2386, 4627, 3920, 21976,
14439, 3668, 291...
## $ pmc_total      (int) 957, 158, 723, 693, 709, 880, 267,
240, 491, 59...
## $ mendeley_total (int) 36, 58, 64, 106, 192, 72, 14, 149,
50, 25, 231,...
```

```
## $ twitter_total  (int) 1, 0, 0, 2, 15, 3, 0, 20, 0, 0, 0,
0, 0, 0, 95,...
## $ figshare_total (int) 12, 33, 9, 10, 19, 6, 10, 11, 12,
23, 25, 28, 1...
```

Notice that we have variables on the DOIs, titles, and metrics from each source. Also notice that these data include metrics from social media and web sources such as Twitter and Wikipedia. One way to explore these data from each source is by using a histogram to see the distribution of metrics of these journal articles we have in our data set. Since we haven't covered a histogram yet, let's create a static one (figure 9.7).

```
altmet %>%
  ggvis(~scopus_total) %>%
  layer_histograms()
```

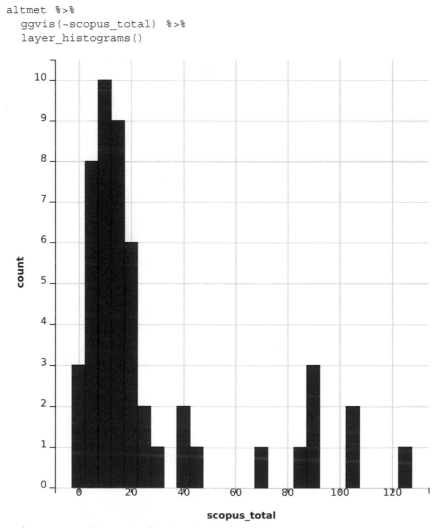

Figure 9.7.   A histogram showing the distribution of Scopus metrics.

To create a histogram, ggvis must first create "bins" in which to group and place the data. This happens behind the scenes in ggvis, but it is worth noting that ggvis has a compute_bin() function that layer_histogram() calls to do the binning. This can be called separately, like so:

```
binned <- altmet %>% compute_bin(~scopus_total)
head(binned)
##   count_ x_ xmin_ xmax_ width_
## 1      3  0  -2.5   2.5       5
## 2      8  5   2.5   7.5       5
## 3     10 10   7.5  12.5       5
## 4      9 15  12.5  17.5       5
## 5      6 20  17.5  22.5       5
## 6      2 25  22.5  27.5       5
```

From here, we could use this binned data frame to set the histogram in a more manual fashion. Bin width is an important parameter in a histogram. To show a distribution of a variable one can miss the shape of the distribution if the bin width is too large or too small. Let's look at our previous plot with a different bin set (figure 9.8).

```
altmet %>%
  ggvis(~scopus_total) %>%
  layer_histograms(width = 15)
```

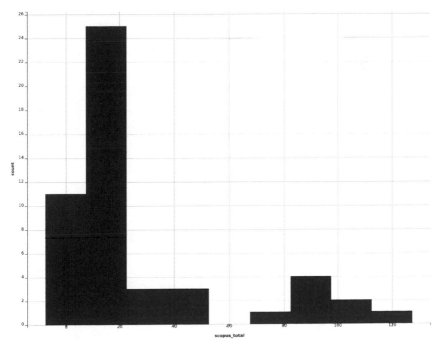

Figure 9.8. A histogram with bin width manually set.

We can see that with a bin width too wide the variable distribution is obscured. Since altering the bin width while exploring the distribution of a continuous variable is such a common task in data exploration, it makes sense to make this an interactive part of the ggvis graphic. We will use an input_slider() for both bin width and center (figure 9.9).

```
altmet %>%
  ggvis(~scopus_total) %>%
  layer_histograms(width = input_slider(0, 50,
    step = 0.10, label = "width"),
    center = input_slider(0, 2, step = 0.05, label =
"center"))
```

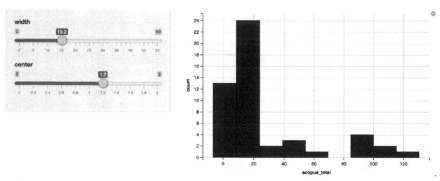

Figure 9.9.   A histogram with interactive user controls for bin width and center.

As we've seen, the bin width strongly affects the shape of the data, and altering this width can lead us to discovering different features in the data that might not have been apparent using default or fixed bins. Another way to get a different sense of the distribution of a variable is through a kernel density plot. These plots are available in ggvis via a layer_density() function. The density layer can produce a number of types of density plots based on different smoothing algorithms, called kernel smoothing. By default, ggvis uses Gaussian smoothing. Let's see what a static version looks like against our Altmetrics data (figure 9.10).

```
altmet %>%
  ggvis(~scopus_total) %>%
  layer_densities()
```

Now let's make this graphic interactive by allowing the user to select different kernel smoothers. This is done by assigning the kernel parameter in the layer_density() function to an input_selector containing various smoothers. Run the code and switch back

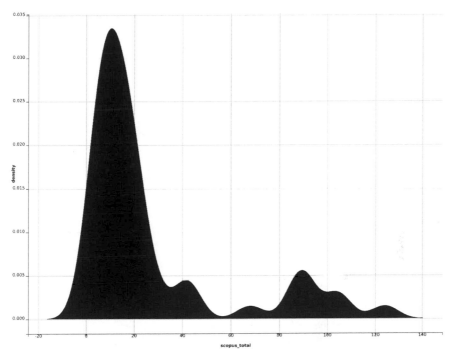

Figure 9.10. A kernel density plot created using the ggvis layer_density() function.

and forth between the different types of kernel smoothers. You can see each kernel produces a different shape and hopefully gives more insight to the data (figure 9.11).

```
altmet %>% ggvis(x = ~scopus_total) %>%
    layer_densities(
        adjust = input_slider(.1, 2, value = 1, step = .1,
label = "Bandwidth adjustment"),
        kernel = input_select(
            c("Gaussian" = "gaussian",
                "Epanechnikov" = "epanechnikov",
                "Rectangular" = "rectangular",
                "Triangular" = "triangular",
                "Biweight" = "biweight",
                "Cosine" = "cosine",
                "Optcosine" = "optcosine"),
            label = "Kernel")
    )
```

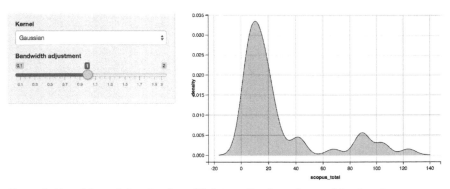

Figure 9.11. A kernel density plot with interactive kernel smoothing input.

DISCUSSION

Because ggvis is currently under development, if you load ggvis from the CRAN repository, you will get this message:

> The ggvis API is currently rapidly evolving. We strongly recommend that you do not rely on this for production, but feel free to explore. If you encounter a clear bug, please file a minimal reproducible example at https://github.com/rstudio/ggvis/issues. For questions and other discussion, please use https://groups.google.com/group/ggvis.

At the time of this writing ggvis is on version 0.42. There are limitations, and as the developers indicate it really shouldn't be run in production. That said, as this chapter has demonstrated, it can be a great tool to explore and get a feel for data. Also, since the aim of ggvis is to be the successor to ggplot2, it's reasonable to assume that learning ggvis will put you in good stead for the future of visualization in R. However, it will be a moving target, and code you write now might need to be altered as the API changes.

Eases Barrier to Web and Interactive Graphics

Building interactive graphics is a thorny proposition for a data professional. A data analyst must prepare the data, perform relevant analysis of the data, and get the data structured so a web application can consume it. The web application then must listen for changes in triggering events and change the visualization. Abstracting these activities so an analyst can focus on the data and using R to analyze the data isn't simple, and many aspects on how best to do this are being worked out now. The ggvis API will be one way this is worked out in R, and it is already showing promise to make it easier to build interactive data visualizations.

Facilitates Clean and Maintainable Code

Because ggvis is plugged into a larger framework of packages that support data pipe-lining, writing clean and maintainable code becomes much easier. In this chapter, we explored how to read in data, reshape it, and then feed those data to ggvis. This is scratching the surface on how this pipelining framework can be utilized. dplyr also allows R users to perform all manner of manipulations on a data set (subset, filter, add new computed variables, summarize grouped data). Put together, one could read a dirty data set, reshape, clean, filter, add computed variables, group by variables, and then visualize in one code chunk sequence. Because thought was put into the con-ceptual underpinnings of the verbs used by these tools (select, filter, gather, mutate), once you learn how to use these on data, they open up an interactive toolbox of data manipulation, analysis, and visualization.

Also, in this chapter we used data that were stored in a CSV file, but dplyr sup-ports reading in data from a database as well. So if your library has data in a relational database, you could use the data pipelining features in ggvis, dplyr, and tidyr to query, select, filter, and visualize all in R. Because of the semantic use of a grammar of graphics and verb-based vocabulary for data manipulation and summarization, revisiting your code in the future won't be as painful. And because it is "code" you won't have to retrace your steps in an interactive tool such as Excel. You might have to change some file names or minor aspects of your code if the source data has changed, but you should be in better shape to adapt to change. Alternately, getting your analysis into R and piping into ggvis allows you to think about how to abstract your code to adapt to change in more automated ways (reports by different years of data or library branches). Using a structured and defined vocabulary of terms related to data preparation and visualization enables you to produce simpler, more compre-hensible and maintainable code.

CONCLUSION

In this chapter we introduced the R visualization package ggvis and its goal to make it easier to create interactive graphics for exploratory data analysis. We walked through how ggvis employs a grammar of graphics in decomposing plotting elements into declarative components. We also demonstrated how ggvis plugs into a larger R ecosystem for creating data pipelines to improve code readability and maintenance. Finally, we created interactive graphics with library-related data and showed how they change when a user changes elements in the graph.

NOTES

1. http://swirlstats.com/.
2. https://github.com/jt14den/rggvis-libdata.
3. http://lagotto.io/.
4. http://API.plos.org/.

REFERENCES

Allaire, J. J., Jeffrey Horner, Vicent Marti, and Natacha Porte. 2015a. *Markdown: "Markdown" Rendering for R.* http://cran.r-project.org/package=markdown.
Allaire, J. J., Joe Cheng, Yihui Xie, Jonathan McPherson, Winston Chang, Jeff Allen, Hadley Wickham, and Rob Hyndman. 2015b. *Rmarkdown: Dynamic Documents for R.* http://CRAN.R-project.org/package=rmarkdown.
Bache, Stefan Milton, and Hadley Wickham. 2014. *magrittr: A Forward-Pipe Operator for R.* http://cran.r-project.org/package=magrittr.
Carchedi, Nick, Bill Bauer, Gina Grdina, and Sean Kross. 2015. *Swirl: Learn R, in R.* http://CRAN.R-project.org/package=swirl.
Chamberlain, Scott, Carl Boettiger, and Karthik Ram. 2015b. *alm: R Client for the Lagotto Altmetrics Platform.* http://CRAN.R-project.org/package=alm.
———. 2015a. *rplos: Interface to the Search "API" for "PLoS" Journals.* https://cran.r-project.org/package=rplos/.
Chang, Winston, and Hadley Wickham. 2015. *ggvis: Interactive Grammar of Graphics.* http://ggvis.rstudio.com/.
Chang, Winston, Joe Cheng, J. J. Allaire, Yihui Xie, and Jonathan McPherson. 2015. *shiny: Web Application Framework for R.* http://cran.r-project.org/package=shiny.
Knuth, Donald E. 1984. "Literate Programming." *Computer Journal* 27(2): 97–111. Oxford, UK: Oxford University Press. doi:10.1093/comjnl/27.2.97.
RStudio Team. 2012. *RStudio: Integrated Development Environment for R.* Boston, MA: RStudio, Inc. http://www.rstudio.com/.
Wickham, Hadley. 2009. *ggplot2: Elegant Graphics for Data Analysis.* New York: Springer. http://www.springer.com/us/book/9780387981406.
———. 2014a. *Advanced R.* Boca Raton, FL: CRC Press.
———. 2014b. "Tidy Data." *Journal of Statistical Software* 59(10). http://www.jstatsoft.org/v59/i10.
———. 2014c. *tidyr: Easily Tidy Data with "Spread()" and "Gather()" Functions.* http://cran.r-project.org/package=tidyr.
Wickham, Hadley, and Romain Francois. 2015. *dplyr: A Grammar of Data Manipulation.* http://cran.r-project.org/package=dplyr.
Wilkinson, Leland. 2005. *The Grammar of Graphics.* New York: Springer.
Xie, Yihui. 2015. *knitr: A General-Purpose Package for Dynamic Report Generation in R.* http://yihui.name/knitr/.

10

Integrating Data and Spatial Literacy into Library Instruction

Charissa Jefferson

As librarians, we are in the information business. However, in our information literacy instruction sessions, we may overlook the fact that all of our information must be informed by data, whether qualitative or quantitative. We may bypass the data set to look for the report narrative or article summary. But what if we took a step back to include data sets in our instruction as an opportunity for our students to create something new with that data set? What if, instead of looking for the article that analyzes the data, we encourage our students to compare or mash-up of the data themselves to come up with their own conclusion? For our students to understand the content, they must be able to understand context. We must take a step back and start at the beginning of the process; before information creation come data. Our literacy instruction begins with data.

All of the higher order thinking skills in Bloom's taxonomy, skills that include analyzing, evaluating, and creating, are achievable by integrating data and spatial literacy instruction into our library instruction sessions (Bloom 1956). This chapter will discuss several examples of projects where spatial literacy gives students the opportunity to understand deeper the content of their curricula by visualizing data in context. Many library patrons are considered novices when it comes to data visualization or map creation. This chapter will discuss the role of the library in geospatial instruction/programs and how to determine information literacy needs and competencies and will suggest mapping software to use to illustrate the process of information creation for various subject applications.

The academic library's role is to support institutional learning outcomes. If we as librarians consider expanding our role to include multiple kinds of literacies, we can better support the curricula. Geospatial data can be used to help explain context for a variety of curricula including, but not limited to, humanities, environmental sciences, health sciences, and social sciences. This chapter will focus on the ways in which many academic libraries are offering their faculty and student patrons access to data visualization methods using maps to support their curricula and will discuss some examples of projects that have allowed for students to evaluate and create knowledge by using spatial data.

BACKGROUND

Data literacy can be defined as being able to analyze and work with quantitative information. People who are data literate must be able to understand how to read a basic spreadsheet's columns and rows. Data literate people can organize and deconstruct the differing information by comparing each of the row's and column's attributions and data points. From a spreadsheet, data literate people can understand the structure and find the outlying data points. Data literate people can detect trends in the data and create the appropriate form of graph, chart, or table to illustrate the numerical information. Additionally, data literate people can describe results of the data set to make statistical arguments and conclusions. An essential component of quantitative literacy is statistical competency because statistics come from raw data. It is important for people to be able to critically evaluate data-related arguments by understanding the process of information creation (Prado and Marzal 2013).

The Association of American Colleges and Universities (AACU), an organization comprising members from higher educational institutions, has created an initiative to evaluate undergraduate learning. VALUE (Valid Assessment of Learning in Undergraduate Education) Rubrics offer assessment tools for sixteen different literacies including quantitative literacy, civic engagement, and global learning. The Quantitative Literacy (QL) VALUE Rubric emphasizes that "[quantitative literacy] is not just computation, not just the citing of someone's data. QL is a habit of mind, a way of thinking about the world that relies on data and on the mathematical analysis of data to make connections and draw conclusions" (AACU 2009). The AACU makes an effort to address analysis of data as an important achievement: "Virtually all of today's students, regardless of career choice will need basic QL skills such as the ability to draw information from charts, graphs, and geometric figures, and the ability to accurately complete straightforward estimations and calculations" (AACU 2009). When a student can draw information *from* charts, graphs, and so on, the student can determine the accuracy of the information by critically evaluating the underlying data. The QL VALUE Rubric measures (1) interpretation and (2) representation of tables, graphs, diagrams, and words; (3) calculation; (4) application/analysis; (5) assumptions; and (6) communication of numbers as evidence.

Upon developing its Data Information Literacy (DIL) program, Purdue University spearheaded a collaborative project involving university libraries to determine the data literacy needs of their patrons through interviews (Carlson et al. 2011). The DIL interviews were initiated by librarians from Purdue University, Cornell University, the University of Minnesota, and the University of Oregon. During the interviews, participants were asked to rate twelve DIL competencies on a five-point Likert scale ranging from "not important" to "essential." Each competency was ranked at least "important" by all participants. However, data discovery and acquisition and data visualization and representation were among those rated most essential by faculty. Data processing and analysis, followed by data management and organization, was ranked highest by the students. Ranked next of most importance was data discovery and acquisition, followed by data visualization and representation, which shared ranking with ethics and attribution and metadata and data description.

The new Information Literacy Framework for Higher Education, created by the Association of Colleges and Research Libraries (ACRL) addresses the concept of information creation as a process in one of its six frames (ACRL 2015). The process of information creation includes each of Bloom's lower and higher order thinking skills, including remembering, understanding, applying, analyzing, evaluating, and creating. Library instruction often focuses on evaluating information. The following competencies are linked to evaluation of information: critiquing, justifying, summarizing, describing, and contrasting. Skills such as synthesizing, categorizing, combining, compiling, composing, generating, modifying, organizing, planning, rearranging, reusing, and rewriting are linked to creation. Integrating data literacy into instruction is one of the best ways for learners to acquire these skills, because learners must learn to choose the appropriate data set by locating the appropriate repository or source of data. Then the student must make an accurate representation of the content in the appropriate format.

SPATIAL LITERACY AND GEOSPATIAL VISUALIZATION

Creating maps is an engaging opportunity to achieve the skill set for data literacy. Exercises in mapping, using geographic information, directly incorporate skills needed for data discovery and acquisition as well as for data visualization and representation. Where data literacy is the foundation, spatial literacy is the channel to accomplish the skills of analyzing, evaluating, and creating.

Spatial literacy is the ability to use geographic information to make decisions. Geographic information often comes in the form of *geocoded* data, which involve finding coordinates using spatial reference points such as zip codes, addresses, and building polygons. In learning activities using geospatial data, students are exposed to data and given the opportunity to create something, in this case a map, to illustrate the data. Maps can be used for cross-disciplinary, interdisciplinary, and disciplinary-specific instruction to help users understand past, present, and predictive data. More important, maps give viewers a perspective of the data that may not be easily communicated in numbers alone. A list of coordinates is seemingly meaningless unless people can see where they are in relation to environmental surroundings and given distance, breadth, and scope.

One of the methods by which spatial literacy is taught is through geographic information systems (GIS). GIS consists of layers of data that contain spatial information and attributes to create maps. Spatial data include the location of something, essentially "where" something is in the world. Two common types of spatial data formats are vector and raster. Raster data represent data using grids and often appear in the form of image files (such as a .jpg file of an aerial photograph). Vector data consist of longitude and latitude coordinates of buildings, trees, boundaries, and bodies of water. GIS vector data can be formatted as shapefiles as used with Esri systems (such as ArcGIS) or KML (Keyhole Markup Language), which can be used with Google Earth (see figure 10.1) (Elliott 2014). Shapefiles are often downloaded as compressed directories (.zip) and consist of a set of files, including (but not limited to) a .dbf file (which includes a table of data), an .shp file (which includes geographic information about the features in the shape file), a .prj file (containing the coordinate system that stores the features), and an .shx file (an indexing file) (see figure 10.2). Shapefile data can be directly edited using OpenOffice or LibreOffice, a free and open source document editing software (see figure 10.3) (Fitzpatrick 2011).[1]

```
<Folder>
  <name>Placemarks</name>
  <description>These are just some of the different kinds of placemarks with
    which you can mark your favorite places</description>
  <LookAt>
    <longitude>-122.0839597145766</longitude>
    <latitude>37.42222904525232</latitude>
    <altitude>0</altitude>
    <heading>-148.4122922628044</heading>
    <tilt>40.5575073395506</tilt>
    <range>500.6566641072245</range>
  </LookAt>
  <Placemark>
    <name>Simple placemark</name>
    <description>Attached to the ground. Intelligently places itself at the
      height of the underlying terrain.</description>
    <Point>
      <coordinates>-122.0822035425683,37.42228990140251,0</coordinates>
    </Point>
  </Placemark>
  <Placemark>
    <name>Floating placemark</name>
    <visibility>0</visibility>
    <description>Floats a defined distance above the ground.</description>
    <LookAt>
      <longitude>-122.0839597145766</longitude>
      <latitude>37.42222904525232</latitude>
      <altitude>0</altitude>
      <heading>-148.4122922628044</heading>
      <tilt>40.5575073395506</tilt>
      <range>500.6566641072245</range>
    </LookAt>
    <styleUrl>#downArrowIcon</styleUrl>
    <Point>
      <altitudeMode>relativeToGround</altitudeMode>
      <coordinates>-122.084075,37.4220033612141,50</coordinates>
    </Point>
</Point>
```

Figure 10.1.   A sample Keyhole Markup Language (KML) file.

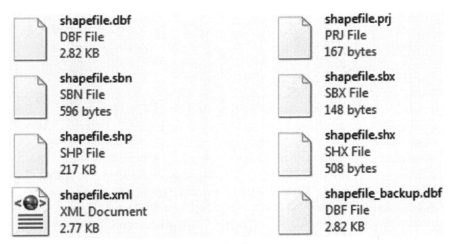

Figure 10.2. An uncompressed shapefile file directory.

STATE_NAME,C,25	STATE_FIPS,C,2	SUB_REGION,C,20	STATE_ABBR,C,2	DRAW,N,3,0
Hawaii	15	Pacific	HI	1
Washington	53	Pacific	WA	2
Montana	30	Mountain	MT	3
Maine	23	New England	ME	4
North Dakota	38	West North Central	ND	5
South Dakota	46	West North Central	SD	6
Wyoming	56	Mountain	WY	7
Wisconsin	55	East North Central	WI	8
Idaho	16	Mountain	ID	9
Vermont	50	New England	VT	10
Minnesota	27	West North Central	MN	11
Oregon	41	Pacific	OR	12
New Hampshire	33	New England	NH	13

Figure 10.3. A shapefile .dbf file opened and being edited using LibreOffice.

In addition to spatial data, attribute data consist of "what" about "where" and "why." Attribute data are often formatted in Excel or CSV or text files and include latitude and longitude, street addresses, and a wealth of detail in architectural description (Elliott 2014). Although spatial data usually refer to points or location elements on a map and are often distinguished from the descriptive information of attribute data, spatial literacy incorporates both spatial and attribute data. This is because the scholarly aspect of GIS in curricula allows for students to describe their geographic information in their project narratives.

Libraries are providing GIS support to fulfill the need within the community to understand spatial information and create something new. By providing GIS services, libraries expand patrons' ability to not only access data and statistics across multiple disciplines but also to view them spatially. Patrons can "manipulate [that data] through queries and analysis to create new information" (Elliott 2014, 9). There are many resources for data sets from governments, organizations, institutional repositories, companies, and user-generated data available in an online open source data repository.

Eva Dodsworth, a librarian on the forefront of GIS services in the library for reference and instruction, wrote the LITA guide "Getting Started with GIS" (2012), which extensively speaks to this. As libraries adopt more tools and technologies to engage patrons in civic engagement and global citizenry, the traditional library reference services have expanded to mapping and georeferencing. Dodsworth explains integrating mapping in reference services by emphasizing georeferencing: "Georeferencing is the procedure used to establish the spatial location of an object (image, map, document, etc.) by linking its position to the earth's surface" (Dodsworth 2012, 11). Ms. Dodsworth also provides an online professional development course for librarians who are interested in gaining technical skills in the area of mapping using GIS open source software such as Google Earth, Google Maps, and Esri products such as ArcGIS Explorer. There are also other open source GIS programs from local governments and smaller organizations with a specific subject focus such as public and urban fruit trees. The open source mapping software can be easily utilized in reference and instruction to increase patron's awareness of their communities and beyond.

Branch, in his article "Libraries and Spatial Literacy: Toward Next-Generation Education," states that spatial literacy ought to be included in library services because it "helps develop critical thinkers and an engaged citizenry" (Branch 2014, 109). He goes on to state that:

> collaboration, collective problem solving, and data sharing are desirable habits for learners to develop through such trends as community informatics, citizen science, constructivism in the classroom, or policy debate. A critical thinker may benefit and develop from a librarian-led data experience; the librarian can pull spatial data sources that already exist and assist the researcher, student, or faculty member in utilizing government data that has been vetted to render a visual data comparison to better argue an intellectual perspective. (Branch 2014, 110)

Branch argues that librarians ought to utilize census data and earth science data in information literacy instruction to impart the important skill of spatial literacy in global citizenry. Because world governments use geospatial data for decision making, students need to learn the skills of understanding maps to problem solve regional and global issues.

The AACU has two VALUE Rubrics that would be useful for assessment of spatial literacy: Civic Engagement and Global Learning. The Civic Engagement

Rubric emphasizes historical and current policies, values, and cultural influences to create cultural awareness through civic identity. The rubric measures (1) diversity of communities and cultures, (2) analysis of knowledge, (3) civic identity, (4) civic communication, (5) civic action and reflection and, (6) civic contexts.

An example of a civic engagement project using spatial literacy skills comes from a participatory mapping project out of the University of Washington where students used their own interpretations of archival "quantitative data with human-centered narratives" (Williams et al. 2014) to think spatially about community culture (Mitchell and Elwood 2012). Inspired from this participatory mapping project, City Digits, a research team created "Local Lotto, a mathematics curriculum that incorporates data collection and analysis methods informed by participatory media projects for use in New York City high schools" (Williams et al. 2014). The students use census data and state lottery data to formulate opinions about the social justice issues the lottery impacts. The section headed Examples of Cases in this chapter will present more detail about these projects.

The AACU Global Learning VALUE Rubric evaluates (1) global self-awareness, (2) perspective taking, (3) cultural diversity, (4) personal and social responsibility, (5) understanding global systems, and (6) applying knowledge to contemporary global contexts.

Maps can illustrate the interdependent global systems of economic, political, social, and physical legacies and their implications for people's lives by providing diverse perspectives. At Hobart and William Smith Colleges, assistant professors Kristen Brubaker, Environmental Studies, and Christine Houseworth, Economics, collaborated in a Mellon Grant–funded project to create a curriculum for social science spatial literacy. Their curriculum provided an understanding of how location could impact economic or other social issues (Brubaker and Houseworth 2014).

EXAMPLES OF CASES

This section describes the curricula some institutions have specifically provided to engage students in data and/or spatial literacy activities. These examples of projects include small to large higher education institutions with a variety of subject-specific instruction in the social or environmental sciences. These projects are examples of how students can utilize open data and open source software to better understand their communities and their disciplines.

Case Study 1: Digital Information Literacy (DIL)

In 2014, in a semester-long data information literacy (DIL) program, spearheaded by Purdue University librarian Jake Carlson, faculty and students were interviewed about their data information needs. In addition to the interviews, participants were asked to rank the importance of competencies, which determined that data discovery and acquisition and data visualization and representation were at least "very important" to participants. The DIL project collaborators then created a "suite of core data information literacy skills" and activities to support the learning objectives (Carlson et al. 2011, 654). The lessons were taught over the course of fifteen weeks. Following is a discussion of the instruction session from week 4, discovery and acquisition, and week 11, data visualization and representation.

From the DIL interviews, discovery and acquisition was found to include such skills as the ability to find data repositories and evaluate the quality of data from them. An interviewee also identified the importance of navigating data use agreements. The instruction session to teach these skills was taught by librarian Marianne S. Bracke at Purdue University. The lesson plan flipped the classroom by having students read a set list of articles prior to the library instruction session. The reading list consisted of resources about data sharing, discovery, and open data. The student learning objectives included an introduction to data sources so that students could (1) "recognize the work that goes into publishing a dataset" and (2) gain the ability to "develop and apply search strategies towards locating and acquiring data sets that are relevant to their research" (Carlson and Bracke 2015).

The activities of the lesson began with a fifteen-minute general discussion of where data come from and how to access them. A forty-five-minute presentation consisted of a demonstration of search strategies for finding freely available data from government and public data repositories. A twenty-five-minute discussion was held on evaluating data for trustworthiness and the consequences of not carefully evaluating data. Students were then given an exercise in which they were instructed to search a specific repository using a specified keyword term or search phrase and then asked to discuss the results. Next, the class was divided into small groups to conduct the same search using the same terms but now in multiple, preselected data repositories. The purpose was for the students to see and discuss the different results between the accessible supplemental data files they found in literature and the data sets they found on the public and government repositories. After the group discussion, students were given time to find data sets related to their own research. The lesson ended with a short paper to allow students to reflect on what they had learned and what might still be unclear. There was also room for suggestions for improvement on the lesson.

Overall, this lesson plan is adaptable for any subject's library lesson on finding data. Once students are given some suggested government and public repositories and they get the overview of how to search within each, they should begin to feel more comfortable identifying sources. Building on that basic understanding, students can then begin to discover discipline-specific open access repositories. Many academic libraries offer online research guides to direct patrons to useful subject-specific open access data repositories. For students, it is just a matter of getting started in the right direction for their research. For example, when students are just beginning to find raw data sets, I recommend using Google's file format search strategy to search for Excel (.xls) files related to their research topics.

The data visualization and representation lesson plan was also led by Marianne S. Bracke. Data visualization competencies include proficiency in using basic visualization tools, and the mechanical skills necessary in learning specific data visualization software programs, including spreadsheet and mapping software. The second component of the data visualization lesson was data representation. This component included not only accurately representing the data in the appropriate visual form as the creator but also understanding those representations that are being presented as a viewer. Skills in this area will allow learners to avoid representations that are misleading or ambiguous. This lesson emphasized how to best communicate findings and convey information effectively.

The student learning outcomes for this lesson plan included the basic understanding of (1) authors' decisions of published data visualizations and (2) what constitutes good or poor examples of data visualizations. The prerequisite to this instruction was that students needed to have found examples of both good and poor representations of data. Then students were asked to provide links to visualizations in articles relevant to their research areas that make the research unclear or clearer.

The instruction session allowed time for student presentations and discussion of those examples of complete or incomplete data visualizations the students found prior to the session. A minute paper followed the instruction session for reflection on what was most effective in the session. Note that the lesson gave the students the opportunity to guide the session based on their insights of how well information was being communicated to them in their fields. There may be room for facilitated guidance from the librarian or professor on suggested software to learn to create visualizations or the incorporation of additional tutorials such as those from Lynda.com. Overall, the lesson was learner centered and involved opportunity for discussion.

Each of these library instruction sessions offered students a basic understanding that data are accessible to them and provided concrete examples of effective communications of data. Other library programs can adopt the general content of these lessons to the context of their subject-specific instruction to tailor them to the specific needs of their students. For example, an instruction session may go into more detail about discipline-specific repositories or search strategies within them. Another instruction session may go into more detail about commonly used graphs or diagrams depending on the reason for displaying the data. Overall, in combination with professors' assignments, library lab instruction can be a fun playground for basic exploration and understanding of creative possibilities.

Case Study 2: Geographic Information Systems (GIS) and Spatial Literacy

Professors Kristin Brubaker in Environmental Sciences and Christine Houseworth in Economics at Hobart and William Smith Colleges collaborated on a Mellon Grant–funded project titled "Teaching Geographic Information Systems and Spatial Literacy in the Social Sciences" (Brubaker and Houseworth 2014). This curriculum combined quantitative economic data with mapping natural science information.

Brubaker and Houseworth used the software GeoDa, an open source geospatial analysis and computational software, which was developed by Arizona State University's geographic data center. GeoDa analyzes statistical patterns. In GeoDa, a data set can be used to map spatial components and then to create a choropleth map to visualize the differences in areas.

The focus of this course was for students to gain experience using a data representation tool that would aid in an understanding of spatial thinking and quantitative data while working with large public data sets. Students were able to explore data sets to find relationships between data in tables. The student learning objective was to gain an understanding of how location can impact social issues, especially economics. The final project consisted of analyzing socioeconomic differences between areas on a map of their creation. Students were able to bridge course work with current events while learning about spatial components.

Pre- and postassessment questionnaires revealed that students had gained an increased understanding of spatial components as related to social issues such as "the importance of considering the characteristics of the region when analyzing economic or political issues" (Brubaker and Houseworth 2014). A second form of assessment evaluated students' final projects to measure comfort with and understanding of the data set.

This project and others at Hobart and William Smith Colleges have led professors to partner with librarians to create course guides. The course guides assist students in learning GIS skills and offer resources for geospatial information. The library offers a GIS service point managed by Rob Beutner in information technology. Mr. Beutner partners with librarians and teaching faculty to provide library instruction activities that enhance the curriculum. In a personal communication to the author, Mr. Beutner explained that he uses georeferencing in his instruction sessions by utilizing plotting points on local chamber of commerce business maps.

Many local governments have open source GIS programs that anyone can use for georeferencing or adding objects such as images. One example of a lesson plan involves having students search online for "GIS" and the name of a city with which they are familiar. Students can create profiles and add layers to their own maps of their cities. For example, the GIS open source map Explore Santa Monica for the city of Santa Monica in California allows users to select landmark public art and library locations. Users can pick points on the maps and add images of the pieces of art or the façades of the buildings. Users can also draw shapes of the buildings, creating KMZ (zipped KML) files. This activity puts the creative ability in the students' hands by having them apply something contextual about their neighborhoods to something concrete such as specific street addresses. Students can share their maps to identify geographic relationships among other students' maps. Some students who have never been to a particular location and will have now seen how important it is for someone else by comparing and contrasting their visualizations. Georeferencing can be incorporated into any instruction session focused on social or cultural issues.

Case Study 3: City Digits: Local Lotto

Another example of a curriculum designed to impact students' understanding of social and cultural communities is the City Digits: Local Lotto project from New York City high schools. The students used data obtained from the New York State Lottery Commission and 2010 Census to "synthesize quantitative and qualitative data to formulate their own opinions about the lottery's social impact" (Williams et al. 2014).

The multimedia narratives students created from this project increased their interactions with their communities and heightened their civic interests. Students learned how to engage and organize the data to analyze the opportunity gaps. Students conducted interviews and collected narratives from lottery players about experiences with the lottery. Students geolocated where the interviews were held and created maps. These maps provided the location points of the interviews led by the students coupled with lottery data about the neighborhoods represented in either bubble charts or choropleths. The bubble chart maps had circles of various sizes representing the amount of money spent on tickets in stores. The choropleth maps visualized the percentage of median household income spent on lottery ticket purchases. The data analysis and representation informed the students' ability to support their opinions of social justice. The pre- and postinterviews with a student focus group and a survey of all students found that students' own opinions about the civic issue came directly from their newfound ability to interpret and represent the data.

The Local Lotto project curriculum was inspired by curriculum from the University of Washington developed by professors of geography Katharyne Mitchell and Sarah Elwood. Their curriculum combined historical texts with spatial thinking. Students were given prompts to think of local historical places, and they utilized archives to learn more information about those places. Students mapped the locations of the historical places and added layers of information to their maps, including images and narratives about the places and their cultural impact on the communities.

DISCUSSION

There are some possible challenges to implementing data literacy or spatial literacy in library instruction. While there are open source data repositories and geographic spatial data freely available online, keeping up the currency and relevancy of the data sets can be difficult. Although data sharing and management incentives and initiatives help researchers publish their data more regularly, not all data sharing is mandated. There may be a lapse in time before researchers share their data and they are accessible to the public for fear of being scooped. Government data are produced regularly depending on the nature and breadth of the surveys. However, although the data may have been recently collected, it takes several months, even years, before the data are available to the public. Sometimes the data available aren't as current as one would hope, thus presenting a challenge to teach the application of data sets on research projects with current events.

Libraries may also consider using subscription databases to incorporate data and spatial thinking into library instruction. At my institution, California State University, Northridge, I have used Data-Planet and PolicyMap. Data-Planet combines government and proprietary data that enable a user to have much more control to layer multiple data sets and create choropleth maps. PolicyMap is effective for political science, public policy, and social science spatial thinking. The challenge of relying on proprietary sources of data is the expense. Because most of the research and analytics of subscription databases are subject specific and can go through a detailed vetting process to meet the competitive intelligence needs of the databases' clients, many of their subscription fees are too high for most public-serving institutions. Overall, "libraries need budgets that allow them to implement data services" (Branch 2014, 112). One possible solution may be that while libraries are assessing the current usage of subscription databases, they could trial a competitive intelligence data analytics database during a time aligned with students' research projects. California State University, Northridge, trialed a proprietary business database, IBISWorld, during the height of project-oriented research assignments. IBISWorld received high usage, and we were able to cancel a database with similar content and cost with substantially lower usage to replace coverage. Overall, the students and faculty are more pleased with this acquisition, and much of our data needs in the subject area have been met with the new database. Students want to use the newer database, and it has made teaching data visualization more effective because of the currency and relevancy of the information, which is packaged in a more user-friendly way. We were lucky that we had the ability to cancel one database and subscribe to another. However, I realize that this option is not always available.

An additional challenge in the area of spatial data literacy involves the training of librarians. While GIS software costs have decreased and many open source software programs are available online, the cost of infrastructure, staffing, and training to offer the services and programs must be considered. As the popularity of GIS increases among patrons and librarians, a geospatially equipped librarian workforce needs initial and ongoing training to meet an inevitably growing demand. Despite the growing role of GIS and geospatial visualization in the profession, many library and information science programs do not incorporate GIS training in the curricula. Some libraries are hiring geospatial data specialists to meet their demands, but they are hiring outside of the library profession because of the lack of specialized training librarians have received in this area. Geospatial thinking is another area in which libraries need to adapt to remain relevant to users' needs. In their article "Geospatial Thinking of Information Professionals," authors Bradley Bishop and Melissa Johnston provide recommendations on how to incorporate geospatial thinking in library science curricula. They suggest that management classes involving strategic planning incorporate an aspect of facility location analysis. The authors also suggest that in specialized reference courses, a portion of the class ought to be devoted to "finding and locating geospatial data" (Bishop and Johnston 2013, 20).

CONCLUSIONS AND FUTURE DIRECTIONS

The future of data competency skills is bright for library services. Future trajectories can align patrons' data needs with library outreach services. As librarians become embedded in more academic courses, there can be possible channels for integration of data and spatial thinking in general education courses and subject-specific curricula. As data librarianship expands, opportunities arise for more training and access to resources and guides among librarians in interest groups in professional associations. As the research life cycle model expands to include data information literacy skills, including data sharing and creation, library services models will open to support the needs of today's and tomorrow's researchers.

NOTE

1. LibreOffice can be downloaded for free from https://www.libreoffice.org/.

REFERENCES

Abresch, John. 2008. *Integrating Geographic Information Systems into Library Services: A Guide for Academic Libraries.* Hershey, PA: Information Science Pub.

Association of American Colleges and Universities (AACU). 2009. *VALUE rubrics.* Accessed October 30, 2015. http://www.aacu.org.

Association of College and Research Libraries (ACRL). 2015. *Framework for Information Literacy for Higher Education.* Accessed October 30, 2015. http://www.ala.org/acrl/standards/ilframework.

Bishop, Bradley Wade, and Melissa P. Johnston. 2013. "Geospatial Thinking of Information Professionals." *Journal of Education for Library and Information Science* 54(1): 15.

Bloom, Benjamin S. 1956. *Taxonomy of Educational Objectives: The Classification of Educational Goals.* New York: Longmans, Green.

Branch, Benjamin D. 2014. "Libraries and Spatial Literacy: Toward Next-Generation Education." *College & Undergraduate Libraries* 21(1): 109–114.

Brubaker, Kristen, and Christina Houseworth. 2014. *Digital Pedagogy Project: Teaching Geographic Information Systems and Spatial Literacy in the Social Sciences.* William and Hobart Smith Colleges. http://www.hws.edu/offices/provost/digital.aspx.

Carlson, Jacob, Michael Fosmire, C. C Miller, and Megan Sapp Nelson. 2011. "Determining Data Information Literacy Needs: A Study of Students and Research Faculty." *Portal: Libraries and the Academy* 11(2): 629–657.

Carlson, Jake, and Marianne S. Bracke. 2015. "Agriculture/Graduate Students/Carlson & Bracke/Purdue University/2014." *Data Information Literacy Case Study Directory* 1(3).

Dodsworth, Eva. 2010. "Indirect Outreach in a GIS Environment: Reflections on a Map Library's Approach to Promoting GIS Services to Non-GIS Users." *Journal of Library Innovation* 1(1): 24.

Dodsworth, Eva. 2012. *Getting Started with GIS: A LITA Guide.* New York: Neal-Schuman Publishers.

Elliott, Rory. 2014. "Geographic Information Systems (GIS) and Libraries: Concepts, Services and Resources." *Library Hi Tech News* 31(8): 8–11.

Fitzpatrick, Charlie. 2011. *Using External Data Tables with ArcGIS Online.* Esri. http://ed-community.esri.com/Resources/ArcLessons/Lessons/U/Using_External_Data_Tables_wit.

Koltay, Tibor. 2015. "Data Literacy: In Search of a Name and Identity." *Journal of Documentation* 71(2): 401–415.

Mitchell, K., and Elwood, S. 2012. "Engaging Students through Mapping Local History." *Journal of Geography* 111(4): 148–157.

Prado, Javier Calzada, and Miguel Ángel Marzal. 2013. "Incorporating Data Literacy into Information Literacy Programs: Core Competencies and Contents." *Libri* 63(2): 123–134.

Williams, Sarah, Erica Deahl, Laurie Rubel, and Vivian Lim. 2014. "City Digits: Local Lotto: Developing Youth Data Literacy by Investigating the Lottery." *Journal of Digital and Media Literacy* 2(2). http://www.jodml.org/2014/12/15/city-digits-local-lotto-developing-youth-data-literacy-by-investigating-the-lottery/.

11

Using Infographics to Teach Data Literacy

Caitlin A. Bagley

Since 2012 librarians at Gonzaga University have begun teaching data visualization elements to their students through the use of infographics. A range of methods have taken place over the course of the past three years, and with these experiences in place this chapter aims to discuss best practices as well as some common pitfalls when attempting to use infographics in lesson planning. Infographics can be an exciting tool to employ in instruction, but as with all new instructional technologies, it takes time to learn and use effectively. Similarly, not all methods are best suited for all classes. During the learning period, instructors discovered that there were times when it was best not to use infographics, such as for more advanced classes or classes that relied heavily on lecture and in-depth work.

While this chapter was being written, librarians were been busy finalizing the Framework for Information Literacy for Higher Education from the Association of College and Research Libraries (ACRL). Keeping this in mind, the author seeks to examine how infographics and data literacy can fit into the ACRL information literacy standards as they currently exist and to offer some thoughts on the way they might fit into future iterations. As no pedagogical method stands alone, it is important to evaluate the methods of instruction and the value they could potentially bring to students before adding them into the curriculum. While data visualization does not and cannot touch on all aspects of the standards, it can provide the instructor with structure and guidance when presenting the idea of using data visualization within instructional programs to a director or dean.

The tools and resources covered in this chapter are largely free or already owned by most academic libraries. In particular, the resources include reference staples such as the *Statistical Abstracts of the United States* and other government publications that most libraries have access to. The federal government has ceased print publication of the abstracts as of 2011, but since then ProQuest has published the annual as a searchable database. Although some librarians (and many patrons) can be intimidated by government documents, data visualization is particularly well suited to the strictures and methods of government data collection, and the use of these collections strengthens both librarian and patron skill levels. Other resources involve freemium web apps such as Piktochart, an infographic generator perfect for students unfamiliar with the concept and new to graphic design. The use of these tools delicately walks the line between hand-holding and allowing students to explore their own creativity without being hampered by preset rules. With these two tools, instructors were able to do the majority of instruction.

BACKGROUND

The Foley Center Library at Gonzaga University is a Jesuit Catholic institution based in Spokane, Washington, that serves a diverse student body of over 8,000 traditional, distant, and online students. Every year, instruction librarians teach a wide span of classes ranging from upper division one-shots to entry to the major- and freshman-level courses. One set of nonacademic classes that they spend a special amount of time on is the Pathways series of classes. These classes differ from traditional freshman classes in that they usually comprise honors students who are new to the university and they have no specific focus other than to develop a cohort of students familiar with the university. Special focus is put on developing a program for them, and in 2012 librarians decided to show students in the Pathways program how to create infographics.

For those readers who are unfamiliar with the concept of infographics, the generally accepted definition is a visual image such as a chart or diagram that is used to represent information or data in a creative way. Although infographics have been around in many forms for some time, only in the past few years have they have come into common use in classroom and other academic settings. In some ways, this is due to generators that make infographics easier to create along with a more general familiarity with them in the populace. In recent years, their use has exploded into lesson plans in libraries and across other curricula at the university level. They represent a quickly and easily understood method of seeing numbers and hard facts for people who, prior to the lesson, may not have felt entirely comfortable with either graphic design or statistics. Many students have remarked that they would not have used these sources had they not learned about them in class.

Another key concept to be aware of is that many infographics are built around templates, blocks, and themes. A template is a blank or prefilled infographic screen that allows users to build their individual infographics. Within Piktochart, the service that we will be exploring here, templates can be created out of blocks so that each template can be as long or as short as desired (see figure 11.1). Each template starts with three blank blocks, which can be added or deleted as needed. Similar to a template, a theme is an infographic that has already had the majority of its design

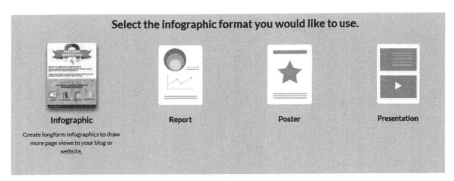

Figure 11.1.   A selection of Piktochart templates.

elements created along particular thematic approaches but leaves spaces for users to add their own information and stylistic choices. Individually, all of these elements were approachable, but combined as a whole, the instructors found that students could easily become overwhelmed. So they made sure that they discussed each element of the infographic. Instructors also relied heavily on Microsoft Excel and Google Spreadsheets at the beginning of the course.

During the time that these classes first began to be taught, professors at the university were looking for creative ways to bring multimodal learning and digital humanities aspects into their teaching styles. Likewise, the librarians wanted to explore new methods for instruction to find ways of teaching that were not static. In particular, with the Pathways classes, the author was struggling to find a way to teach an academic class without a fixed topic and without repeating ideas that the students would most likely receive in future library instruction. Prior to giving infographic lessons, instruction had centered on projects such as creating videos and gamification in the library. A precedent had been set for the Pathways classes to be energetic and fun but with an academic lesson hidden within.

When deciding what to teach to the students, the librarians decided to represent underused databases that were not typically shown in instruction, so they reviewed database usage statistics to identify such databases. During a time of increased costs and decreased budgets, librarians used this opportunity to promote databases that they knew students could benefit from. Eventually the librarians decided to settle on the ProQuest Statistical Abstract of the United States. They did so because it was a new database to the library with which many librarians were unfamiliar and because it had been a reference staple prior to its publication as an electronic resource. Students often see statistics and large data sets as intimidating, so the librarians were concerned that it would not be possible to teach the new database in a fifty-minute time slot. Infographics were suggested as a potential solution. Relatively quick and heavily reliant on data, they seemed like they would make the perfect bridge between trying to teach a relatively new database while maintaining a sense of fun to encourage students to get involved with the library beyond their initial introduction to it.

CASE STUDY: INSTRUCTIONAL DESIGN

Over the course of the fall 2012 semester, the library had eight sections of Pathways courses to teach, each section with between fifteen and twenty students. Taught in a classroom with full computer support, it seemed like teaching infographics to these students would go smoothly. After all, the classes were smaller, each student had his or her own computer, and as many instructors rationalized, these were young students who would be the most tech savvy and get it immediately.

Designing the course took several bouts of trial and error, during which instructors had to face the reality of how much time certain aspects of the tools actually took versus how much time they thought they would take. Instructors knew they only fifty minutes of time and keeping it within the time constraints seemed difficult. Many of the instructors were used to spending the whole class time on just one database demonstration. To consider teaching a database, a website, and a new type of graph seemed excessive. Despite these initial concerns, the plan was broken up into the following time chunks:

10 minutes of introduction/explanation
10 minutes on the Statistical Abstract
10 minutes of active instruction on Piktochart
10 minutes of working time
10 minutes for presentation/wrap-up
50 minutes of total instruction time

While the major structure of the instruction never changed much, there were several adjustments to how much time was needed in each area. It is important to point out that the problems with the timing of the lesson would not have become clear if it had not been for the practice sessions and demos before the actual lesson. They gave instructors critical time to rearrange and reformat the class to meet expectations.

It was assumed that the Statistical Abstract would be the hardest part of the lesson to teach and would therefore need the most instruction time. However, in reality, this appeared to be an easy topic to address for students due to a number of factors. The initial assumption was that students would need to download the individual tables from the database to manipulate the data within. In actuality, the students rarely needed all of the data held within the spreadsheets. Using large amounts of data often confused students or even confused the point that they were trying to make. Sometimes downloading large files made students think they needed more information than was truly required. It was often far simpler to spend time discussing with students one-on-one what the point was that they were actually trying to make. Frequently, their true motives differed vastly from what they were searching. The Statistical Abstract was always used as a starting point, but this frequently led to discussions about from where the source material was drawn and where to gather similar information. One of the more helpful features about the Statistical Abstract is that it sources its information in hyperlinks when available so that students could frequently follow through to the original agency that had reported the information. Over time this led to discussions about the many varied branches and agencies of the government as well as discussion on the authority of sources. If students failed to find the specific information they were looking for in the Statistical Abstract, they could often find something similar to what they wanted in a linked agency. Using the seeds of the sourcing, from there they could extrapolate better locations from which to search, including state and federal agencies. While not every student needed to expand beyond the Statistical Abstract, it served as a good opening discussion model for the rest of the class, especially for entry-level students who might not have been exposed previously to this level of research. The majority of students used the Statistical Abstract for their data source if only because sourcing the information and citing it became easier when it was provided for the students right within the item record of their research. Comparing this to finding or creating full citations for outside sources, many opted to use the resources at hand. One of the greater problems was that a significant portion of students lacked a deep understanding of how to read spreadsheets. Considering that this was a class that relied heavily on spreadsheets, this was a deeply terrifying revelation.

It had been assumed that most students would have a working knowledge of most Microsoft Office products including Excel. However, this was alarmingly not the case. Many students had only surface-level interaction with the products prior to coming into class. In particular, the concept of rows and columns was fuzzy to the students. While most students understood that information needed to be placed in the individual rows and columns in an ordered fashion, many had trouble understanding that these rows and columns corresponded to one another. For example, many students were unaware that information needed to be labeled on both column and row or being unaware that you could not put information from an x-axis into a y-axis column. These initial frustrations were difficult to explain for instructors who had not come prepared to discuss the basics of spreadsheets. On top of this quandary, the problem often arose during work within the Piktochart module, which varied just enough from typical spreadsheets that confusion was quick to arise (discussed below).

This trouble with spreadsheets put fear into the minds of instructors, as the main tenet of data visualization involves interpreting data in visual ways to highlight and reveal new or previously unseen truths. Yet many students seemed to lack this visual style or even the impetus to add interpretation to it. Sometimes, leading questions had to be asked of the students, where instructors would prompt students by asking, "How do you think they gathered this information?" or "Why do you think more people did X than Y?" and even "What would be the best way to show that?" While instructors were not directly informing students on how to build and design their infographics, they did use these questions to stimulate free thinking and promote thinking beyond what they saw directly on the computer. Sometimes diagramming brainstorming methods on the blackboard was the best option to visualize what instructors desired for their students. Indeed, this occurred only in a minority of instances, but it happened with enough frequency that instructors felt that this should be in the arsenal of any prepared teacher to know when and when not to gently prompt students to go further in their research. The end goal is that students will reach unanticipated conclusions from this research. When students come to a project with a fixed idea of what they want to say, they fail to bring a willingness to embrace the possibility of a different or unknown outcome, which inherently precludes learning.

There were two immediate adaptations brought on by paying attention to how students were receiving the information and watching the struggle points. The first was to have instructors make their students sign up for a Piktochart account prior to attending class. Although it was a relatively simple and quick process, it did eat up time in an already limited class session. Most students were willing to create the accounts prior to class, and as an added bonus some of them were curious and played around with the tools at that time so that they had at least a general idea of how to use them. The other adaptation that ended up saving the most time was in creating a step-by-step handout to go along with the instruction. The handout went over the process of where to find each database and each step the students needed to do. While it did lead to some students jumping ahead and working on their own ahead of the rest of the class, for the majority of students it gave them a referral point to look at if they became lost in the presentation or had to refer back to a prior step. An added benefit is that this then makes the instruction cover multifaceted ways of learning styles such as visual, kinetic, and tactile learning. Since not all students learn the same way, it is important to give them several options beyond a static presentation, especially within a class that stresses multimodal learning.

Typically, demonstrating the Statistical Abstract was not the hardest part of the lesson, which was a surprise. The instructor would spend about ten to fifteen minutes discussing how to access the database and how to search it. Sometimes, they would pass around older physical copies of the Statistical Abstract to illustrate how it had changed and in particular to point out to the students how the indexing language worked so that students had a better idea of what their search parameters would be. While students may not have gained direct information from the physical copies of the Statistical Abstract, they did gain insight into the structure of the content that was not necessarily clear from the search interface. The majority of the instruction on the Statistical Abstract ended up being less on the specifics of how to search in the database and more on what users could find in the database versus what they could not. In the first trial runs, most of the test users had been other staff members well versed in searching techniques. These users had quickly grasped the general idea of what statistics were needed and made their own infographics with ease. With students, however, there was often a temptation to take the entire table and dump it into Piktochart without any analysis or contemplation on the meaning or context of the data held within. Some would try to directly copy and paste what they saw on the screen and then be confused when they ended up with garbled information.

Sometimes, this required a consultation with the librarian in which the librarian asked probing questions about why the student had wanted to make an infographic on that topic and what information the student thought was really useful out of all the information. After a quick discussion, students were usually able to see that they needed to use a little more evaluation in how they presented their information.

Choosing Infographic Software

At the time of implementation there were (and remain) many varied infographic content generators. With a wealth of options, in some ways it was difficult to choose one that prevailed over the others. However, librarians looked for a few key details when they chose a website for students to work from. The first issue was cost. The librarians at Gonzaga had funding to pay for a small one-time subscription fee for a site, but they did not want to use it unless it was for a site that went above and beyond other free options. The other thing they took into consideration was ease of use. There were many professional-grade websites for graphic designers and those who had more skill than the average user. The content they generated was beautiful, but it also required a higher level of skill than most entry-level students would have. One source they continued to return to as they researched was Piktochart.com. This service seemed to offer the appropriate levels of content and ease of use that they felt most students would be able to handle. A freemium site, Piktochart offered both free accounts and paid accounts with extras tacked on. Although they looked into buying a subscription from Piktochart, at the time of instruction, the site lacked the ability to offer IP address–specific access. Instead, they could have created individual accounts for each student who would use the program, but ultimately, the library felt that this would not have met their needs. Considering this would require making over a hundred individual accounts, this seemed like it would rapidly become unmanageable. They wanted the service to be available to all of their student body, not just a select few who happened to be taking one specific course. Piktochart's pay scale is structured as Free for a basic account, $150/year for the Lite account, and $290/year for the Pro account. Its education licenses are $120 for thirty individuals for four months. After some discussion, it was decided that the free accounts provided by Piktochart would offer the best support for what the students needed to create their infographics. One serious complaint that comes up frequently with Piktochart is its lack of serious education licenses that would enable an entire campus to log on through a proxy or group code. While their current educational licenses do fulfill a need, they are lacking in depth of coverage that the typical classroom environment would need.

Although librarians at Gonzaga chose Piktochart as their choice of infographic generator, there are a number of options to be considered currently on the market. The most frequently mentioned are Piktochart, Infogr.am, Easel.ly, and Canva. Each has its own unique strengths and weaknesses, and aside from a few items of note later on, often the choice comes down to instructor preference. While they offer similar service and the same end product, they can be difficult to navigate when you are more familiar with one style over another.

As shown in table 11.1, all of the top contenders are freemium products. A freemium service generally means that the base versions are free and you have the option to pay for higher quality services and more content. Many of the services featured here are not specifically designed for educational use. When infographic generators were new to the field, they relied heavily on clip art and cartoon-like images that were easy to source. Even in the past year, imaging options have advanced to such a point that they no longer rely solely on clip art and basic imagery; instead they are now highly photograph reliant, including rich, high-resolution imagery, along with options to upload your own content. Canva, for example, shows previews of available images and offers the option to pay a dollar per image. These prices may seem cheap but can quickly add up. When demonstrating this product to students, it is important to mention pricing options and alternative free services.

Table 11.1. Comparison of infographic software

Software	Cost per month	Pros	Cons	Sharing options
Piktochart	Free/$15/$29	Easy-to-start templates	Harder to use without a template	Download and social media pushing
Infogr.am	Free/$15/$42/$166	Detailed tutorials	Not an entry-level platform	Aspect ratios tailored to social media platforms
Easel.ly	Free/$3	Best pricing options	Little training in how to use	Can choose resolution to download in and republish later
Canva	Free/Paid Options	Highly graphical	Focused more on marketing than information	Detailed downloading options. Pushes only to Facebook and Twitter.

ASSESSMENT

One of the biggest points of discussion when thinking of how to design the lesson revolved around how to judge and assess creativity. The instructors knew they could not require students to be perfect at this on their first attempt, but they did want infographics to have a few specific elements. Although the ideal of a perfect infographic could not be dictated, there were a few tenets that we all felt each infographic should contain. In the expanding and evolving world of infographics, there has been much debate over how to teach and effectively use such tools. Some instructors, such as Abilock and Williams (2014), have a line of questioning that they prefer their students follow called an Infographic Question Matrix, which builds on addressing most effective areas. Others, such as Richard Saul Wurman (1989), rely on acronyms such as LATCH (location, alphabet, time, category, and hierarchy). Bearing these two ideas in mind, the librarians elected to create their own model. These were the items written on the white board and on the handout so that each student knew what was expected of his or her end product. They were as follows (see figure 31 in the photospread):

- A title
- One graph/chart
- A citation
- Images/clip art
- Explanatory information on data

Although there were numerous other things the instructors would have wanted in an idealized infographic, they felt it was best to keep the requirements to a smaller number so that students would not feel overwhelmed with too much information and too many new technologies. Time was also a huge factor. Had the class taken place over a longer period of time or several days there would likely have been more requirements. In the best-case scenarios of the class after it had spread to other professors, the students would have a clear objective and audience to which they could direct these infographics. Lacking these things often gave students a small hurdle. It was not that they did not have anything to say but rather that they did not have a clear direction in which to point what they had to say. Particularly in the original Pathways classes, it became clear that having a directed topic was a necessity and that prompts were needed to give direction. Sometimes this allowed for breaking up students into small groups of two or three to have them work together to research a common topic (see figure 31 in the photospread).

TECHNICAL CONSIDERATIONS

As noted above, one of the major, unexpected hurdles to deal with when first presenting the topic was scalability. Most of the instructors, having grown up and using Microsoft Excel frequently in professional environments, assumed that their students would also understand how to input information in a spreadsheet. While all students had used Microsoft Excel before, instructors found that the degree to which the students had used it did not necessarily match up with the skill level needed for the course. The most common issues dealt with a basic misunderstanding of how columns and rows interacted with each other, in particular realizing that these columns and rows would relate directly to their x- and y-axes within their graphs. Understandably, many students were inputting information in a manner that would make the spreadsheet inherently readable to human readers but often proved to be unreadable or incoherent to machines when translating it to graphs. Much time was spent correcting students and showing them that they needed to move entire rows or columns. Likewise, many failed to understand how information would be relayed onto a graph, in that they would scale their information so that the numbers would look disproportionately small or large by putting information on the wrong axis. Usually these mistakes could be spotted before they were committed to a final form, but this required the instructors to spend the majority of their time walking around the classrooms and checking in with individual students to monitor their progress. In a class of twenty or more students this could sometimes take up the majority of instructional time. Initially, these classes were taught with two instructors so there would be a backup in case there were too many questions for one instructor to handle alone. Since first debuting this course that practice has changed to only one instructor per class. Although the individual problems have not changed that much from class to class, the instructors have become more experienced in handling the problems and now feel competent to teach the class alone.

A lingering problem with using Piktochart involves the fact that it works best in Mozilla Firefox and Chrome but many students default to using Internet Explorer. At the start of every class, students were reminded that the preferred Internet browser for the course was Firefox, but there were always one or two students who simply did not hear or ignored the directions. It is unlikely that this problem will ever be completely resolved unless Internet Explorer should suddenly become compatible with Piktochart. The best bet is to be aware of the issue so that when the problem arises you know how to handle it. The most frequent problem is that using Internet Explorer with Piktochart tends to cause the browser to either drag down performance, freeze, or in the worst scenario, crash. One of the nicer features of Piktochart is that it automatically saves all work. In the event of crashes or having to restart machines, users can log back into Piktochart in a different browser and restart where they left off. A good way to prevent the problem is to mention that everyone should use Firefox or Chrome when students are logging in to their computers.

Another small annoyance about Piktochart are inconsistencies within the product when creating chart types (see figure 31 in the photospread). In the best-case scenario, the program should allow users to input multiple types of charts that they can choose from including icon matrices, gauges, and progress bars, which students are often not as familiar with. Information can be manually added directly or can be imported from CSV or Excel files (.xls) or Google Spreadsheet. While individually many of the students had the capability to understand and important the information via CSV or .xls files, in practical terms the time limitations of the class did not allow for the teachers to teach every student how to do this. Frequently, data were manually imported into Piktochart's in-house spreadsheets. Yet not all students had access to the same types of charts as their classmates. This was a problem that instructors could see no obvious evidence for why one student would get preference over another. At first glance it seemed as though it might be a difference between browsers or even operating systems, but the instructors have never been able to fully determine what causes these inconsistencies. Since 2012, when we first began to roll this out, this problem has slowly receded, and now most students have the same default charts when they first sign up. The best guess instructors can offer for this discrepancy would be that these new types of charts were phased rollouts that were randomly assigned to new accounts before the finalized versions went site wide. While it would appear that this problem has been temporarily resolved, it is something that is always on the back burner during instruction as something to deal with should it pop up. Considering that this is a free resource that provides a powerful tool, users must take what they are given, but when choosing, there are other options out there that an instructor might want to consider before settling with Piktochart. There were and remain many other viable options for generating infographics, but instructors have generally felt that the limitations of Piktochart are small compared to the abilities it offers. Likewise, the other options considered were frequently not as user friendly nor did not offer the breadth of services wanted for students (see figure 32 in the photospread).

As the course shifted from being one taught in a nonacademic setting to being specifically requested by professors for their own individual courses, the librarians had to think of a way for it to still work in a now deliberately academic setting. The time constraints in place were already fairly inflexible, and it did not seem likely that in most cases there would be more class time. However, it became clear that while the Statistical Abstract was a stellar database for a nonacademic class on this subject, it was not always the best solution when students had course-specific subjects that were not necessarily targeted by the database. English, business, and some science classes began to adopt the lesson plan in droves, but each had its own unique demands. In some cases, professors were fine with instructors continuing to provide instruction with the Statistical Abstract, but especially with English classes they wanted other options. In a typical English 101 class, an instructor would go over basic search construction while using EBSCO's Academic Search Complete. Initially instructors had hoped that they would be able to use this database as a replacement for the Statistical Abstract. Unfortunately, while it had data sets hidden within the articles, most students did not want to put in the effort to fully explore the articles or they would not choose with careful deliberation, instead choosing the first article that matched their keywords. Had the instructors been able to do this over multiple days in embedded instruction, this plan likely would have worked because there would be more time for discussion about sourcing materials and choosing appropriate resources. Very little embedded instruction takes place with the infographics lessons, so ultimately the instructors elected to work with tools from the Census or Gale's Opposing Viewpoints database, which frequently covered the types of arguments that freshmen were offered and gave sourcing for their data sets that students could use. Subject specialists often knew of databases or websites that would give advanced scholars the information that we were seeking, but that would not be appropriate for a freshman with little research experience. It was a balancing act of exposing them to new information without overwhelming them.

DISCUSSION

The initial infographics project for freshman students new to the university was a resounding success in many ways. Word of the lesson spread from professor to professor, and it became a common request from professors regardless of whether their specific class had initially been targeted to receive that type of instruction. Infographics is now taught not only to freshmen but also to English 101 courses, business students, and communications students, among other populations. While the lesson has proved popular across campus, there were some concerns that the lesson would get overblown and eventually students would receive instruction in it more than once or simply move on beyond the topic, having done it already in other courses. Preventing these occurrences is a special pet project of the instructors in that each instructor tries to tailor his or her lessons to each class and make it unique no matter how many times a student may have been in the library. There was some initial hesitation to make sure that even these infographics lessons would end up becoming unique in their own way, whether by focusing on a specific type of data or whether it was by going into a more detailed talk about design elements for the infographics. Many instructors chose to incorporate infographics into multimodal lesson plans, often having the students use the infographics as a final project to sum up a semester's worth of research into a presentable project. In particular, professors who were seeking to add digital humanities elements to their courses were impressed by the infographics, and they felt that this project was perfectly matched to melding their digital requirements with their research needs.

Assessing the end product of the infographics initially offered some amount of confusion. While some students would turn in almost astounding infographics that offered comprehensive thought, beautiful pictures, and great composition, there were also students who turned in infographics that seemed to offer no thought process or simply seemed as though the student was not engaged with the project and was merely going through the motions with it. Given such wildly variable end products, instructors debated for a while whether this had been a successful project. Indeed, although professors were excited about the project, the library instructors wanted to ensure that this was also an exciting project for the students as well. Overall, consensus and reports from the students said that the students were enjoying the project. Feedback came from firsthand, face-to-face interactions and emailed follow-up from instructors and students. It was not uncommon to see students later in the semester and hear them say, "Hey! You're that infographics lady!" Similarly, this familiarity with librarian instructors encouraged students to feel welcome and relaxed at the library because they knew a friendly face. While many students had been in the library before coming to their orientations, many expressed that they were uncomfortable using services such as reference, whereas after instruction they were more comfortable in the space overall.

Although part of assessment involved ensuring that each infographic had the elements listed above as part of the necessary requirements, assessment still needed to be more than a simple checklist. Some discussions have revolved around the library's need for annual assessment. One way that instructors hope to incorporate instruction assessment is to have professors submit the infographics to librarians after class and have them build a rubric and norming session to see how successful the infographics truly were in effectively communicating to the students the particular strengths of the assignment. Items up for debate on the rubric would be creativity (use of color, imagery, etc.), citation, data accuracy, and time. This may vary depending on what instructors end up preferring in their own teaching styles, but we wanted to ensure that all infographics were judged based on the same basic elements. Once a semester's worth of infographics have been gathered, library instructors can spend time reviewing and assessing just what has come of these projects. Depending on your institution, you may need to gather institutional review board approval or a student release form for these data.

While using infographics in class is not necessarily the most straightforward assignment, if instructors have the time to plan their lessons carefully, they should be able to convey their own sense of excitement to their students along with what their individual desires for and needs from their students could be. One librarian took it on herself to find books and reference materials on graphic design and used them in her lesson plans to incorporate better creativity and more appealing infographics. With these small variations, infographics instruction began to vary. One instructor might truly excel at explaining graphic design and ways to choose colors and imagery, while another instructor might have strengths that rely mostly on statistics and data literacy. While both of these skill sets are invaluable to a class on infographics, inconsistent instruction can over time create wildly differing classes. It was important to ensure that while some instructors might be stronger at teaching different aspects of the class, they were all relying on the same basic plan. This ensures that while details of individual classes might be different, all students are still receiving the same quality and level of education, appropriate to where they are in their educational process. It is an easy step to overlook when scheduling and organizing, but it is a vital step that cannot be forgotten, no matter the class.

CONCLUSION

The overall consensus from both students and faculty was that this project was perceived as fun and engaging, and while not necessarily a task that students would immediately associate the library with, it helped them to learn about resources that they otherwise would never have known about. While this project was focused mostly on the use of the Statistical Abstract, it was easily adapted to other databases, particularly around class-specific research such as business and engineering.

Piktochart is undertaking the process of creating a mobile-friendly app, and instructors are hopeful that in the future they will be able to use this application in the classroom. Although not all students have tablets and smartphones, increasingly the numbers of students who do not have these items can be offset by the numbers of tablets that the library already has available for checkout. This would give students the ability to not only learn how to decipher and disseminate information using mobile technology, but it would also help instructors learn to adapt to increasingly swift changes in the technological field. Indeed, just as there is room for growth in terms of mobile applications, instructors always watch for new and better infographics sources in case there is a way to improve the lesson plan. Just because something works does not mean we should ignore it and leave it alone without reassessing its power over time. Sometimes what was effective in the beginning of use, as time goes on is no longer relevant or needed by students. Continuous assessment allows instructors to see where their strengths and weaknesses with a particular subject area might be. Currently, the mobile app is best just for viewing infographics that have already been created, but there is hope that future versions will be in-app creator friendly.

Teaching nonacademic courses can be a challenge for any library instructor. While these instructors were used to arriving with new ideas each year for this course, as this class was taught over a string of semesters to different expanding groups, instructors began to see that this was a powerhouse tool that was worth investing time in. So many new instruction techniques can appear as the buzzword-like activity of the week and result in a sense of burnout about new ideas. This project helped renew the passion that many felt about instruction. It can be worth trying out new things, as this was a stellar project that could easily be translated into a number of environments. The library instructors would recommend this for a wide range of audiences, although those more familiar with the details of data visualization might find this project to be too simple for them. This makes an excellent beginner's project for those who are new to data literacy and would enjoy having a threshold project to introduce them to the topic. While there are certainly more in-depth ways to take advantage of a project like this, it can be viewed as an entry-level way to bring data visualization to students who may be unfamiliar with the concept.

REFERENCES

Abilock, Debbie, and Connie Williams. 2014. "Recipe for an Infographic." *Knowledge Quest* 43(2): 4655.

Wurman, Richard Saul. 1989. *Information Anxiety.* 1st ed. New York: Doubleday.

Appendix

The following pages list and describe the data visualization technologies discussed in this book.

Technology	Type	Description	Supported Operating Systems, Browsers, and Software	Associated Libraries and Tools	Examples of Associated File Extensions	Proprietary?
ArcGIS	Software	Suite of geospatial visualization and GIS tools.	Windows, Mac OS X, Linux (ArcGIS Server)		(see Shapefile below)	Yes
CSS3	Stylesheet language	Display, formatting, and style information for web pages and web data visualizations. Can be edited using plain text editors and IDEs.[1]	All modern Internet browsers[2]		.css	No
CSV	Data format	Comma Separated Values; stores data delimited by commas.		Excel, Apple Numbers, Open/LibreOffice	.csv	No
Git	Software	Command-line version control system.	Windows, Mac OS X, and Linux	GitHub	.gitignore	No
Google Analytics API	Software / API	API for querying website usage data gathered from Google Analytics, returning data for visualization in JSON format.	All modern Internet browsers			Yes
Google Charts API	Software / API	API JavaScript library for rendering charts and graphics for display.	All modern Internet browsers			Yes
Google Earth	Software	Freely downloadable geospatial visualization software.	Windows, Mac OS X, and Linux		.kml, .kmz, .csv, .txt, shapefiles	Yes
Google Maps	Software/API	API JavaScript library for manipulating geospatial data and rendering map data for display.	All modern Internet browsers		.kml, .kmz	Yes
HTML5	Markup language	Markup for rendering content on the web. Can be edited using plain text editors and IDEs.	All modern Internet browsers		.html	No
JavaScript	Programming language	Commonly used for client-side development with extensive functional libraries, including many data visualization libraries.	Windows, Mac OS X, Linux, and all modern Internet browsers	D3.js, Socket.IO, Raphael, JSON	.js	No

Name	Type	Description	Platform	Associated tools	File extension	Open source
JSON	Data format	JavaScript Object Notation; commonly used to return structured data for visualization. Can be edited using plain text editors and IDEs.			.json	No
jVector Map	Software / API	Mapping and geospatial visualization plug-in.	All modern Internet browsers			Yes
KML	Data format	Keyhole Markup Language; designed for representing geospatial data information for use with Google Earth.	Google Earth		.kml, .kmz	Yes
Library of Congress Viewshare/ Recollection	Software	Installation of open-source Recollection software[3] used for generating visualizations related to digital collections.	All modern Internet browsers			No
Node.js	Software	JavaScript runtime environment designed for creating network applications.	Windows, Mac OS X, and Linux			No
Open Refine	Software	A data cleanup and analysis tool.	Windows, Mac OS X, and Linux		.csv, .txt, .tsv, .xls/.xlsx, .json, .xml, .rdf, etc.	No
Python	Programming language	General purpose programming language with extensive libraries used for manipulating and analyzing data.	Windows, Mac OS X, and Linux	csvkit	.py	No
R	Programming language	Designed for use with data, statistics, and graphics.	Windows, Mac OS X, and Linux	Deducer (graphical user interface), stringj, dplyr, stringr, ggvis	.R, .Rproj, .RData	No
Raster File	Data format	Graphics format designed to represent data using a grid.			.jpg, .tiff, .gif, .png	No
RStudio	IDE	A graphical user interface (GUI) for use with the R programming language.	Windows, Mac OS X, and Linux			Yes
Scalar	Software	Open-source, digital authoring platform designed for scholarly publishing.	Linux			No

(continued)

Technology	Type	Description	Supported Operating Systems, Browsers, and Software	Associated Libraries and Tools	Examples of Associated File Extensions	Proprietary?
Shapefile	Data format	Geospatial data format designed for use with Esri's ArcGIS software and other geospatial visualization tools.		ArcGIS	.dbf, .shp, .prj, .shx	Yes
SQL	Programming language (Structured Query Language)	Structured Query Language; designed to store, retrieve, and manipulate data in a relational database.	Microsoft, Mac OS X, Linux	MySQL, SQLite, Microsoft SQL Server		No
UNIX	Operating system	Operating and command-line software system.	Linux	Sort, pipe, uniq, sed		No
Vector File	Data format	Graphics format designed to represent images using polygons.			.svg, shapefiles	No
VOSviewer	Software	Bibliometric visualization software.	Windows, Mac OS X, operating systems with Java support			Yes
XML	Markup language (eXtensible Markup Language)	eXtensible Markup Language; designed for data and metadata encoding.	Can be edited using plain text editors, IDEs, or software such as Oxygen XML Editor		.xml	No

1. Integrated development environments designed for reading and editing computer code such as Sublime Text (https://www.sublimetext.com/).
2. Modern browsers include Internet Explorer, Chrome, Firefox, and Safari.
3. The source code for Recollection is freely available to download (http://sourceforge.net/projects/loc-recollect/).

Index

About the Editor

Lauren Magnuson is systems and emerging technologies librarian at California State University, Northridge. Her interests include PHP, Python, analytics, and data visualization, as well as promoting open-source technology in academic libraries. Lauren has an MA in information science and an MEd in educational technology, both from the University of Missouri, as well as a BA in philosophy from Tulane University.

About the Contributors

Godmar Back is associate professor of computer science at Virginia Tech, where he has been doing research and teaching in computer science since 2004. Dr. Back obtained his PhD from the University of Utah and worked as a postdoctoral scholar at Stanford University. His research interests are diverse, including operating systems, virtualization, programming languages, scientific computing, web technology, and library information systems. He is an active collaborator with librarians in the area of advancing library technology to ensure that modern technology can find its way into the library sphere. Since 2007, he has been involved in the LibX project, providing technical supervision and input. His most recent library research is the LibFX project, which visualizes real-time use of the Summon discovery system at Virginia Tech.

Annette Bailey is the assistant director for Electronic Resources and Emerging Technology Services for the Jean Russell Quible Department of Collections and Technical Services at Virginia Tech. Bailey serves on the program planning committee for the ER&L Conference. She codeveloped the open-source LibX plug-in, for which she received the 2007 LITA Brett Butler Entrepreneurship Award. She won a National Leadership Grant in 2006 for LibX and in 2008 for LibX 2.0. In 2013, Bailey won the Library Journal Movers and Shakers award as a Tech Leader. Her current research is the LibFX project to visualize real-time library resource usage of the Summon discovery system.

Caitlin A. Bagley is an assistant professor and instruction librarian at Gonzaga University. She received her MLS from Indiana University. She is the author of *Makerspaces: Top Trailblazing Projects* and has also been published in *Introduction to Cloud Computing: A LITA Guide to Social Information Research*. She is interested in the intersection between technology and education and firmly believes that libraries and librarians should be leaders in this area. She lives in Spokane, Washington.

Tim Dennis is data services and collections librarian for the UCSD Library. In this role, Tim supports data-intensive research with specialized, point-of-need assistance on data science tools and best practices in reproducible research. Tim teaches workshops on various statistical and programming topics that include data preparation, representation, and visualization and computing with data. Tim works closely with the UCSD Research Data Curation program to make data and digital scholarship openly discoverable and reusable. Tim joined UCSD in spring 2015, after fifteen years at UC Berkeley, where he helped to plan, launch, and run the UC Berkeley Library Data Lab. At Berkeley, Tim provided a variety of research data services that included research design, statistical tool instruction, data discovery, management, and analysis. Tim obtained a MIMS degree from UC Berkeley's School of Information and a BA in sociology from Millsaps College in Jackson, Mississippi.

Charissa Jefferson is business and data librarian at California State University, Northridge. She earned her MLS from the University of North Texas, her MA in cultural studies from Claremont Graduate University, and her BA in women's studies from California State University, Long Beach. Ms. Jefferson's research interests include information literacy and assessment.

Kenny Ketner is a 2003 graduate of the University of Chicago (BS in computer science) and has worked as a programmer for over fifteen years. He has written software for government, private companies, and individuals. He has been a programmer for the Texas Tech University Libraries since 2008 and currently serves as their software development manager. Kenny is the cocreator of Occam's Reader, the first library-developed method of loaning ebooks through interlibrary loan. He enjoys working on projects that propel academic libraries into the future. Kenny's hobbies include comics, retro video games, board games, computer music, writing, and activism.

Stephen Kutay is digital services librarian and research fellow at California State University, Northridge, where he oversees digital collections and digital preservation. He holds a bachelor of science in music and a master of library and information science from the University of California at Los Angeles. Steve has previously worked at the UCLA Library and the Los Angeles Philharmonic Association Archives. In addition to digital heritage, his professional interests include academic information systems, personal information management, and usability/user experience design. Steve has presented and published articles in the area of academic digital asset management and curation.

Ryan Litsey is associate librarian for document delivery at Texas Tech University and a graduate of Florida State University with a degree in library and information sciences. He has spent the majority of his academic career developing groundbreaking technologies that have endeavored to transform resource sharing. Both Occam's Reader and the stats tracking system OBILLSK have changed the way ILL librarians are able to share the resources of their respective institutions. He is active in the American Library Association and is the associate editor for the *Journal of Interlibrary Loan, Document Delivery & Electronic Reserve*. His academic research is in resource sharing, predictive analytics, and anticipatory commerce.

Scott Luker received his bachelor of arts in music performance and composition from Texas Tech University. He began his self-taught computer programming experience early in life at the age of ten. While pursuing his degree, he also worked full-time to obtain professional experience in computer programming. Scott is currently a programmer/analyst at Texas Tech University Libraries, where he develops library software and web-based applications to enhance patron services. His research interests include mobile application development, augmented reality integrations, and media-based solutions.

Emily Mitchell is webmaster librarian for SUNY Oswego's Penfield Library, where she also serves as liaison to the Computer Science and Electrical and Computer Engineering departments. She has an MLS from Indiana University and an MA in educational technology from Central Michigan University.

Eric Phetteplace is systems librarian at California College of the Arts, where his primary duties are maintaining and developing websites, an institutional repository, and an integrated library system. Previously, he was emerging technologies librarian at Chesapeake College in Maryland. In 2015, he was a fellow at the inaugural Institute of Open Leadership organized by Creative Commons. He holds a bachelors of arts and sciences in English and mathematics from Stanford University and a masters of library and information science from the University of Illinois at Urbana-Champaign. In his spare time, he plays the card game Netrunner and fiddles with code on GitHub.

David Edward Polley is social sciences librarian at Indiana University-Purdue University Indianapolis (IUPUI). He has an MLIS from Indiana University and a background in political science. Prior to joining IUPUI, he worked as a researcher at the Cyberinfrastructure for Network Science Center in the School of Informatics and Computing at Indiana University, Bloomington. He is interested in open-access publishing, open data, social science, and data visualization.

Roger Taylor is assistant professor at SUNY Oswego in the Psychology Department and Human Computer Interaction program. In addition to data visualization, his research focuses on uncovering the relationships between students' learning and their emotional (i.e., affective) states. The research goals include refining psychological theory and developing educational applications such as emotionally adaptive learning environments.

Angela Zoss began work as Duke University's first data visualization coordinator in 2012. While developing this new position, she created new library workshops on visualization; hosted an annual student data visualization contest; consulted with students, researchers, and faculty; and helped to introduce visualization concepts and tools into many courses. She co-organizes a weekly talk series on visualization and is collaborating within and outside the Duke community to improve instructional and technical support for visualization projects. She has taught courses and presented on visualization services and techniques for regional and national library and data science conferences. She holds a master of science in communication from Cornell University and is pursuing a doctorate in information science from Indiana University. Her research interests include informetrics, network science, human-computer interaction, and visualization literacy.

PROFESSIONAL

MYP